A M E R I C A
AUTOMOBILE
COLLECTIONS
A N D   M U S E U M S

"We are all tied to the automobile by history,
by business, by emotion. The automobile
deserves to be preserved and remembered."
—William F. Harrah

A M E R I C A N
AUTOMOBILE
COLLECTIONS
A N D   M U S E U M S

A GUIDE TO U.S. EXHIBITS

MICHAEL MORLAN

From the **American Travel Themes** series

BON A TIRER
publishing

**American Automobile Collections
 And Museums**
A Guide To U.S. Exhibits

ISBN: 1-878446-10-X

Library of Congress Catalog
Card Number 92-70150

Catalog number AAC-1
SA-JE-CM

Printed in the U.S.A.
Printed on acid-free paper

First Edition
10 9 8 7 6 5 4 3 2 1

From the **American Travel Themes** series

Publisher: Joseph E. Zanatta

Technical Editor: Douglas Morlan

BON A TIRER
publishing

PO Box 3480
Shawnee, KS 66203
913-236-4828

Table of Contents

ACKNOWLEDGEMENTS 8
INTRODUCTION 9
ALABAMA
International Motorsports Hall of Fame
(Talladega) 11
ALASKA
Museum of Alaska Transportation &
Industry (Wasilla) 15
ARKANSAS
Museum of Automobiles (Morrilton) 16
Reed's Museum of Automobiles
(Hot Springs) 18
CALIFORNIA
Behring Auto Museum (Danville) 19
Deer Park Car Museum (Escondido) 23
Dennis Mitosinka's Classic Cars
(Santa Ana) 27
Hayes Antique Truck Museum
(Woodland) 28
Natural History Museum of Los Angeles
County (Los Angeles) 31
San Diego Automotive Museum
(San Diego) 32
San Sylmar-Merle Norman Classic Beauty
Collection (San Sylmar) 34
Silverado Classic Car Collection (Napa) 35
Towe Ford Museum (Sacramento) 36
COLORADO
Forney Transportation Museum
(Denver) 41
Front Wheel Drive Auto Museum
(Brighton) 44
Royal Gorge Scenic Railway Museum
(Canon City) 45
DISTRICT OF COLUMBIA
National Museum of American History 46
FLORIDA
Bellm's Cars & Music of Yesterday
(Sarasota) 48
Birthplace of Speed Museum
(Ormand Beach) 51
Collier Automotive Museum (Naples) 52

Don Garlits Museum of Drag Racing
(Ocala) 56
Elliot Museum (Stuart) 59
GEORGIA
Antique Auto and Music Museum
(Stone Mountain) 60
Pebble Hill Plantation (Thomasville) 62
IDAHO
Old Idaho Penitentiary (Boise) 63
Vintage Wheel Museum (Sandpoint) 64
ILLINOIS
Bortz Auto Collection (Gurnee) 65
Dale's Classic Cars (Mt. Vernon) 66
Grant Hill Auto Museum (Galena) 68
Gray's Ride Through History Museum
(W. Frankfort) 69
Hartung's Auto Museum (Glenview) 70
Max Nordeen's Wheels Museum
(Woodhull) 71
McDonald's Museum (Des Plaines) 72
Mississippi Valley Historic Auto Club
Museum (Quincy) 74
Museum of Science & Industry
(Chicago) 75
Volo Antique Auto Museum (Volo) 78
Wheels O'Time (Dunlap) 80
INDIANA
Auburn-Cord-Duesenberg (Auburn) 81
Elwood Haynes Museum (Kokomo) 85
Indianapolis Motor Speedway Hall of
Fame Museum (Indianapolis) 86
S. Ray Miller Classic Auto Museum
(Elkhart) 90
Studebaker National Museum
(South Bend) 92
Wayne County Historical Museum
(Richmond) 94
IOWA
Duffy's Collectible Cars (Cedar Rapids) 95
Olson Linn Museum (Villisca) 97
Schield International Museum
(Waverly) 98

IOWA-Cont.
Van Horn's Antique Truck Museum
  (Mason City) 99
KANSAS
Reo Antique Auto Museum (Lindsborg) 101
Wheels & Spokes (Hays) 103
MAINE
Boothbay Railway Village (Boothbay) 105
Coles Land Transportation Museum
  (Bangor) 107
Jay Hill Antique Auto Museum (Jay) 108
Owls Head Transportation Museum
  (Owls Head) 109
Seal Cove Auto Museum (Seal Cove) 113
Stanley Museum (Kingfield) 114
Wells Auto Museum (Wells) 115
MASSACHUSETTS
Edaville Railroad (Carver) 117
Heritage Plantation (Sandwich) 118
Museum of Transportation (Brookline) 119
MICHIGAN
Alfred P. Sloan Museum (Flint) 121
Automotive Hall of Fame (Midland) 123
Detroit Historical Museum (Detroit) 124
Domino's Classic Car Collection
  (Ann Arbor) 125
Gilmore-Classic Car Club Museum
  (Hickory Corners) 126
Henry Ford Museum & Greenfield
  Village (Dearborn) 130
Motorsports Hall of Fame (Novi) 134
Poll Museum of Transportation (Holland) 135
R.E. Olds Transportation Museum
  (Lansing) 137
Ypsilanti Antique Auto, Truck & Fire
  Museum (Ypsilanti) 139
MISSOURI
Autos of Yesteryear (Rolla) 140
Kelsey's Antique Cars (Camdenton) 141
National Museum of Transport
  (St. Louis) 142
Patee House Museum (St. Joseph) 144
MONTANA
Oscar's Dreamland (Billings) 145
Towe Ford Museum (Deer Lodge) 146

NEBRASKA
Chevyland USA (Elm Creek) 151
Hastings Museum (Hastings) 152
Sawyer's Sandhills Museum
  (Valentine) 153
Stuhr Museum (Grand Island) 154
NEVADA
Imperial Palace Auto Collection
  (Las Vegas) 155
Liberace Museum (Las Vegas) 158
National Auto Museum (Reno) 159
NEW HAMPSHIRE
Grand Manor Antique & Classic Car
  Museum (Glen) 164
NEW JERSEY
Space Farms (Beemerville) 166
NEW YORK
Auto Memories (Arkville) 167
BMW Gallery (New York) 168
Collectors Cars Museum (Freeport) 169
Himes Museum of Motor Racing
  Nostalgia (Bay Shore) 170
Old Rhinebeck Aerodrome (Rhinebeck) 171
Wilson Historical Museum (Wilson) 172
NORTH CAROLINA
Backing Up Classics (Harrisburg) 173
C. Grier Beam Truck Museum
  (Cherryville) 175
Greensboro Historical Museum
  (Greensboro) 176
North Carolina Transportation Museum
  (Spencer) 177
Richard Petty Museum (Randleman) 179
OHIO
Canton Classic Car Museum (Canton) 180
Carillon Historical Park (Dayton) 182
Frederick C. Crawford Auto-Aviation
  Museum (Cleveland) 184
National Road/Zane Grey Museum
  (Norwich) 188
Pro Team Classic Corvette Collection
  (Napoleon) 189
OKLAHOMA
Chickasha Automobile & Transportation
  Museum (Chickasha) 190

Lewis Museum (Lawton) 191
Museum of Special Interest Cars
    (Shawnee) 193
OREGON
'77 Grand Prix Museum (Portland) 194
PENNSYLVANIA
Alan Dent Antique Car Museum
    (Lightstreet) 195
Boyertown Museum of Historic Vehicles
    (Boyertown) 197
Gast Classic Motorcars (Strasbourg) 198
JEM Classic Car Museum (Andreas) 200
State Museum of Pennsylvania
    (Harrisburg) 202
Station Square Transportation Museum
    (Pittsburgh) 203
Swigart Museum (Huntingdon) 204
SOUTH CAROLINA
Schoolhouse Antiques Museum
    (Liberty) 205
Stock Car Hall of Fame/Joe Weatherly
    Museum (Darlington) 206
SOUTH DAKOTA
Museum of Wildlife, Science & Industry
    (Webster) 207
Pioneer Auto Show & Antique Town
    (Murdo) 208
TENNESSEE
Car Collectors Hall of Fame
    (Nashville) 211
Dixie Gun Works (Union City) 213
Elvis Presley Automobile Museum
    (Memphis) 214
Music Valley Car Museum-Cars of
    the Stars (Nashville) 216
Smoky Mountain Car Museum
    (Pigeon Forge) 219
TEXAS
Alamo Classic Car Museum
    (New Braunfels) 220

Bolin Wildlife Exhibit & Antique
    Collection (McKinney) 221
Central Texas Museum of Automotive
    History (Rosanky) 222
Panhandle-Plains Historical Museum
    (Canyon) 223
Pate Museum of Transportation
    (Fort Worth) 224
UTAH
Bonneville Speedway Museum
    (Wendover) 226
Classic Cars International
    (Salt Lake City) 227
Union Station Museum (Ogden) 229
VERMONT
Westminster MG Car Museum
    (Westminster) 230
VIRGINIA
Glade Mountain Museum (Atkins) 231
Historic Car and Carriage Caravan
    (Luray) 232
Roaring Twenties Antique Car Museum
    (Hood) 235
U.S. Army Transportation Museum
    (Fort Eustis) 236
WASHINGTON
Lynden Pioneer Museum (Lynden) 237
WISCONSIN
Brooks Stevens Auto Museum
    (Mequon) 238
David V. Uihlein Antique Race Car
    Museum (Cedarburg) 240
Dells Auto Museum (Lake Mills) 241
FWD Museum (Clintonville) 242
Hartford Heritage Auto Museum
    (Hartford) 243
Zunker Auto Museum (Manitowac) 244
BIBLIOGRAPHY 246
PHOTOGRAPH CREDITS 247
INDEX 248

Acknowledgements

Putting together a book such as *AMERICAN AUTOMOBILE COLLECTIONS AND MUSE-UMS* requires considerable travel, correspondence and assistance. The work load is lessened considerably when the research phase passes smoothly. This occurred while compiling *AMERICAN AUTOMOBILE COLLECTIONS AND MUSEUMS* due to the friendly, professional people encountered. My sincere thanks to all the owners, directors, curators, public relations managers and other personnel of the collections and museums listed inside.

Several people went out of their way to provide help and I give special thanks to Donald Alberstadt (Collier Automotive Museum), Dale Anderson (Hartford Heritage Auto Museum), Harvey Anderson (Gilmore-Classic Car Club Museum), Dave Baker (International Motorsports Hall of Fame), Tim Belden (Canton Classic Car Museum), Eleanor Billey (S. Ray Miller Antique Car Museum), Gregg Buttermore (Auburn-Cord-Duesenberg Museum), Patricia Byron (Old Idaho Penitentiary), Greg Capitano (Don Garlits Museum of Drag Racing), Judith DeMott (Owls Head Transportation Museum), Jackie Frady (National Automobile Museum), Jean Gast (Gast Classic Motorcars Exhibit), Ann Grube (Frederick C. Crawford Auto-Aviation Museum), Lee Hartung (Hartung's Automotive Museum), Don Hays (Hays Antique Truck Museum), Heddy Herncane (Swigart Museum), Martin Himes (Himes Museum of Motor Racing Nostalgia), Sandra Houston (Alfred P. Sloan Museum), Robert Hurley (Domino's Classic Car Collection), Robert Knapp (Deer Park Auto Museum), Georgana Kos (Volo Auto Museum), Sally Law (Bellm's Cars & Music of Yesterday), Harry Loder (JEM Classic Car Museum), Deborah Lucien (Museum of Science and Industry), Skip Marketti (Auburn-Cord-Duesenberg Museum), George Martin (R.E. Olds Transportation Museum), Cameron McCrady (Behring Auto Museum), Johnny McDonald (San Diego Automotive Museum), Ann McIntosh (Henry Ford Museum), Terry Michaelis (Pro Team Classic Corvette Collection), Todd Morgan (Elvis Presley Automobile Museum), Jeanne Palermo (Carillon Historical Park), Jim Peel (Pate Museum of Transportation), Pete Peters (Imperial Palace Auto Collection), Martha Powell (Indianapolis Motor Speedway Hall of Fame Museum), Ron Radecki (Studebaker National Museum), Naomi Roth (Museum of Transportation), Beth Satter (Grand Manor Antique & Classic Car Museum), Cornelia Spain (Historic Car & Carriage Caravan), Andrew Towe (Towe Ford Museum), Margaret and Lloyd Van Horn (Van Horn's Antique Truck Museum), Roger White (National Museum of American History), Dick Williams (Classic Cars International).

Thanks to family and friends for encouragement during this project and for understanding the time required. Thanks to Joe Zanatta for another interesting undertaking.

Introduction

A trip to America's automobile museums is not an entirely geographical trip, but one through time and history that permits the traveler to see the results of the automotive evolution, embodied in the wheeled creations of backyard inventors, American industry and the world's finest craftsmen and artisans.

AMERICAN AUTOMOBILE COLLECTIONS AND MUSEUMS is not the usual road map pulled from the glove compartment or desk. And it's not the typical guide book focusing on a geographical area. As the title indicates, this book focuses on the auto collections and museums spread across the country. For those who enjoy a glimpse of a historically significant car, an exotic prototype or that memorable "special" car, this guide is hopefully the roadmap to many successful sidetrips and vacations.

AMERICAN AUTOMOBILE COLLECTIONS AND MUSEUMS was created to help the car enthusiast locate museums and cars of particular interest, as well as address the practical needs of the traveler, such as directions, operating hours and admission cost.

The criteria for inclusion in AMERICAN AUTOMOBILE COLLECTIONS AND MUSEUMS is that a facility serves to educate the visitor as well as preserve automobiles, artifacts and memorabilia. In a few cases the criteria were bent or expanded; for instance, several collections devoted to trucks are included. Also included are some facilities where the automobile collection is not the sole attraction. In those instances, additional information is provided that may be helpful to those in the family with other interests.

For various reasons some collections are not included. Facilities operating as sales outlets are not included, unless there is an overriding reason, such as an interesting car on permanent display. Some owners of private collections specifically asked not to be included, preferring anonymity. And information on a few collections could not be obtained before publication; hopefully, they will be included in the next edition.

The universe of automobile collections and museums is everchanging. Each year two or three facilities open and a like number close. If you know of any museums or collections that should be listed in AMERICAN AUTOMOBILE COLLECTIONS AND MUSEUMS, please write to the author in care of the publisher.

A special note for the reader who is in the trip planning stage. The operating days and times provided inside are as accurate as possible when the book was printed. However, it is wise to call ahead and verify days and hours of operation, particularly during the off-season and around holidays. Many collections are operated by small staffs and changes in operation can occur quickly.

CONTENTS

Many museums are miles from towns, shops and other facilities that provide the normal conveniences for travelers. And an appropriate tour may take hours, if not the better portion of a day. This guide attempts to anticipate questions the visitor might have concerning the logistics of a visit. The guide lists museums and exhibits alphabetically by state. The information in each entry provides the following information:

- Mail address; phone number.
- General information about the museum. This will vary according to the identity of the museum. The auto collection may be part of a larger facility, in which case, any pertinent information is also included.
- Information concerning unique or significant autos on display.
- Directions to the museum, generally from the major highways near the museum.
- Admission cost.
- Hours of operation — subject to change for special events and holidays. Some museums request that you call ahead and they are noted.
- Museum notes — whether there is a gift shop and if film can be purchased; whether there is a restaurant nearby; brochure availability.
- List of automobiles — listed by manufacturer, model and body style. The list was compiled by information provided by the museums and by onsite inspection. Many museums rotate their cars to provide "fresh" exhibits for regular patrons, so call the museum if interested in a particular car. Some museums preferred not to have their cars listed.

Throughout the book are snippets of facts included in the museum listings as well as in the photograph captions. These are provided as entertaining and educational sidebars for the reader interested in automotive history.

ACCURACY

The information is as accurate as possible at time of publication, but as in other museums, certain pieces may be removed for restoration or returned to a private owner. And some museums will cease operation for various reasons. If a particular car or item is of interest, call the museum.

The information presented in this book was obtained from museums and research sources. Unfortunately, in an industry as vast and old as the automotive industry, data is distorted, altered and lost, resulting in disputed information. Please write to the author if a correction is needed regarding a museum or sidebar information.

MUSEUM ETIQUETTE

Here are a few notes for the inexperienced museum visitor. Just as in museums of fine art, the watchword for all visitors is DON'T TOUCH, unless invited. Thousands of dollars are spent during the restoration process preparing and finishing the car's surfaces. Scratches and other damage caused by fingernails, jewelry, buttons and zippers are expensive to repair. Exercise caution when getting a close look. Unless specifically approved, don't open doors, hoods or trunks, or attempt to operate any devices on the cars. When in doubt, always ask first. Any admonitions regarding children around shiny objects that resemble the family car should be self-evident.

ACCESS FOR THE HANDICAPPED

Efforts to provide detailed information concerning the accommodation of handicapped persons proved impossible to include in useable form. While most museums and exhibits accommodate the handicapped, exactly what constitutes "handicap accessible" remains ill-defined and troublesome for unique facilities such as auto museums. For detailed information, contact the museum.

International Motorsports Hall of Fame

4000 Speedway Boulevard, P.O. Box 1018, Talladega, Alabama 35160
(205) 362-5002

Opened in 1983, the International Motorsports Hall of Fame is the brainchild of Bill France, Sr., who was the moving force in organizing NASCAR, the National Association for Stock Car Auto Racing. NASCAR has become the preeminent stock car racing association in the country with team sponsors fielding multi-million dollar racing teams. France's efforts transformed what was a regional sport into a series of nationally televised races that showcase brightly colored cars emblazoned with corporate names identifying products from soap to chewing tobacco.

France wanted a facility to commemorate the achievements in stock car racing as well as other forms of motorsports. The complex now consists of four buildings housing over 100 vehicles. Along with the Motorsports Hall of Fame are areas devoted to the ARCA (Automobile Racing Club of America) Hall of Fame, Quarter Midgets Hall of Fame, Western Auto/NASCAR Mechanics Hall of Fame, World Karting Hall of Fame, and the Alabama Sportswriters Hall of Fame.

For anyone interested in auto racing, there is much to see. Sir Malcolm Campbell's *Bluebird* set the world land speed record of 335 mph in 1935 at Daytona Beach. Richard

This Buick Regal was driven on NASCAR tracks by stock-car racing great Bobby Allison, now retired. Also exhibited is a Ford Thunderbird driven by Davey Allison, Bobby's son and a current star.

Sir Malcolm Campbell drove a series of vehicles named Bluebird *to several land speed records. The* Bluebird *on display was driven at Daytona Beach, Florida, and set a record of 305 mph. The car weighed approximately 5 tons when fully loaded, including 1,000 lbs. of ballast to reduce wheel spin generated by the V-12 aircraft engine. Dual wheels were attached to both ends of the rear axle. Each 18-ply, 37-inch-diameter tire cost $1,800 and had to be discarded after each run due to abrasive wear from the beach sand.*

Petty's STP Dodge Charger won 31 races and 16 pole positions. The Budweiser Rocket Car set the current land speed record of 739.666 mph, breaking the speed of sound during the run. Don Garlits' *Swamp Rat XII* was the first dragster to exceed 240 mph in a quarter-mile drag race, doing so in 1968. The various Halls of Fame document the achievements of the honorees in their respective motorsport areas.

The Hall of Fame is located adjacent to Talladega Superspeedway. Tours of the race-track are also available.

DIRECTIONS TO MUSEUM: From I-20 eastbound take Exit 168 and follow signs. From I-20 westbound take Exit 173 and follow signs.

ADMISSION COST: Adults $5.00; senior citizens $4.50; children (7-17 yrs.) $4.00.

HOURS OF OPERATION: Open daily 9am-5pm. Closed New Year's Day, Easter morning, Thanksgiving and Christmas.

MUSEUM NOTES: There is a restaurant nearby. The Hall of Fame has a gift shop and film is available.

A brochure is available.

On December 17, 1979, Stan Barrett drove the Budweiser Rocket Car to a land speed record of 739.66 mph, becoming the only land vehicle to exceed the speed of sound at ground level. The car reached 400 mph in three seconds on the record-run at Edwards Air Force Base, California. The main rocket engine produced 48,000 horsepower, while the auxiliary rocket engine, from a Sidewinder missile, produced 12,000 horsepower.

Display Automobiles

NOTE: This is only a partial list of vehicles on display. Most race cars are listed according to driver's name.

Adcox Chevrolet Monte Carlo
Allison, Bobby, AMC Matador
Allison, Bobby, Buick
Allison, Davey, Ford Thunderbird
Allison, Donnie, Ford Torino
AMC, 1966, AMX Prototype
AMC, 1972, Javelin
Arrington Chrysler Imperial
Baker Dodge Daytona
Bonnett Chevrolet
Bouchard Buick
Budweiser Rocket Car
Campbell Bluebird
Chevrolet, 1936, Coupe
Chevrolet, 1968, Corvette
Chevrolet, 1968, Yenko Camaro
DeLorean, 1981
Dodge, 1970, Daytona

Eagle Indy Car
Earnhardt Chevrolet Monte Carlo
Elliot Ford Thunderbird
Farmer Ford Torino
Flock Mercury
Ford, 1919, Indy Car
Ford, 1931, 2dr Sedan
Ford, 1932, Roadster
Ford, 1939, Coupe
Garlits Swamp Rat 23 Dragster
Hackman Ford Escort
Hartman Dodge Charger
Hillin Buick
Issac Dodge Daytona
Kurtis-Novi Indy Car
Moroso Oldsmobile
Nemechek Buick
Oldsmobile, 1955, Convertible

Two stock car racing legends were responsible for the success of number "22". The talents of driver "Fireball" Roberts and engine builder Smokey Yunick won many races with Pontiac "22", the first stock car to win a 500 mile race at an average speed over 150 mph.

Packard, 1937, 4dr Sedan
Petty Dodge Charger
Plymouth, 1970, Barracuda Convertible
Plymouth, 1970, Superbird
Pontiac, 1987, Grand Prix
Pontiac Trans Am Pace Car

Porsche, 1989, 962
Roberts Pontiac
Smith Oldsmobile
Stovall Oldsmobile
Waltrip Chevrolet

Museum of Alaska Transportation & Industry

P.O. Box 870646, Wasilla, Alaska 99687
(907) 376-1211

Alaska presents formidable barriers to any traveler with its imposing terrain and harsh weather. Growth in Alaska is directly related to the capability of the transportation system. The museum documents the story of transportation in Alaska through displays of cars, trucks, trains, aircraft, boats, tools, dog sleds, farm equipment and other artifacts.

Among the vehicles displayed is a 1923 Dodge Touring that was used by President McKinley during his visit to Alaska in 1924. There are also eight fire trucks exhibited, most of them built by American LaFrance.

DIRECTIONS TO MUSEUM: From Parks Hwy. turn onto Rocky Ridge Rd. at milepost 46.5. Turn left onto Neuser Museum Dr. and go 3/4 mile to museum.

ADMISSION COST: Adults $3.00; children $1.50.

HOURS OF OPERATION: Open Tuesday-Saturday 10am-4pm. Closed Sunday and Monday.

MUSEUM NOTES: There is a restaurant nearby and a gift shop onsite. Film is available.

A brochure is available.

Display Automobiles

American LaFrance, 1921, Fire Truck
American LaFrance, 1942, Fire Truck
American LaFrance, 1948, Fire Truck
American LaFrance, 1957, Fire Truck
Cadillac, 1964, Hearse
Cadillac, , Ambulance
Chevrolet, 1943, Fire Truck
Chevrolet, 1974, Suburban
Chrysler, 1966, Town & Country
Dodge, 1923, Touring

Ford, 1926, Model A
Ford, 1929, Truck
GMC, 1953, Bus
Hupmobile, 1930
Nash, 1950, Ambassador
Plymouth, 1937, Truck
Seagrave, 1940, Fire Truck
Seagrave, 1942, Ladder Fire Truck
Studebaker, 1947, Truck
Western States, 1967, Fire Truck

Museum of Automobiles

Route 3, Box 306, Morrilton, Arkansas 72110
(501) 727-5427

The museum presents fine automobiles owned by collectors in the United States and abroad.

Winthrop Rockefeller, the late, former governor of Arkansas, founded the museum and many of the cars are from the Rockefeller collection.

Because the cars are privately owned, the cars on display are subject to change. Call the museum for information on a specific car or an update on the cars on display.

DIRECTIONS TO MUSEUM: From I-40 take Exit 108 and follow Hwy. 9 south to Hwy. 154. Turn west on Hwy.154 and travel approximately 9 miles to museum.

ADMISSION COST: Adults $4.00; children (6-17 yrs.) $2.00.

HOURS OF OPERATION: Open daily 10am-5pm. Closed Christmas.

MUSEUM NOTES: A restaurant is nearby. The museum has a gift shop and film is available.

A brochure is available.

Display Automobiles

Auburn, 1932, 4dr Brougham
Bantam, 1940, Speedster
Buick, 1909, Model F

Cadillac, 1949, Convertible Coupe
Cadillac, 1951, Fleetwood 75
Cadillac, 1959, Eldorado Convertible

1933 Dodge Coupe. *Dodge built over 106,000 of its 1933 models, placing it fourth on the best-selling list for that year.*

1923 Climber Touring. *Built in nearby Little Rock from 1919 to 1924, only 200 Climbers were constructed (the museum's is one of two known to exist). Insufficient production and lack of funds forced bankruptcy in 1923. Some cars were built in 1924 from leftover parts.*

Cadillac, 1967, Fleetwood 75
Chevrolet, 1924, Touring
Chevrolet, 1936, Pickup Truck
Chrysler, 1926, Royal Sport Coupe
Climber, 1923, 6-50 Touring
Cord, 1928, L-29 Cabriolet
Cord, 1936, 810 Phaeton
Cretors, 1914, Popcorn Wagon
Dodge, 1933, Coupe
Essex, 1927, Boattail Speedster
Ford, 1914, Model T Speedster
Ford, 1915, Model T Coupelet
Ford, 1923, Model T Touring
Ford, 1926, Model T Touring
Ford, 1929, Model A Sedan
Ford, 1929, Model A Station Wagon
Ford, 1929, Model A Town Car
Ford, 1932, Model A Victoria
Ford, 1932, Phaeton
Ford, 1936, Roadster
Ford, 1938, Club Cabriolet
Ford, 1940, 2dr Sedan

Ford, 1955, Thunderbird
Hudson, 1938, Convertible
Kaiser, 1949, Convertible Sedan
Kaiser, 1954, Darrin
Lincoln, 1939, Zephyr Coupe Sedan
Lincoln, 1946, Continental
Maxwell, 1917, Touring
Metz, 1913, Runabout
MG, 1952, TD Roadster
Oldsmobile, 1905, French Front
Packard, 1936, Business Coupe
Packard, 1937, Town Car
Paige, 1912, Beverley Touring
Plymouth, 1932, Roadster
Plymouth, 1934, Sedan
Railton, 1936, Tourer
Rolls-Royce, 1929, Phantom I Coupe
Smith, 1916, Motor Wheel
Studebaker, 1923, Coupe
Terraplane, 1934, Coupe
Wills Sainte Claire, 1921

Reed's Museum of Automobiles

714 Central Avenue, Hot Springs, Arkansas 71901
(501) 321-1166

The museum is owned by the Tommy Reed family and presents a broad range of cars, ranging from Ford Model Ts to a Rolls-Royce. Also found are automotive-related artifacts and equipment, as well as historical items.

A significant portion of the collection is made up of Cadillacs, with three of them built in the 1950s. Cadillac introduced the tailfin to automobile styling with the 1948 Cadillac models, but the 1950s saw the greatest use of the style. What began as modest protuberances on the rear fenders, evolved in 1959 to garish projections with rocket-like taillights attached. Cadillac unveiled the Eldorado in 1953. Derived from a show car, the "Eldo" became the star of the line, and is highly sought after by collectors.

DIRECTIONS TO MUSEUM: The museum is in downtown Hot Springs.

ADMISSION COST: Adults $4.50; children $3.00

HOURS OF OPERATION: Open Mid-March through October daily 9am-5pm, until 9pm during summer. Call ahead during winter.

MUSEUM NOTES: There is a restaurant nearby. Film is not available.

A brochure is available.

Display Automobiles

Buick, 1928, Roadster
Cadillac, 1904
Cadillac, 1932, Roadster
Cadillac, 1954, Eldorado Convertible
Cadillac, 1956, DeVille
Cadillac, 1958, Eldorado Seville
Cadillac, 1966, Eldorado Convertible
Cadillac, 1973, Eldorado Convertible
Cadillac, 1975, Mirage Pickup Truck
Chevrolet, 1931, Cabriolet
Chevrolet, 1932, Coupe
Chevrolet, 1933, Eagle Cabriolet
Chrysler, 1929, Loche Cabriolet
Datsun, 1968, 1600 Roadster
Ford, 1917, Model T Pickup Truck

Ford, 1918, Model T
Ford, 1923, Model T Touring
Ford, 1929, Model A Pickup Truck
Ford, 1931, Model A Roadster
Ford, 1947, Convertible
Ford, 1961, Thunderbird
Ford, 1965, Thunderbird Convertible
Ford, 1966, Thunderbird Convertible
Lincoln, 1954, Capri
Lincoln, 1959, Continental Convertible
Marmon, 1927, Roadster
Packard, 1934, Limousine
Packard, 1937, Coupe
Rolls-Royce, 1928, Cabriolet
Smith, 1917, Motor Wheel Flyer

Behring Auto Museum

3750 Blackhawk Plaza Circle, Danville, California 94506
(510) 736-2280

The Behring Auto Museum is adjacent to the University of California at Berkeley Museum. Both museums benefit from funds provided by the Behring-Hofmann Educational Institution. The auto museum building and most of the auto collection were gifts of Kenneth E. Behring, a real estate developer. The W.E. Miller Transportation Research Library, the largest library devoted to auto and transportation topics on the West Coast, is located at the Behring Auto Museum.

Showcased is a priceless permanent collection of classic and rare automobiles, as well as significant cars on loan from foreign collections. The collection is comprised of cars from the turn-of-the-century to the 1960s.

1936 Mercedes-Benz 540K. *The 540K offered the driver high-speed cruising in luxurious style. Capable of 106 mph, the Mercedes was powered by an eight-cylinder, supercharged engine with a displacement of eight liters (488 cubic inches).*

1976 McClaren Indy Car. *Johnny Rutherford drove this Offenhauser-engined McClaren to victory in the rain-shortened Indianapolis 500 race in 1976.*

Among the noteworthy cars in the collection are a 1936 Mercedes-Benz 540K, a 1926 Daimler made of German silver for an Indian potentate, a 1935 Cadillac V-12 Aerodynamic Coupe, the 1975 McClaren that won the 1976 Indianapolis 500 and a 1910 Mercer Speedster.

Mercer built Speedsters in 1910 only. The museum's Speedster is the last known to exist. Mercer production began in 1910 in Trenton, New Jersey, which is in Mercer County, as a continuation of the Walter Automobile Company. Mercers were high-priced, fast automobiles, capable of carrying Ralph dePalma and Barney Oldfield on record-setting drives. But management and ownership problems resulted in a short life span. Production was discontinued in 1924, except for a few cars constructed from leftover parts. An attempted resurrection in 1929 failed during the onset of the Depression.

DIRECTIONS TO MUSEUM: From I-680 exit onto Sycamore Valley Rd. Drive east 4 miles on Sycamore Valley Rd., which becomes Camino Tassajara. Museum is in Blackhawk Plaza near intersection of Camino Tassajara and Blackhawk Rd.

ADMISSION COST: Adults $5.00; senior citizens and children $3.00. Tickets packages are available for both museums.

HOURS OF OPERATION: Open Tuesday, Thursday, Saturday and Sunday 10am-

5pm. Open Wednesday and Friday 10am-9pm. Call ahead for holiday schedule.

MUSEUM NOTES: There is a cafe onsite and restaurants nearby.

A brochure is available.

Display Automobiles

Adler, 1938, Competition
Alfa Romeo, 1931, Flying Star
Argonaut, 1958
Auburn, 1934, V-12 Sedan
Auburn, 1935, Roadster
Auburn, 1936, Labordette
Autocar, 1913, Gas Truck
Ballot, 1924, Speedster
Bentley, 1928, 8 Liter
Bentley, 1938, 4.25 Roadster
Bignan, 1923, Speedster
BMW, 1967, 2000CS
Bugatti, 1927, Speedster
Bugatti, 1932, Grand Prix Race Car
Bugatti, 1932, Type 50T
Bugatti, 1937, Type 57SC
Bugatti, 1939, Type 57C Sports Roadster
Buick, 1953, Roadmaster
Cadillac, 1906, Tulip Tourer
Cadillac, 1931, V-12
Cadillac, 1931, V-16 Custom
Cadillac, 1935, V-12 Aerodynamic
Cadillac, 1938, V-16
Cadillac, 1957, Eldorado
Chevrolet, 1933, Roadster
Chevrolet, 1953, Corvette
Chevrolet, 1955, Bel Air
Chevrolet, 1965, Corvette
Chrysler, 1928, 80
Chrysler, 1931, Waterhouse
Chrysler, 1946, Town & Country
Cord, 1929, L-29
Cord, 1937, Beverly Sedan
Daimler, 1926, Salon
Delage
Delahaye, 1948
DeLorean, 1981
Duesenberg, 1923, Model A
Ford, 1927, Model T Popcorn Truck
Ford, 1951, Country Squire
Ford, 1955, Crown Victoria
Ford, 1955, Thunderbird
Ford, 1958, Edsel

Ford, 1962, Thunderbird
Ford, 1965, Mustang
Franklin, 1910
Franklin, 1928, Sedan
Hispano-Suiza, 1924, Tulipwood
Hispano-Suiza, 1925, Monza HB6
Hispano-Suiza, 1926, Carriage
Hispano-Suiza, 1926, H6B
Hispano-Suiza, 1935, J-12 Pillarless
Horch, 1937, 853
Horch, 1937, Parade Car
Horch, 1938, 853
Horch, 1938, Roadster
Hudson, 1917, Super-6
Hudson, 1949, Convertible
Isotta Fraschini, 1928, Tipo 8A LeBaron
Jaguar, 1933, SS1 Tourer
Jaguar, 1948, Mk IV
Lagonda, 1939, Drophead V-12
Lanchester, 1910, Limousine
Lea Francis, 1951, 4 Seater
Leon Bolle, 1897, Tri-car
Leon Duray, 1917, Indy Race Car
Lincoln, 1930, 7 Passenger
Lincoln, 1934, V-12 Aerodynamic
Lincoln, 1941, Lowey
Lincoln, 1957, Premiere
Maserati, 1948, Grand Prix Race Car
Maybach, 1938, SW38
McClaren, 1975, Indy Race Car
Mercedes-Benz, 1929, Model SS
Mercedes-Benz, 1936, 540K
Mercedes-Benz, 1937, 320 Cab A
Mercedes-Benz, 1937, 500K
Mercedes-Benz, 1939, 540K
Mercedes-Benz, 1958, 300SC
Mercer, 1910, Speedster
MG, 1961, A Roadster
Minerva, 1929, Type AK
Nash-Healey, 1953, Roadster
Oldsmobile, 1901, Curved Dash
Packard, 1920, Limousine
Packard, 1930, Convertible Sedan

Packard, 1931, Phaeton
Packard, 1933, Roadster
Packard, 1933, Roadster
Packard, 1938, Limousine
Packard, 1939, 120 Darrin
Panhard, 1906, Tourer
Plymouth, 1953, Belmont
Plymouth, 1957, Fury Limited
Rolls-Royce, 1910, Hotel Taxi
Rolls-Royce, 1910, Silver Ghost
Rolls-Royce, 1925, Silver Ghost
Rolls-Royce, 1927, Phantom 1

Rolls-Royce, 1955, Silver Dawn
Rolls-Royce, Barclay
Rolls-Royce, Hooper
Rolls-Royce, Park Wood
Ruxton, 1933, Demonstrator
Sears, 1911, High-Wheeler
Stutz, 1912, Bearcat
Talbot
Talbot-Lago, 1951, Grand Sport
Triumph, 1947, Swallow
Tucker, 1948, 4dr Sedan

Deer Park Auto Museum

29013 Champagne Boulevard, Escondido, California 92026
(619) 749-1666

The museum adjoins the Deer Park Winery, thereby offering the visitor the opportunity to sample spirits and view the largest collection of American convertibles in the world. A wine tasting room, a wine shop, a market/deli, a park and a gift shop, which has an extensive selection of model kits for sale, are also located at Deer Park.

Almost all of the cars in the collection are convertibles or "open" cars. The first cars were predominately windowless, or open. Gradually, enclosed bodies became more prevalent, and appreciated, given the inadequate or nonexistent heaters of the day. But the pleasure of an open car remained and the convertible was developed, allowing the driver to raise or lower a canvas top. Canvas, however, had to be replaced after a few years and could be vandalized easily. So, Ford begat the Skyliner, a convertible hardtop that provided open-air motoring plus the security and durability of steel. Introduced in 1957, the Skyliner's articulated powered top separated into segments that folded into the trunk. The museum has two 1957 Skyliners on display from a production run of more than 20,000. Sales declined the next two years with less than 13,000 built in 1959, which was the last year for Skyliner production.

1928 Ford Model A Sport Coupe. *The Model A was first built in 1928. The only similarities with the previous model T were the L-head, four-cylinder engine and front and rear transverse, semi-elliptic springs. The Model A was another Ford triumph, selling over five million from 1928 until the appearance of the V-8 in 1932.*

1957 Ford Skyliner. *The Skyliner's retractable top provided the owner an open car for fair-weather cruising, as well as the security of an enclosed, metal top. Sacrificed, however, was use of the trunk, which was where the top resided when down. The Skyliner cost approximately $350 more than a convertible. Insufficient sales prompted Ford to drop the model after 1959.*

DIRECTIONS TO MUSEUM: From southbound I-15 exit onto Gopher Canyon Rd. and travel east to Champagne Blvd. Turn right onto Champagne Blvd. and follow to Deer Park.

From northbound I-15 exit onto Mountain Meadow Rd. and travel east to Champagne Blvd. Turn left onto Champagne Blvd. and follow to Deer Park.

ADMISSION COST: Adults $4.00; senior citizens $2.00; children under 12 yrs. free.

HOURS OF OPERATION: Open daily 10am-6pm in summer, 10am-5pm in winter. Closed New Year's Day, Thanksgiving and Christmas.

MUSEUM NOTES: Deer Park operates a delicatessen. There is a gift shop and film is available.

A brochure is available.

Display Automobiles

Amphicar, 1965
Benz, 1886, Velo
Buick, 1908, Model 10
Buick, 1929, Master 25th Anniversary
Buick, 1941, Phaeton
Buick, 1950, Riviera
Buick, 1950, Roadmaster
Buick, 1953, Skylark 50th Anniversary
Buick, 1958, Roadmaster
Buick, 1959, Electra
Buick, 1959, Le Sabre
Buick, 1960, Electra 225

1957 Chrysler 300C 2dr Hardtop. *The Chrysler 300 was introduced in 1955 in a package that provided both power, style and luxury. Subsequent model years were identified by a suffix letter. The 1965 "L" was the last letter-series 300 built (Chrysler also built lesser 300 Series models). The letter-series 300s are the most sought after Chryslers of their era.*

Buick, 1960, Le Sabre
Buick, 1962, Skylark
Buick, 1972, GS455
Buick, 1975
Cadillac, 1953, Eldorado
Cadillac, 1959, Eldorado
Cadillac, 1959, Limousine
Cadillac, 1960, Eldorado
Cadillac, 1960, Limousine
Cadillac, 1962, Eldorado
Cadillac, 1962, Limousine
Cadillac, 1976
Chevrolet, 1956, Corvette
Chevrolet, 1957, Bel Air
Chevrolet, 1959, Bel Air
Chevrolet, 1963, Corvair Monza
Chrysler, 1931, Roadster
Chrysler, 1948, Woody
Chrysler, 1957, 300C
Chrysler, 1960, Imperial
Chrysler, 1962, 300
Chrysler, 1982
Crosley, 1949, Hot Shot
Dodge, 1955, Custom Royal Lancer

Edsel, 1958, Citation
Ford, 1915, Model T Speedster
Ford, 1928, Sport Coupe
Ford, 1929, Hot Rod
Ford, 1949, Custom
Ford, 1953, Crestline 50th Anniversary
Ford, 1957, Skyliner
Ford, 1957, Thunderbird
Ford, 1965, Mustang
Ford, 1983, Mustang
Franklin, 1928, Runabout
Hudson, 1950, Pacemaker
Indy Race Car, 1966
Kaiser-Darrin, 1954
Lincoln, 1959, Continental
Lincoln, 1946, Cabriolet
Lincoln, 1957, Premiere
Lincoln, 1962
Mercedes-Benz, 1968, 250SL
Mercury, 1955, Montclaire
Mercury, 1971, Cougar
MG, 1959, A Roadster
MG, 1967, B Roadster
Muntz-Jet, 1955

Nash, 1950, Rambler
Nash, 1956, Metropolitan
Nash-Healey, 1953
Oldsmobile, 1903, Curved Dash
Oldsmobile, 1953, Fiesta
Packard, 1935, Model 120
Packard, 1941, Model 110A
Packard, 1949, 50th Anniversary
Packard, 1951, 24th Series
Packard, 1954, Carribean

Plymouth, 1969, Roadrunner
Pontiac, 1953, Chieftain
Pontiac, 1964, GTO
Studebaker, 1915, Touring
Studebaker, 1950, Champion
Studebaker, 1950, Pickup Truck
Studebaker, 1952, Champion 100th
   Anniversary
Studebaker, 1959, Pickup Truck
Studebaker, 1960, Pickup Truck

Dennis Mitosinka's Classic Cars

619 E. 4th Street, Santa Ana, California 92701
(714) 953-5303

The Mitosinka collection focuses on cars built after World War II. There are, however, several pre-war cars of interest, namely a 1929 Hispano-Suiza built for the King of Spain and a 1929 Rolls-Royce Phantom I Playboy.

On display is a 1957 Pontiac Bonneville convertible equipped with the rare fuel injection engine option. Although fuel injection was only offered two years, its availability, along with the introduction of a new V-8 engine in 1955, indicated to buyers that Pontiac was shedding its mundane mantle. Bunkie Knudsen became Pontiac general manager in 1956, and he, along with Pete Estes and John DeLorean, changed the staid image of Pontiac. Powerful engines, stock car racing and aggressive styling positioned Pontiac squarely in the youth market when "baby boomers" reached car-buying age. The Pontiac GTO that started the "muscle car" era in 1964 was the product of the Pontiac team of the mid-1950s, and was subsequently responsible for Pontiac's climb to number three carmaker in the 1960s.

DIRECTIONS TO MUSEUM: From I-5 exit onto 4th St. and travel west to facility.

ADMISSION COST: Adults $2.00; senior citizens and children $2.00.

HOURS OF OPERATION: Call ahead.

MUSEUM NOTES: There is a restaurant nearby and a gift shop onsite. Film is not available.

Display Automobiles

Armstrong Siddeley, 1946
Cadillac, 1954, Deville Coupe
Cadillac, 1954, Eldorado Convertible
Cadillac, 1960, Eldorado Seville
Chevrolet, 1932, Roadster
Chevrolet, 1969, Camaro Convertible
Chrysler, 1934, Airflow
Chrysler, 1962, 300 Convertible
Chrysler, 1962, 300H Hardtop
Daimler, 1963, SP250 Roadster
Delahaye, 1946, 135M Convertible
Facel Ford, 1952, Custom Coupe
Ford, 1949, Custom Convertible
Ford, 1965, Thunderbird Convertible

Ghia, 1963, 1500 Coupe
Hispano-Suiza, 1929, Convertible
Jaguar, 1973, XK-E Convertible
Lincoln, 1931, Sedan
Lincoln, 1955, Capri Convertible
Lincoln, 1964, Continental Convertible
Nash, 1950, Airflight Convertible
Nash, 1951, Airflight Convertible
Oldsmobile, 1962, F-85 Jetfire Coupe
Packard, 1948, Super 8 Convertible
Pontiac, 1957, Bonneville Convertible
Rolls-Royce, 1929, Phantom I Playboy
Spohn, 1952, Custom Convertible
Studebaker, 1951, Champion Convertible

Hays Antique Truck Museum

2000 E. Main Street, P.O. Box 2347, Woodland, California 95695
(916) 666-1044

With over 120 trucks, the Hays Antique Truck Museum is the largest museum specializing in trucks in the country. The bulk of the collection was manufactured before 1940, which means many are equipped with wooden wheels and hard rubber tires characteristic of early trucks.

For the auto enthusiast, the museum provides an opportunity to view some of the trucks built by well-known auto makers. Chevrolet, Dodge and Ford are widely known for their trucks, and examples are on display. Other car manufacturers that also built trucks, and are on display, include Studebaker, Reo, Packard, Pierce-Arrow, Kissel, Maxwell, White and Velie.

DIRECTIONS TO MUSEUM: The museum is located off of I-5 on County Rd. 102.

ADMISSION COST: Adults $3.00; children $1.00.

HOURS OF OPERATION: Open Monday-Friday 8am-4pm; Saturday and Sunday 9am-3pm. Closed New Year's Day, Christmas Eve and Christmas.

MUSEUM NOTES: There is a restuarant nearby. Film is not available.

A brochure is available.

Display Trucks

Acme, 1929, 5 1/2-Ton Chassis
Aetna, 1916, 2 1/2-Ton Chassis
Alco, 1910, 3 1/2-Ton Chassis
All American, 1919, 1-Ton Chassis
Armleder, 1924, 1 1/2-Ton Chassis

Atterbury, 1930
Autocar, 1919, 1 1/2-Ton Flatbed
Autocar, 1926, 2-Ton Flatbed
Bethlehem, 1923, 2-Ton Chassis
Brockway, 1927, 2 1/2-Ton Chassis

Early trucks were not equipped with the comforts of today's trucks. The driver wrestled a stubborn steering wheel and bounced along on solid-rubber tires while exposed to the elements.

1930 Linn. *This unique truck is a 1930 Linn dump truck. Note the half-track rear drive.*

C.T. Electric, 1916, 5-Ton Flatbed
Chevrolet, 1929, 1 1/2-Ton Flatbed
Chevrolet, 1930, Pickup Truck
Chevrolet, 1935, Pickup Truck
Chevrolet, 1941, 1 1/2-Ton Dump Truck
Chicago, 1918, 2 1/2-Ton Stakebed
Clark, 1925, 1/2-Ton Dump Truck
Clydesdale, 1920
Coleman, 1925, 2-Ton Chassis
Commerce, 1919, 1-Ton Grain Truck
Dart, 1918, 2-Ton Chassis
Day Elder, 1921, 2-Ton Chassis
De Martini, 1925, 2-Ton Chassis
Dearborn, 1921, 1 1/2-Ton Chassis
Defiance, 1921
Denby, 1917, 1 1/2-Ton Chassis
Detroit Motor Wagon, 1911
Diamond T, 1929, 1 1/2-Ton Chassis
Diamond T, 1937, 1 1/2-Ton Tank Truck
Diamond T McDonald, 1946, 3-Ton Flatbed
Doane, 1918, 6-Ton Flatbed
Dodge, 1930, 1/2-Ton Express
Dodge, 1936, 1 1/2-Ton Stakebed
Dodge, 1941, 1 1/2-Ton Chassis
Douglas, 1917, 2 1/2-Ton Chassis
Duplex, 1923, Chassis

Fageol, 1919, 4-Ton Chassis
Fageol, 1927, 2 1/2-Ton Chassis
Fageol, 1929, 1-Ton Chassis
Fageol, 1930, 3 1/2-Ton Chassis
Fageol, 1938, 3 1/2-Ton Flatbed
Fargo, 1933
Federal, 1917, 1 1/2-Ton Chassis
Federal Knight, 1925, 1-Ton Express
Fisher, 1926, 1 1/2-Ton Chassis
Ford, 1920, 1-Ton Chassis
Ford, 1925, 1-Ton Flatbed
Ford, 1928, 1-Ton Flatbed
Ford, 1932, 1 1/2-Ton Dump Truck
Ford, 1938, 1 1/2-Ton Flatbed
Freightliner, 1949, Tractor
FWD, 1918, 3-Ton Chassis
Galloway, 1908, 1/2-Ton Flatbed
Garford, 1916, 2-Ton Tank Truck
Gary, 1921
GMC, 1922, 2-Ton Chassis
GMC, 1924, 5-Ton Chassis
Gotfredson, 1922, 3-Ton Chassis
Graham Brothers, 1929, 3-Ton Flat Body
Gramm-Bernstein, 1919, 3 1/2-Ton Chassis
Hawkeye, 1925
Hug, 1930, 3 1/2-Ton Dump Truck

Indiana, 1927, 1 1/2-Ton Stakebed
Inertnational, 1912, Pickup Truck
International, 1922, 3-Ton Chassis
International, 1929, 3-Ton Chassis
International, 1947, Paddy Wagon
International, 1948, 2-Ton Dump Truck
Jumbo, 1919, 2 1/2-Ton Flatbed
Kelly Springfield, 1914
Kenworth, 1930, 3-Ton Dump Truck
Kenworth, 1954, Half Cab
Kenworth, 1955, Half Cab
King Zeitler, 1919, 2-Ton Chassis
Kissel, 1914, 2-Ton Flatbed
Kissel, 1916, 2-Ton Chassis
Kleiber, 1918, 3 1/2-Ton Flatbed
Knox, 1901, 1/2-Ton Flatbed
Koehler, 1916, 1-Ton Chassis
L.A. Trailer, 1918, 2-Ton Chassis
Larrabee, 1923, 1-Ton Chassis
Linn, 1930, Half-Track Dump Truck
Locomobile, 1914, Chassis
Maccar, 1919
Mack, 1918, 1 1/2-Ton Chassis
Mack, 1920, 2 1/2-Ton Tank Truck
Mack, 1921, 2 1/2-Ton Log Truck
Mack, 1922, 3 1/2-Ton Chassis
Mack, 1922, 7 1/2-Ton Chassis
Mack, 1925, 2 1/2-Ton Beet Truck
Mack, 1929, 10-Ton Chassis
Mack, 1947, 10-Ton Chassis
Marmon Herrington, 1940, 1 1/2-Ton Chassis
Master Jr., 1920, 1 1/2-Ton Chassis
Maxwell, 1916, 1-Ton Chassis
McDonald, 1922, 6-Ton Flatbed
McDonald, 1947, 3-Ton Stakebed
Menominee, 1917, 1-Ton Express
Moreland, 1927, 3-Ton Boom Truck
Moreland, 1929, 3-Ton Winch
Moreland, 1929, 5-Ton Chassis
Nash, 1919, 1-Ton Chassis
Nash Quad, 1918, 2-Ton Flatbed
Nelson Le Moon, 1915, Chassis
Old Reliable, 1921, 2 1/2-Ton Flatbed
Oldsmobile, 1919, 1-Ton Grain Truck
Oneida, 1917, 1-Ton Chassis
OshKosh, 1922, 2 1/2-Ton Chassis
Packard, 1910, 2-Ton Chassis
Packard, 1911, 2-Ton Flatbed
Packard, 1918, 3 1/2-Ton Flatbed
Paige, 1920
Parker, 1919, 3 1/2-Ton Chassis

Patriot, 1920, 1 1/2-Ton Chassis
Peterbilt, 1939, 5-Ton Tractor
Peterbilt, 1946, 5-Ton Tractor
Pierce-Arrow, 1918, 2-Ton Flatbed
Pierce-Arrow, 1919, 5-Ton Flatbed
Powell, 1955, Pickup Truck
Randolph, 1911, 1-Ton Flatbed
Relay, 1929, 3-Ton Chassis
Reliance, 1910
Reo, 1928, 3-Ton Chassis
Republic, 1919, 2-Ton Chassis
Riker, 1917, Fire Truck
Rowe, 1921, 2 1/2-Ton Chassis
Rugby, 1928, 1-Ton Stakebed
Ruggles, 1924, 1-Ton Chassis
Sampson, 1922, 1-Ton Chassis
Sandow, 1915, 1 1/2-Ton Chassis
Schacht, 1928, 4-Ton Dump Truck
Sears, 1909
Service, 1921, 5-Ton Chassis
Signal, 1916, 1 1/2-Ton Chassis
Standard, 1920, 5-Ton Chassis
Sterling, 1923, 1 1/2-Ton Chassis
Sterling, 1941
Sterling, 1953, 10-Ton Chassis
Stewart, 1920, 2-Ton Chassis
Stoughton, 1927
Studebaker, 1902, Electric Car
Studebaker, 1946, 1-Ton Flatbed
Titan, 1927
Traffic, 1920, 2-Ton Chassis
Transport, 1918, 2-Ton Stakebed
United, 1927, 2-Ton Chassis
USA, 1918, 5-Ton Flatbed
Velie, 1919, 3 1/2-Ton Chassis
Walker Electric, 1918, 2 1/2-Ton Chassis
Walter Snowfighter, 1925, 7 1/2-Ton
   Snowfighter
White, 1914, 5-Ton Crane
White, 1917, 3-Ton Flatbed
White, 1920, 5-Ton Chassis
White, 1924, Chassis
White, 1927, 1 1/2-Ton Bus
White, 1929, 3-Ton Chassis
White, 1956, Tractor
White Hickory, 1921, 2 1/2-Ton Chassis
Wilcox, 1919
Winther, 1917, 6-Ton Log Truck
Winther Marwin, 1920
Wolverine, 1918, 1-Ton Chassis
Yellow-Knight, 1927, 1-Ton Express

Natural History Museum of Los Angeles County

900 Exposition Boulevard, Los Angeles, California 90007
(213) 744-3466

On display in the museum are exhibits concerned with the natural history of California and the Southwest. Areas of interest include dinosaurs and fossils, marine life, mammals, birds, gemstones and minerals, plus many hands-on exhibits.

At publication, the museum is exhibiting a 1902 Oldsmobile. All other cars in the museum's collection, approximately 74 cars, are in storage until a new building is constructed at the corner of Wilshire Boulevard and Fairfax Avenue. Scheduled completion is 1993. In addition to the museum's collection, Hollywood cars, race cars, prototype and experimental vehicles on loan will be displayed.

Contact museum for opening date and visitor information.

1932 Duesenberg Model J. *The body of the museum's Duesenberg Model J was built by Murphy, one of several coach builders that constructed bodies on the Model J chassis. The chassis alone cost $8,500 to $9,500, with a total cost of approximately $13,000, sometimes more.*

San Diego Automotive Museum

2080 Pan American Plaza, Balboa Park, San Diego, California 92112
(619) 231-2886

The museum is located in Balboa Park, which is a complex of museums, theaters, exhibit buildings and entertainment facilities that address areas of interest for virtually everyone.

The museum's collection is broad-based with cars from all decades of auto production. Some cars are significant due to their influence in automotive evolution, while some are unique by virtue of their design, engineering or meteoric lifespan.

In the museum's inventory is a car that fits most of the aforementioned points, the Tucker. Creation of the car by Preston Tucker was depicted in the 1989 movie *Tucker*. Although not as radical as Tucker's original plans, the Tucker automobile built in 1948 was altogether different than the typical car of the day. Three headlights provided illumination at night — the center headlight turned in the direction the car was steered. An air-cooled helicopter engine that was converted to liquid-cooling provided power. The heater system used an independently controlled pump so heat was available when the engine wasn't running. Other features included four-wheel independent suspension, disc brakes and a safety windshield. But Preston Tucker's ambition of becoming a major auto builder was cut short by financial and legal problems that led to extensive court battles. Although Tucker eventually won in court, the company couldn't overcome its financial problems and the assets were liquidated. Only 51 Tucker cars were built.

DIRECTIONS TO MUSEUM: The museum is located off of Park Blvd. in the museum area of Balboa Park. Facilities throughout the park provide maps.

1948 Tucker 4dr Sedan. *Alex Tremulis designed the sleek body of the Tucker. The flowing lines were distinctively different from the bulbous shapes of its contemporaries. The top of the unique doors occupied a portion of the roof area, a style next seen on the 1963 Corvette and not uncommon today.*

ADMISSION COST: Adults $4.00; senior citizens $3.00; 13-17 yrs. $2.50; 6-12 yrs. $1.00. Ticket packages are available in the gift shops throughout Balboa Park that offer savings on multi-museum tickets.

HOURS OF OPERATION: Open daily 10am-4:30pm. Every fourth Tuesday of month free. Closed New Year's Day, Thanksgiving and Christmas.

MUSEUM NOTES: There are restaurants in the park. Film can be purchased in the gift shop.

A brochure is available.

Display Automobiles

Allard, 1953, Model J2
AMX III, 1967
Barnel, 1971, Gordini Race Car
Bentley, 1927, Tourer
Benz, 1886
Brewster-Ford, 1934, Sedan de Ville
Cadillac, 1906, Coupe
Chrysler, 1935, Airflow
Cord, 1937, 812 Beverly Salon
Corvette, 1954
Crane-Simplex, 1916, Tourer
Crofton, 1960, Bug
DeLorean, 1977
Elva, 1960, Formula Junior Race Car
Fiat, 1959, Jolly
Ford, 1905, Model B
Ford, 1910, Model T
Ford, 1930, Model A Town Sedan
Ford, 1931, Model A Victoria
Holsman, 1907
Hudson, 1950, Commodore 8 Convertible
Hunt, 1910
Indy Race Car, 1981
International Harvester, 1907

International Harvester, 1910
Isotta Fraschini, 1929, Castagna
Lincoln, 1956, Continental
Lincoln, 1968, Presidential Limousine
Lincoln, 1992, Mark X Prototype
Mercedes, 1902
Mercedes-Benz, 1937, 170
Mercedes-Benz, 1938, 540K Cabriolet
Mercury, 1948, Woody
Messerschmidt, 1954, K-175
MG, 1954, TF Roadster
Pegaso, 1956, Z102
Pierce-Arrow, 1915, Town Car
Pierce-Arrow, 1933, Silver Arrow
Porsche, 1963, Model C
Renault, 1982, R5 Turbo
Rolls-Royce, 1931, Phaeton Phantom I
Scorpion, 1956
Standard, 1934, Model 9
Star, 1922, Speedster
Stutz, 1914, Bearcat
Thomas, 1906, Flyer
Tucker, 1948, 4dr Sedan
Unser, 1981, Indy Race Car

San Sylmar-Merle Norman
Classic Beauty Collection

15180 Bledsoe Street, Sylmar, California 91342
(818) 367-1085; Tour Reservations (818) 367-2251

As might be expected of a collection underwritten by a cosmetics company and the company's co-founder, J.B. Nethercutt, the theme of the collection is characterized by beauty, in particular, the display of fine functional art in opulent surroundings. From gold leaf ceilings to marble columns to crystal chandeliers, the structure is no less stunning than the prized possessions contained within. Along with the auto collection is one of the world's largest and finest assemblages of orchestrions and music boxes, as well as other beautiful artifacts.

The auto collection contains over 200 cars. Only a portion are on display, but the cars are rotated regularly. The cars are showcased in two rooms, the Grand Salon showroom containing a variety of classic cars and the Rolls-Royce Room featuring examples of the distinguished marque.

The Rolls-Royce Room, with its extensive collection of Rolls-Royce automobiles, offers the visitor an opportunity to view the evolution of one of the most recognized and respected marques in the world. The progenitor of the line was the Royce auto built by Frederick Royce in Manchester, England, in 1904. Needing a sales organization, Royce contracted with Charles Rolls' company to sell the car, with Rolls stipulation that the car be named the Rolls-Royce. In 1906 the companies merged. The Rolls-Royce became the vehicle of choice for the elite of the world, and the company never lost money from the time of its founding until 1971 (problems in aircraft engine manufacturing bankrupted the company in 1971). In Springfield, Massachusetts, Rolls-Royce of America constructed cars from 1919 to 1935. Overshadowed by the English firm and lacking funds, the U.S. company sold its assets to Pierce-Arrow in 1936.

DIRECTIONS TO MUSEUM: From I-5 exit onto Roxford and travel east on Roxford to San Fernando Rd. Turn right onto San Fernando Rd. and follow to Bledsoe St. Turn left onto Bledsoe St. and follow to San Sylmar.

From I-210 exit onto Polk and travel west on Polk to Glenoaks Blvd. Turn right onto Glenoaks Blvd. and follow to Bledsoe St. Turn left onto Bledsoe St. and follow to San Sylmar.

ADMISSION COST: Free.

HOURS OF OPERATION: Tours at 10am and 1:30pm.

MUSEUM NOTES: Admission is by tour only. Call for tour reservations; calling well ahead is recommended. There is a restaurant nearby. Film is not available.

A brochure is available.

Silverado Classic Car Collection

Napa, California
(707) 224-6735 or 224-7732

The collection has several interesting cars on display including: the 1953 Buick Skylark hardtop prototype — the only one built; a 1947 Chevrolet woody convertible — one of five known; the 1955 Devin sports car judged "most beautiful" at Seattle World's Fair; a 1969 Dodge California Highway Patrol car; a Corvette-powered 1957 Devin; a 1930 Ford Model A racer with aluminum "boattail" speedster body.

Special emphasis is placed on woodys and vintage race cars. The cars exhibited are rotated periodically.

DIRECTIONS TO MUSEUM: Call Silverado for directions.

HOURS OF OPERATION: By appointment only.

ADMISSION COST: Adults $3.00; senior citizens $2.00; children $1.00.

MUSEUM NOTES: There are many restaurants in Napa. Film is not available onsite

Towe Ford Museum

2200 Front Street, Sacramento, California 95818
(916) 442-6802

In 1986 the California Vehicle Foundation brought a large portion of the Towe Ford collection from Montana (also found in this book) for display in Sacramento. Opened in
1987, the museum has on display the most complete collection of Ford cars and trucks
in the world. Virtually every model year from 1903 through 1971 is on display.

Henry Ford's greatest achievement was the Model T. But before he started his spectacular ascent to the top, there were two failed attempts at car manufacturing. In 1899
Ford was in charge of producing cars for the new Detroit Automobile Company, but no
cars were built and the company folded in 1901. In 1901 the Henry Ford Company
was organized, but Ford failed to construct a car for sale and left the company. The financiers decided to stay in business and renamed the firm Cadillac Automobile Company, the ancestor of today's Cadillac Division of General Motors. The third try was the
charm for Henry Ford. He again found backers for his dream of producing automobiles,
and in 1902 the Ford and Malcolmson Company was organized (in 1903 renamed the
Ford Motor Company). The company was moderately successful at producing and selling cars during its early years. Then in 1908 the company's fortunes rose spectacularly
with the unveiling of Henry's dream car, the Model T.

1947 Ford V-8 Sportsman. *Ford only built 2,274 of the Sportsman model and few survive
today. The top is hydraulically actuated and wood adorns the doors and rear quarter-panels. It
was the most expensive model of the 1947 Fords, with a price tag of $2,282.*

1940 Ford Station Wagon. *This Ford woody carried a price tag of $875. The last 60 hp V-8 was built in 1940. The engine was conceived in 1937 as the base engine of the Standard line, with the bigger 85 hp V-8 engine available as an option in the Standard line and as the base engine in the Deluxe line. Buyers weren't interested in the small V-8, however, and in 1941 the base engine for Standard models became a 90 hp inline six-cylinder.*

DIRECTIONS TO MUSEUM: From the north on I-5: Exit at J St. and turn right onto 3rd St. Follow 3rd St. then turn right onto O St. Follow O St. to Front St. and turn left onto Front St.

From the south on I-5: Exit onto Broadway and follow Broadway to Front St. Turn right onto Front St.

From the west on Bus. I-80: Take Downtown Sacramento Exit (Capitol Ave.). Cross the Tower Bridge and immediately turn right onto Front St.

From the east on Bus. I-80: Exit onto 10th St. then turn left onto 11th St. Follow 11th St. to Broadway and turn right onto Broadway. Follow Broadway to Front St. and turn right onto Front St.

ADMISSION COST: Adults $5.00; senior citizens $4.50; students: high school $2.50; grade school $1.00.

HOURS OF OPERATION: Open daily 10am-6pm. Closed New Year's Day, Thanksgiving and Christmas.

1936 Jaguar SS 4dr Sedan. *Jaguars were originally built as a model in the car line of SS Cars Ltd., an outgrowth of the Swallow Sidecar Company. Jaguar did not become a marque until 1945. The museum's Jaguar was one of only 136 built, and a winner in car show competition.*

MUSEUM NOTES: There is a restaurant nearby. Film is available in the gift shop.

A brochure is available.

Display Automobiles

Buick, 1938, 4dr Sedan
Cadillac, 1903, Model A
Cadillac, 1947, Limousine
Chevrolet, 1928, Coach
Chevrolet, 1967, Camaro
Dodge, 1915, 4dr Touring
Edsel, 1958, Sedan
Edsel, 1959, Station Wagon
Edsel, 1960, 4dr Sedan
Ford, 1903, Model A Runabout
Ford, 1904, Model B Touring
Ford, 1905, Model C Runabout
Ford, 1905, Model F Touring
Ford, 1906, Model K Touring
Ford, 1906, Model N Runabout
Ford, 1907, Model R Runabout

Ford, 1908, Model S Runabout
Ford, 1908, Model T Touring
Ford, 1909, Model T Touring
Ford, 1910, Model T Touring
Ford, 1911, Model T Torpedo
Ford, 1911, Model T Touring
Ford, 1912, Model T Touring
Ford, 1913, Model T Express Wagon
Ford, 1913, Model T Touring
Ford, 1914, Model T Runabout
Ford, 1915, Model T Couplet
Ford, 1915, Model T Town Car
Ford, 1917, Model T Touring
Ford, 1917, Model T Truck
Ford, 1918, Model T Touring
Ford, 1919, Model T Sedan

Ford, 1920, Model T Touring
Ford, 1921, Model T Runabout
Ford, 1922, Model T Coupe
Ford, 1923, Model T 4dr Sedan
Ford, 1923, Model T Roadster
Ford, 1923, Model TT Fire Truck
Ford, 1925, Model T Coupe
Ford, 1926, Model T 2dr Sedan
Ford, 1926, Model T Coupe
Ford, 1926, Model T Roadster
Ford, 1926, Model TT Truck
Ford, 1927, Model T Touring
Ford, 1928, Model A Pickup Truck
Ford, 1928, Model A Sport Coupe
Ford, 1928, Model AR 2dr Sedan
Ford, 1929, Model A Briggs 4dr Sedan
Ford, 1929, Model A Mail Truck
Ford, 1929, Model A Phaeton
Ford, 1929, Model A Pickup Truck
Ford, 1929, Model A Roadster
Ford, 1929, Model A Station Wagon
Ford, 1929, Model A Town Car
Ford, 1929, Model AA Truck
Ford, 1929, Model AA Truck
Ford, 1930, Dump Truck
Ford, 1930, Model A 2dr Sedan
Ford, 1930, Model A Coupe
Ford, 1930, Model A Phaeton
Ford, 1930, Model A Pickup Truck
Ford, 1930, Model A Station Wagon
Ford, 1930, Model A Town Sedan
Ford, 1931, Model A 2dr Sedan
Ford, 1931, Model A 4dr Town Sedan
Ford, 1931, Model A Cabriolet
Ford, 1931, Model A Phaeton
Ford, 1931, Model A Pickup Truck
Ford, 1931, Model A Roadster
Ford, 1931, Model A Victoria
Ford, 1931, Model A-400 Convertible Sedan
Ford, 1931, Model AA Fire Truck
Ford, 1931, Model AA Mail Truck
Ford, 1932, Model B 2dr Sedan
Ford, 1932, Model B 4dr Sedan
Ford, 1932, Model B Cabriolet
Ford, 1932, Model B Coupe
Ford, 1932, Model B Roadster
Ford, 1932, Model B Station Wagon
Ford, 1932, Model B-400 Convertible Sedan
Ford, 1933, 4dr Sedan
Ford, 1933, Cabriolet
Ford, 1933, Coupe

Ford, 1933, Phaeton
Ford, 1933, Roadster
Ford, 1934, 2dr Sedan
Ford, 1934, Phaeton
Ford, 1935, 4dr Sedan
Ford, 1935, Phaeton
Ford, 1935, Pickup Truck
Ford, 1936, Cabriolet
Ford, 1936, Convertible Sedan
Ford, 1936, Roadster
Ford, 1936, Station Wagon
Ford, 1937, 2dr Sedan
Ford, 1937, Convertible Sedan
Ford, 1937, Coupe
Ford, 1937, Phaeton
Ford, 1937, Pickup Truck
Ford, 1938, 2dr Sedan
Ford, 1938, Phaeton
Ford, 1939, 2dr Sedan
Ford, 1939, Convertible Sedan
Ford, 1940, 2dr Sedan
Ford, 1940, Coupe
Ford, 1940, Station Wagon
Ford, 1941, 4dr Sedan
Ford, 1941, Coupe
Ford, 1941, Pickup Truck
Ford, 1942, 2dr Sedan
Ford, 1942, Jeep
Ford, 1946, 4dr Sedan
Ford, 1946, Convertible Coupe
Ford, 1947, Sportsman
Ford, 1948, 4dr Sedan
Ford, 1949, Station Wagon
Ford, 1950, 4dr Sedan
Ford, 1951, 2dr Sedan
Ford, 1952, 2dr Sedan
Ford, 1955, Thunderbird
Ford, 1957, Skyliner
Ford, 1958, 4dr Sedan
Ford, 1960, 4dr Sedan
Ford, 1961, Falcon
Ford, 1962, 2dr Sedan
Ford, 1963, Hardtop
Ford, 1964, Convertible
Ford, 1965, Mustang
Ford, 1967, Falcon
Ford, 1967, Mustang
Ford, 1969, Hardtop
Ford, 1970, Maverick
Ford, 1971, Pinto
Ford, 1972, Military 4dr Sedan

Ford, 1976, Thunderbird
Jaguar, 1936, SS
Lincoln, 1957, Continental
Lincoln, 1963, Continental
Lincoln, 1970, Continental
Mercury, 1939, Sedan
Mercury, 1941, Coupe

Mercury, 1959, 4dr Sedan
Mercury, 1967, Cougar
Mercury, 1970, 4dr Sedan
Pontiac, 1953, Ambulance
Simplex, 1937, Model H
Star, 1922, 4dr Touring Sedan
Studebaker, 1950, 4dr Sedan

Forney Transportation Museum

1416 Platte Street, Denver, Colorado 80202
(303) 433-3643

The Forney Transportation Museum is housed in the historic former power station for the Denver trolley system. The site also marks the birthplace of Denver. Traders and trappers congregated at the confluence of the South Platte River and Cherry Creek establishing a community that evolved into Denver.

The museum has on display carriages, farm machinery, engines, trolleys and railroad equipment. Several pieces of railroad rolling stock are presented including the immense "Big Boy" steam locomotive, the largest of its type in the world.

The collection is vast and includes all the more familiar marques: Ford, Chevrolet, Studebaker, Packard, Lincoln, Cadillac, etc. Distributed through the collection are examples of rarely seen marques, such as Searchmont, Muntz, Nyberg, Messerschmitt, Metz, Knox, Jewett, Empire, EMF, Cole, Apperson and Steyr. Noteworthy celebrity cars include a Kissel Gold Bug Roadster owned by Amelia Earhart and a Rolls-Royce owned by Prince Aly Kahn.

DIRECTIONS TO MUSEUM: From I-25 southbound take Exit 212C onto Central St. Follow Central St. and turn left onto 15th St. Follow 15th St. and turn right onto Platte St.

From I-25 northbound take Exit 211 to Water St. Follow Water St. to Platte St.

ADMISSION COST: Adults $4.00; senior citizens $3.00; students $2.00; children $1.00.

HOURS OF OPERATION: Open daily in summer 9am-5pm and winter 10am-5pm.

MUSEUM NOTES: There is a restaurant nearby. The museum has a gift shop, but film is not available.

A brochure is available.

Display Automobiles

Aero Car, 1959
AMC, 1972, Hornet 4dr Sedan
Apperson, 1915, Jack Rabbit Touring
Auto-Buggy, 1916
Bradley, 1974, GT Kit Car
Brewster, 1934, Town Sedan
Brush, 1910, Roadster
Buick, 1912, Touring
Buick, 1920, Touring

Buick, 1921, Opera Coupe
Buick, 1939, Limousine
Buick, 1939, Model 39-31 Limousine
Buick, 1951, Super 4dr Sedan
Cadillac, 1905, Touring
Cadillac, 1915, Sedan
Cadillac, 1923, V-8 Touring
Cadillac, 1938, Hearse
Cadillac, 1949

Cadillac, 1966, Station Wagon
Cadillac, 1968, Brougham 4dr Hardtop
Cadillac, 1976, Bi-Centennial Philadelphia
    Limousine
Chevrolet, 1926, Coupe
Chevrolet, 1929, 4dr Landau Sedan
Chevrolet, 1962, Convertible
Chrysler, 1947, New Yorker
Citroen, 1957, Voiture
Citroen, 1963, Club Coupe
Cole, 1918, Roadster
Cord, 1937, Sedan
Crosley, 1950, Hot Shot
Daimler, 1951, Model DE36 Limousine
DeSoto, 1949, 4dr Sedan
Detroit Electric, 1914, Opera Coupe
Dodge, 1921, 4dr Sedan
Dodge, 1926, Model B 4dr Sedan
Dodge, 1929, Sedan
Dodge, 1962, Dart 2dr Hardtop
Edsel, 1958, Station Wagon
EMF, 1912, Touring
Empire, 1909, Touring
Essex, 1921, Coupe
Fiat, 1923, Model 505 Limousine
Ford, 1905, Model F
Ford, 1915, Model T Touring
Ford, 1924, Model T 2dr
Ford, 1926, Model T Coupe
Ford, 1930, Model A Roadster
Ford, 1936
Ford, 1941, Coupe
Ford, 1957, Thunderbird
Ford, 1968, Thunderbird 4dr Hardtop
Ford, 1970, Mustang Boss 302
Franklin, 1905
Franklin, 1918, Touring Chummy
Franklin, 1931, 4dr Sedan
Hispano-Suiza, 1923, Victoria Touring
Hudson, 1911, Touring
Hudson, 1915, Model 6-40 Touring
Hudson, 1915, Roadster
Hupmobile, 1922, Roadster
International, 1909
Isetta, 1958, Motorcoupe
Jaguar, 1950, Convertible
Jewett, 1924, Touring
Kissel, 1917, Double Eagle Touring

Kissel, 1921, Model 45 Touring
Kissel, 1923, Gold Bug Roadster
Kissel, 1924, Brougham
Kissel, 1927, Roadster
Knox, 1904
Lincoln, 1927, 4dr Sedan
Lincoln, 1937, Model K Roadster
Lincoln, 1941, Zephyr
Lincoln, 1947
Lincoln, 1954, Hardtop
Locomobile, 1900, Dos-E-Dos
Locomobile, 1901, Steamer Runabout
Marmon, 1922, Model 34 Touring
Marmon, 1930, 4dr Sedan
Maxwell, 1906, Roadster
Mercedes-Benz, 1928, Model K Limousine
Mercury, 1950, 4dr Sedan
Messerschmitt, 1955
Metz, 1912, Roadster
Moon, 1925, Sedan
Moon, 1926, Touring
Muntz, 1954, Roadster
Nash, 1958, Convertible
Nyberg, 1910, Roadster
Oldsmobile, 1904, Roadster
Oldsmobile, 1963, 4dr Sedan
Oldsmobile, 1964, Jetstar
Overland, 1910, Speedster
Overland, 1913, Touring
Packard, 1908, Limousine
Packard, 1937, Hearse
Packard, 1937, Model 1073 Convertible
Packard, 1940, Limousine
Packard, 1941, Model 110 Coupe
Packard, 1950, 4dr Station Wagon
Packard, 1953, 4dr Sedan
Packard, 1954, Sedan
Peugeot, 1923, Quadrilette Roadster
Pierce-Arrow, 1925, Sedan
Pierce-Arrow, 1934, V-12 Model 1248A
    Limousine
Plymouth, 1949, 2dr Coupe
Pontiac, 1962, Catalina
Rambler, 1908, Model 53 Touring
Renault, 1912, Opera Coupe
Renault, 1919, Cabriolet
Renault, 1961, Dauphine
Reo, 1909, Roadster

Reo, 1923, Touring
Rolls-Royce, 1927, Phantom I 4dr Sedan
Rolls-Royce, 1928, Silver Ghost Limousine
Rolls-Royce, 1938, Windover Sedan
Samson, 1923, Truck
Saxon, 1914, Roadster
Scripps-Booth, 1919, Touring
Searchmont, 1901, Touring
Sears, 1906
Stephens, 1922, Sport Touring

Steyr, 1935
Studebaker, 1927, 4dr Sedan
Studebaker, 1963, Hawk Gran Turismo
UNIC, 1903, Taxi
Vauxhall, 1912, Limousine Randoulet
Whippet, 1928, Bantam Roadster
White, 1911, Touring
White, 1913, Bus
Winton, 1922, 7-Passenger Sedan

Front Wheel Drive Auto Museum

250 N. Main Street, Brighton, Colorado 80601
(303) 659-6536 (evenings)

This is the only auto museum to feature only front-wheel-drive cars. The museum documents the development of front-wheel-drive power systems through displays of cars, drive systems, photographs and drawings.

Front-wheel-drive was one of the configurations used by early auto makers, but it did not gain the popularity of the typical front-engine, rear-drive layout. Technology, popularity and economy have generated a resurgence of front-wheel-drive cars and the museum offers interesting information on the pros and cons of past and present front-wheel-drive systems.

DIRECTIONS TO MUSEUM: The museum is 0.3 mile north of Bridge St. on Main St.

ADMISSION COST: Free.

HOURS OF OPERATION: By appointment only.

MUSEUM NOTES: There is a restaurant nearby. Film is not available.

A brochure is available.

Display Automobiles

Berkeley, 1958
BSA, 1934, Three-wheeler
Citroen, 1970, Mehari

Emeryson, 1959, F250
Gregory-Porsche, 1950

Royal Gorge Scenic Railway Museum

1193 Fremont, Road 3A, Cañon City, Colorado 81212
(719) 275-5485

The magnet for most visitors to the area is the nearby Royal Gorge, with the world's highest suspension bridge. The museum is a portion of Royal Gorge Country, the Old West's largest theme park. Attractions in the park include a restored mining town, horse and stagecoach rides, daily gun fights, gold panning, train rides and Western entertainment.

The car collection contains several examples of the Ford Model A. Ford lost its claim for number one car builder in 1927 when the Ford factory shut down to retool for Model A production. After resolving production problems in 1928, Ford regained the top slot in 1929. The museum has three 1931 Model As, the last year of production for the Model A, and the year Ford built its 20-millionth automobile. The museum's Victoria is an example of bodywork constructed outside Ford. Victoria bodies were built by Briggs and by Murray. The top of the Briggs body was made of canvas, while steel and rubberized fabric form the top of the Murray body.

DIRECTIONS TO MUSEUM: The museum is located along road leading to the Royal Gorge.

ADMISSION COST: Adults $3.00; senior citizens and children $2.00.

HOURS OF OPERATION: June-August: open daily 8am-8pm. May, September and October: open daily 9am-5pm. Closed remainder of year.

MUSEUM NOTES: There is a restaurant in the park as well as nearby outside the park. The park has gift shops and film is available.

A brochure is available.

Display Automobiles

Cadillac, 1956, Sedan
Chevrolet, 1950, Station Wagon
Chevrolet, 1963, Convertible
Ford, 1915, Model T Speedster
Ford, 1929, Model A Pickup Truck
Ford, 1929, Model AA Truck
Ford, 1930, Model A Coupe
Ford, 1930, Model A Sedan
Ford, 1931, Model A Pickup Truck
Ford, 1931, Model A Roadster
Ford, 1931, Model A Victoria
Ford, 1934, Roadster
Ford, 1956, Sedan
Ford, 1956, Thunderbird
MG, 1952, TC Roadster
Plymouth, 1948, Woody Station Wagon

National Museum of American History

14th Street & Constitution Avenue, N.W., Washington, D.C. 20560
(202) 357-2700

The Smithsonian Institution's National Museum of American History is the national showcase and storehouse for significant artifacts and memorabilia that reflect the American experience. No other nation has been impacted as significantly by the development of the automobile as the United States. The museum presents an overview of the history of the automobile in America through displays of cars and related artifacts.

In the course of making a buying decision during the early 1900s, two major factors a car buyer would consider were the reliability and power of the cars on the market. The common benchmarks used to gauge these attributes were the distance the car would traverse and the speed it could attain. The 1903 Winton in the museum's collection earned high marks for reliability when it became the first car to travel coast-to-coast. The car transported Dr. H. Nelson Jackson and his chauffeur Sewell Croker from San Francisco to New York. The feat, along with other demonstrations of Winton reliability and speed, boosted sales and positioned the company among the top manufacturers of the day.

1893 Duryea Motor Carriage. *The Duryea Motor Carriage was the first American-built car powered by a gasoline engine to run in America. The car was constructed and driven in Springfield, Massachusetts, by Frank Duryea, although Charles Duryea, Frank's brother, is credited with starting the project before moving to Peoria, Illinois. As the name implies, the car is a modified horse-drawn carriage. A single-cylinder 4 hp engine provides power to a rear wheel through a friction drive system. The driver operated a tiller bar to steer the vehicle.*

Along with the cars found in the Road Transportation Hall are items such as service station equipment, road and street surfaces, traffic signals and bus fare boxes. Early American carriages, coaches, buggies and bicycles are also on display.

DIRECTIONS TO MUSEUM: The museum is located on Constitution Ave. between 12th and 14th Sts., N.W., on the National Mall adjacent to the other Smithsonian museums. The museums are marked on most Smithsonian literature, on map markers on the Mall, and on detailed maps of Washington, D.C. The best means of transportation is the subway system.

ADMISSION COST: Free.

HOURS OF OPERATION: Open daily 10am-5:30pm, except closed Christmas. Hours may be extended during summer.

MUSEUM NOTES: A cafeteria and a gift shop are located in the museum. Film is available.

A brochure is available.

Display Automobiles

Chevrolet, 1928, National 2dr Sedan
Dudgeon, 1866, Steam carriage
Duryea, 1893
Ford, 1913, Model T Touring
Garlits, 1987, *Swamp Rat XXX* Dragster
Haynes, 1894
Larson, 1988, Oldsmobile Drag Race Car

Liberty Brush, 1912, Runabout
Oldsmobile, 1903, Curved Dash Runabout
Pontiac, 1984, Petty Race Car
Sears, 1911, Model P Delivery Car
STP-Hawk, 1968, Indy Race Car
Volkswagen, 1972, Super Beetle
Winton, 1903, Touring

Bellm's Cars & Music of Yesterday

5500 N. Tamiami Trail, Sarasota, Florida 34243
(813) 355-6228

Bellm's presents two collections that are totally different. Of interest to the readers of this guide is the auto collection that numbers over 170 cars. And as stated in the name of the museum, there is also a collection of musical artifacts, which includes more than 2,000 music devices such as calliopes, hurdy-gurdies, music boxes, and a 30-foot Belgian organ. There is also a penny arcade and turn-of-the-century artifacts.

The auto collection contains most of the more familiar marques, Ford, Chevrolet, Oldsmobile and Rolls-Royce, as well as some not as familiar, including a car manufactured relatively recently, the Bricklin. Entrepreneur Malcolm Bricklin undertook manufacture of a "safe" sports car after distributing the Suburau 360, which was deemed unsafe by *Consumer Reports*. The plastic-bodied SV-1 fulfilled the safety criteria, but quality problems, especially with sealing the gull-wing doors, drove up manufacturing costs. The car was sold in 1974 and 1975, but overwhelming costs drove Bricklin to request additional money from the province of New Brunswick, the financial backer for the two Bricklin factories in the province. The government refused a new loan and foreclosed. Bricklin gave up manufacturing, and subsequently arranged importation of another foreign car, the Yugo.

DIRECTIONS TO MUSEUM: Bellm's is located on US 41 (Tamiami Trail Rd.) on the north side of Sarasota near the airport.

ADMISSION COST: Adults $7.50; children (6-12 yrs.) $3.75.

1932 Auburn Boattail Speedster. *Alan Leamy designed the classic Auburn Speedster with its characteristic boattail shape. The car looked fast, and was, offering the performance of the speedy Stutz Bearcat at 60 percent the Stutz' cost.*

1906 McIntyre. *The W.H. McIntyre Company built numerous models based on the highwheeler design during the early 1900s. The company failed when "conventional" designs prevailed, and although the company came out with a design similar to other manufacturers, the stigma of the highwheeler design put off buyers.*

HOURS OF OPERATION: Open Monday-Saturday 8:30am-6pm; Sunday 9:30am-6pm. Open all year.

MUSEUM NOTES: There is a restaurant nearby. Bellm's has a gift shop and sells film.

A brochure is available.

Display Automobiles

American Austin, 1930
Auburn, 1932, Boattail Speedster
Autocar, 1906
Bantam, 1939
Bricklin, 1978
Buick, 1930
Buick, 1938
Buick, 1957
Buick, 1962
Buick, 1971
Cadillac, 1908
Cadillac, 1963, Convertible
Carter, 1908
Chevrolet, 1963

Chevrolet, 1966, Corvair
Chevrolet, 1970, Corvette
DeLorean, 1981
DeSoto, 1936, Airflow
DeSoto, 1958
Edsel, 1958
Ford, 1906, Model N
Ford, 1910, Model T
Ford, 1925, Model T Depot Hack
Ford, 1956, Thunderbird
Ford, 1957, Skyliner
Ford, 1962, Thunderbird
Ford, 1963, Pickup Truck
Ford, 1964 1/2, Mustang

International Harvester, 1911, Truck
Jeepster, 1940
Lincoln, 1937, Zephyr
Lincoln, 1952, Convertible
Lincoln, 1966, Continental
Marion, 1905
McIntyre, 1906
Metropolitan, 1950
Moon, 1926
Oldsmobile, 1903

Olin Scimitar, 1959
Pierce-Arrow, 1923
Rambler, 1904
Rolls-Royce, 1921
Rolls-Royce, 1923
Studebaker, 1950
Studebaker, 1963, Avanti
Studebaker, 1963, Hawk
Templer, 1918
Waverly Electric, 1911

Birthplace of Speed Museum

160 East Granada, Ormond Beach, Florida 32176
(904) 672-5657

The Birthplace of Speed Museum was established to preserve the racing heritage of the area encompassing Ormond and Daytona Beaches.

The hard sand beaches that run for miles along the Atlantic Ocean provided a smooth, unbroken surface for record-setting attempts and racing. Attention was first drawn to the beach in 1902 when Ransom Olds and Alexander Winton dueled for the speed record. Both claimed to achieve 57 mph, but no victor was established. Olds drove his single-cylinder *Pirate*, while Winton drove his four-cylinder *Bullet I*. Thirty-three years later, Sir Malcolm Campbell drove the famous *Bluebird* to a speed record of 276 mph. The sand was also the birthplace for NASCAR, the National Association of Stock Car Racing. The museum presents artifacts and memorabilia that document the racing and speed record attempts that occurred on the area's sand beaches.

DIRECTIONS TO MUSEUM: From I-95 take Exit 88 and travel east approximately 7 miles. Museum is on right.

ADMISSION COST: Adults $1.00; children 50¢.

HOURS OF OPERATION: Open Tuesday-Saturday 1-5pm. Closed major holidays.

MUSEUM NOTES: There is a restaurant nearby. The museum has a gift shop, but film is not available.

A brochure is available.

Collier Automotive Museum

2500 S. Horseshoe Drive, Naples, Florida 33942
(813) 643-5252

The Collier Automotive Museum is dedicated to the preservation and restoration of high performance, sports, sports racing and racing automobiles.

The museum is divided into five galleries with specific themes: Sports and Sports Racing Cars; American Racing Cars; Cars of "Conspicuous Consumption;" Grand Prix Racing Cars; and Porsche Racing Cars.

Fifty of the cars on display were formerly a part of the significant Briggs Cunningham collection. Cunningham was a noted racer and car builder during the 1950s. Several of the cars Cunningham built and entered in the Le Mans race are on display. The museum is named in honor of the Collier brothers, who founded the Automobile Racing Club and, coincidentally, raced with Cunningham.

The display of Porsches is one of the largest outside the Porsche museum in Stuttgart, Germany. Porsche is one of the famous names identified with high performance sports cars and auto racing. Ferdinand Porsche was born in Austria in 1875 and after working for Daimler and Steyr, started his design firm in 1930. Among the projects Porsche worked on prior to World War II were the Volkswagen, "people's car," and the successful Auto-Union Grand Prix cars. In 1949 Porsche became an auto maker with the intro-

Porsche RS61L Spyder *(foreground)* and Porsche RS60 Spyder. *The Collier Museum highlights the racing prowess of Porsche as exemplified by the display of these two early 1960s sports car racing champions.*

1958 Porsche-Behra Formula II Race Car. *Jean Behra was Ferrari's number one Grand Prix driver in 1959. The previous year, Behra purchased then modified a Porsche Formula II car. At the hands of another driver, Behra's car won the important race at Reims in 1959. Among the cars defeated by Behra's car were cars entered by Behra's employer, Enzo Ferrari, who was not pleased that he had lost to a car entered by his own Grand Prix driver.*

duction of the 356, the first of a famous line of sports cars. Ferry Porsche had joined his father's company in 1930, and succeeded him as company leader when the elder Porsche died in 1952. During the 1960s, 1970s and 1980s, Porsche grew as a prominent, often dominant, force in high performance sports cars and auto racing.

DIRECTIONS TO MUSEUM: From I-75 take Exit 16 and travel west on Pine Ridge Blvd. Turn left onto Airport Pulling Rd. and travel to Horseshoe Dr. Turn right onto Horseshoe and follow to museum.

ADMISSION COST: Adults $6.00; children (5-12 yrs.) $3.00.

HOURS OF OPERATION: Open Tuesday-Sunday 10am-5pm. Open Monday 10am-5pm December-April. Closed major holidays.

MUSEUM NOTES: There is a restaurant nearby. A gift shop is located at the museum. Film is available.

A brochure is available.

Display Automobiles

Alfa Romeo, 1934, 8C 2300 Mille Miglia
Arrows, 1988, A10B Formula I Car
Ballot, 1919, Indy Race Car
Bentley, 1926, Speed Model, Vanden Plas

Bentley, 1930, Speed Six, Vanden Plas
Bentley, 1931, Corsica
Bentley, 1931, Vanden Plas
Bentley, 1933

1928 Hispano-Suiza H6c Boulogne. *Built in France and Spain, Hispano-Suiza ranked among the best luxury cars in the world. The sporty H6c was built by the French branch of the company.*

Bentley, 1939
BMW, 1938, 328
Bu-Merc, 1939
Bugatti, 1933, Super Sport Type 55
Cadillac, 1950, Le Mans *Le Monstre*
Cadillac, 1950, Le Mans Racer
Chevrolet, 1962, Corvette Grand Sport
Cisitalia, 1950, Tipo 202 Pinin Farina
Cooper, 1959, Formula I Car
Cunningham, 1920, V4 Record Car
Cunningham, 1951, C-1 Prototype
Cunningham, 1952, C-3 Vignale Coupe
Cunningham, 1952, C-4R
Cunningham, 1952, C-4RK
Cunningham, 1953, C-5R
Cunningham, 1955, C-6R
Delage, 1927, Grand Prix Car
Duesenberg, 1930, J LeBaron Phaeton
Duesenberg, 1935, SSJ
Elva Porsche, 1963
Ferrari, 1948, 166 Spyder Corsa
Ford, 1968, GT-40

Gurney, 1967, Eagle
Hispano-Suiza, 1912, T-15 Alfonso XIII
Hispano-Suiza, 1928, H6c
Jaguar, 1955, D-Type
Jaguar, 1962, XK-E
Jorgensen-Eagle, 1975, Indy Race Car
March, 1984, 84C Indy Race Car
Maserati, 1961, Tipo 60 "Birdcage"
Mercedes, 1914, Grand Prix Car
Mercedes, 1923, Targa Florio 28/95
Mercedes-Benz, 1929, SSK 38/250
Mercer, 1912, 35-C Raceabout
MG, 1934, K-3 Magnette
MG, 1935, PA/PB Special Body
Osca, 1954, MT-4 Sports Racer
Packard, 1929, Speedster
Packard, 1933, Dietrich Sports Phaeton
Peugeot, 1913, Coupe de l'Auto Voiturette
Pierce-Arrow, 1915, Model 48 Victoria
Porsche, 1948, 356 SL Gmund Coupe
Porsche, 1956, 550A Spyder
Porsche, 1958, GT Carrera Speedster

Porsche, 1958, RSK Spyder
Porsche, 1960, Abarth-Carrera GTL
Porsche, 1960, RS-60 Spyder
Porsche, 1964, 904 Carrera GTS
Porsche, 1965, 356C 1600SC Coupe
Porsche, 1966, 906
Porsche, 1967, 910/6
Porsche, 1968, 911R
Porsche, 1969, 908LH
Porsche, 1969, 917PA Can-Am Race Car
Porsche, 1970, 914/6 GT
Porsche, 1970, 917K

Porsche, 1971, 908/3 Spyder
Porsche, 1971, Martini 917K
Porsche-Behra, 1958, Formula II Car
Renault, 1907, Type AA Vanderbilt Semi-Racer
Rolls-Royce, 1914, Silver Ghost
Scarab, 1958, Sports Racer
Simplex, 1914, Speed Car
Sprint Car, 1930, Duesenberg Engine
Stutz, 1929, Blackhawk BB Speedster
Sunbeam, 1929, Sunbeam, Super Sport
Vanwall, 1958, Formula I Car
Vauxhall, 1927, Velox 30/98

Don Garlits Museum of Drag Racing

13700 S.W. 16th Avenue, Ocala, Florida 32676
(904) 245-8661

The advent of the automobile quickly provided yet another means to fulfill the competitive needs of human nature. As soon as cars demonstrated they could produce power without coming apart, some adventurous driver no doubt said "let's open her up and see what she'll do!" Get two adventurous drivers together and a race resulted. Popularly known as "drag racing," racing cars from a standing start is one of the oldest forms of auto racing, and in its current form, one of the most popular, both in participation and attendance.

King of the drag strip for over three decades was "Big Daddy" Don Garlits. Garlits started racing professionally in the 1950s and was a moving force in the evolution of drag racing from a regional, grass-roots sport of homebuilt street rods to the corporate-sponsored, high-tech, televised sport of today. Garlits felt that much of the history of drag racing was being lost, so he and his wife, Pat, formed the museum's organization and opened the museum in 1984.

The focus of the facility is the collection of Garlits' dragsters. There are over twenty of the famous Garlits "Swamp Rat" dragsters, most were champions and at the front of the sport's technical evolution. Cars driven by other drag racing stars are also on display, ranging from "funny cars" to high performance street cars.

DIRECTIONS TO MUSEUM: From I-75 take Exit 67 to Rt. 484.

ADMISSION COST: Adults $7.50; children (3-12 yrs.) $3.00.

HOURS OF OPERATION: Open daily 9am-5:30pm. Closed Christmas.

MUSEUM NOTES: A restaurant is located nearby. There is a gift shop and film is available.

A brochure is available.

The Mooneyes *dragster of Dean Moon was a potent competitor during early 1960s drag racing. The lighter* Mooneyes *won its share of top eliminator races against its heavier, tire-smoking adversaries.*

Display Automobiles

Beadle, 1984, Funny Car *Blue Max*
Big Al, 1966, Funny Car
Breedlove, 1964, Streamlined Dragster
Bucher, 1973, Dragster
Buick, 1922, Coupe
Cadillac, 1979, Eldorado
Chassis Research, 1959, Dragster
Chevrolet, 1925, Truck
Chevrolet, 1969, Corvair
Chione/Chione, 1970, Go-Kart
Chrysler, 1987, Fifth Avenue
Cook & Bedwell, 1957, Dragster
Cousino HS, 1970, Jet Dragster
Dodge, 1931, Sedan
Dodge, 1932, Coupe
Dodge, 1966, Coronet
Dodge, 1966, Coronet Hemi
Dodge, 1967, Coronet
Dodge, 1968, Coronet Hemi
Dodge, 1969, Charger 500 Hemi
Dodge, 1970, Challenger Hemi
Dodge, 1976, Truck
Dodge, 1990, Dakota Truck
Dragmaster, 1962, Nelson
Ford, 1926, Model T Touring
Ford, 1927, Model T Roadster
Ford, 1928, Pickup Truck
Ford, 1932, Coupe
Ford, 1932, Model AA Roadster
Ford, 1932, Roadster Street Rod
Ford, 1935, Convertible
Ford, 1936, Roadster
Ford, 1937, Coupe
Ford, 1937, Pickup Truck
Ford, 1937, Roadster
Ford, 1939, Coupe
Ford, 1939, Roadster
Ford, 1940, 2dr Sedan
Ford, 1940, Convertible
Ford, 1940, Customized Convertible
Ford, 1940, Winfield Coupe
Ford, 1941, Roadster
Ford, 1949, 2dr Sedan
Ford, 1950, Crestliner
Ford, 1951, Crestliner
Ford, 1966, Mustang Convertible
Garlits, 1955, Flathead Dragster
Garlits, 1956, *Swamp Rat I*
Garlits, 1961, Dragster

Garlits, 1964, *Wynnsjammer*
Garlits, 1965, Dart Funny Car
Garlits, 1966, Slingshot
Garlits, 1967, Slingshot
Garlits, 1968, Tantor
Garlits, 1969
Garlits, 1970, Slingshot
Garlits, 1971, Dragster
Garlits, 1972, *Wynnsliner*
Garlits, 1972, Hanna Body
Garlits, 1973, Dragster
Garlits, 1975, Dragster
Garlits, 1975, Jungle
Garlits, 1976, Dragster
Garlits, 1978, Dragster
Garlits, 1980, *Godzilla*
Garlits, 1981, Dragster
Garlits, 1983, Dragster
Garlits, 1983, Turbine
Garlits, 1985, Dragster
Garlits, 1987, Dragster
Goeske, 1965, AA/Fuel Coupe
Hudson, 1954, Hornet
Ivo, 1959, Twin-Engine Dragster
Johnson, 1956, Streamlined Dragster
Johnson, 1960, Streamliner
Jones, 1962, *Magwinder*
Kalitta, 1965, Dragster
Karamesines, 1958, Dragster
Karamesines, 1966, *Silver Bullet*
Kraft, 1941, Dragster
Laws, 1979, Motorcycle
Liberman, 1972, Vega Funny Car
Logghe, 1964, Streamliner
Loukas-Preising, 1964, Funny Car
Lozier, 1915, Speedster
Lynwood, 1959, Dragster
Malone, 1960, Sidewinder Dragster
McEwen, 1976, Corvette Funny Car
McNamara, 1971, Andretti
Mercury, 1942, Convertible
Mercury, 1950, Coupe
Mercury, 1950, Customized
Metz, 1913, Roadster
Metz, 1914, Speedster
MG, 1954, TF Roadster
Mitsubishi, 1986, Pickup Truck
Moon, 1959, Dragster
Moon, 1960, Bonneville Racer

Muldowney, 1980, Dragster
Peters, 1952, Dragster
Peterson, 1974, Streamliner
Phelps, 1970, Rocket Dragster
Plymouth, 1962, 2dr
Plymouth, 1973, Duster
Pollutionizer, 1960, Allison
Prudhomme, 1969, Slingshot
Prudhomme, 1970, Dragster
Prudhomme, 1970, Wedge Dragster
Prudhomme, 1973, Barracuda Funny Car
Prudhomme, 1989, *Skoal Bandit*
Pulse, 1986, Motorcycle
Robinson, 1971, *Tinker Toy VI*

Roth, 1965, *Yellow Fang*
Schmitz, 1970, Mini-Dragster
Scott, 1955, Dragster
Silver-Dollar, 1960, Dragster
Speed-Sport, 1957, Roadster
Storza-Carpinello, 1962, *Patrician*
Studebaker, 1948, Pickup Truck
Sullivan, 1957, *Pandemonium*
Vandal, 1964, Dragster
Volkswagen, 1950
Volkswagen, 1974, Kharman-Ghia
Wiebe, 1970, Slingshot
Willys, 1937, Coupe
Willys, 1941, Coupe

Elliott Museum

825 N.E. Ocean Boulevard, Stuart, Florida 34996
(407) 225-1961

The museum serves to chronicle the accomplishments of Sterling Elliott and his son, Harmon Elliott. Between them, 225 patents were issued to the Elliotts. Several of their inventions are displayed, including the first knot-tying machine and the first addressing machine. Housed in the museum are artifacts depicting American lifestyles, as well as the Gracious Living Wing, which presents collections of fine artifacts.

The auto collection comprises several interesting cars, most of which bear the nameplates of luxury cars such as Mercedes-Benz, Rolls-Royce, Lincoln, Cadillac, Stutz, Bentley, Packard and Jaguar.

Sterling Elliott built a quadricycle while he owned his bicycle company in Watertown, Massachusetts. The vehicle had several innovations, such as a rear axle differential and a non-turning front axle. The Stanley brothers owned the photographic dry plate factory next to Elliott and became interested in the powered possibilities of the quadricycle. They bought Elliott's bicycle company and went on to develop their steampowered cars. Elliott concentrated on his addressing machine.

DIRECTIONS TO MUSEUM: In Stuart follow E. Ocean Blvd. to Hutchinson Island, then follow N.E. Ocean Blvd. to museum.

ADMISSION COST: Adults $2.50; children (6-13 yrs.) 50¢.

HOURS OF OPERATION: Open daily 1-4pm.

MUSEUM NOTES: There is a restaurant nearby. The museum has a gift shop onsite, but film is not available.

A brochure is available.

Display Automobiles

Austin, 1932, Racer
Bentley, 1956
Cadillac, 1902, Roadster
Chevrolet, 1928, Model AB
Cunningham, 1953, C-3
Detroit Electric, 1913, Opera Coupe
Fiat, 1960, 600 Sedan
Ford, 1909, Model T Touring
Ford, 1930, Model A Roadster
Ford, 1956, Thunderbird
Hupmobile, 1907, Model 20 Speedster
    Runabout
Jaguar, 1954, Roadster
Lincoln, 1930, Model L Town Car

Maxwell, 1907, Touring
Mercedes-Benz, 1958, 190SL Roadster
MG, 1961, A Roadster
Moline, 1909, Model M Touring
Oldsmobile, 1905
Packard, 1914, Touring
Rauch & Lang Electric, 1915
Reo, 1903, Roadster
Roamer, 1914
Rolls-Royce, 1924, Silver Ghost Phaeton
Rolls-Royce, 1929
Stanley, 1902, Steamer
Stutz, 1923, Roadster

Antique Auto And Music Museum

Stone Mountain Park, Stone Mountain, Georgia 30086
(404) 498-5600

Exhibited in the museum are antique cars, Americana and musical devices, such as juke-boxes, player pianos and nickelodeons.

Several of the cars in the museum are rarely seen elsewhere, such as Saxon, Milburn, Car-Nation, Mitchell and Crow-Elkhart. The Austrian-built Grofri roadster, French-built Fugier, Ford Model C (AA commercial engine) and Brough are the only examples known to exist.

Also on display is a car built in Atlanta, the 1920 Hanson. George Hanson started production in 1918 using Continental engines and other components built by outside suppliers to assemble five models — touring, roadster, sport, sedan and coupe. The company produced approximately 850 cars before faltering in 1925.

DIRECTIONS TO MUSEUM: The museum is located in Stone Mountain Park, which is just east of Atlanta and may be entered from US 78.

ADMISSION COST: A $5.00 fee per car is charged for entrance to Stone Mountain Park. Additional cost for museum admission: adults $2.50; children $1.50.

1911 Hupmobile Touring. *In 1911 a little over 6,000 Hupmobiles were sold, and the founder of the company, Robert Hupp, left after a dispute with the company's financiers. The firm proved moderately successful through the 1920s and 1930s, but car production ceased in 1940 when the company declared bankruptcy.*

HOURS OF OPERATION: June-August: open daily 10am-8pm. September-May: open daily 10am-5pm. Closed Christmas.

MUSEUM NOTES: There are restaurants nearby. Film is available in the gift shop.

A brochure is available.

Display Automobiles

Brough, 1904
Buck Rodgers, 1939, Movie Car
Buick, 1908, Model X
Cadillac, 1907
Car Nation, 1913, Roadster
Chevrolet, 1931, 2dr Sedan
Chevrolet, 1966, Corvair Convertible
Chevrolet, 1978, Corvette
Crow-Elkhart, 1912, Model 52
Ford, 1904, Model C Touring
Ford, 1925, Model T Truck
Ford, 1931, Model A
Ford, 1933, Model C Roadster
Ford, 1938, 2dr Coupe
Franklin, 1905
Fugier, 1895
Grofri, 1927, Roadster
Hanson, 1920, Touring

Hupmobile, 1911
LaSalle, 1939, 4dr Convertible
Lincoln, 1936
Martin, 1928
Maxwell, 1909, Model A
Midget Racer, 1937
Milburn, 1920, Electric
Mitchell, 1910, Touring
Nash, 1955, 2dr Hardtop
Oldsmobile, 1902, Curved Dash
Oldsmobile, 1904, Pie Wagon
Peerless, 1917, Touring
Saxon, 1917, Roadster
Sears, 1908
Sprint Car, 1946
Stanley, 1905, Steamer
Tucker, 1948, 4dr Sedan

Pebble Hill Plantation

P.O. Box 830, Thomasville, Georgia 31779
(912) 226-2344

Groundwork for Pebble Hill Plantation was laid by owner Thomas Jefferson Johnson in the 1820s. Johnson also founded the town of Thomasville and authored the bill that created Thomas County. Successive owners have added to Pebble Hill's grandeur and notoriety. Presidents and royalty have visited this expansive example of plantation living. The plantation was willed for public viewing by Mrs. Elisabeth Poe, the last owner.

Many of the buildings on the grounds are open, including the garage that houses the auto collection. The collection reflects the luxury and utilitarian vehicles that were used on the Plantation prior to 1978.

DIRECTIONS TO MUSEUM: The Plantation is approximately 5 miles south of Thomasville and 20 miles north of Tallahassee on US 319.

ADMISSION COST: Grounds (includes garage but not house tour): adults $2.00; children $1.00. House (includes grounds): adults $5.00; children under 7 yrs. not admitted to house tour.

HOURS OF OPERATION: Open Tuesday-Saturday 10am-5pm; Sunday 1-5pm. Last house tour begins at 4pm. Closed Monday. Closed in September after Labor Day. Closed Thanksgiving, Christmas Eve and Christmas.

MUSEUM NOTES: The garage is open all hours, but viewing the house is by tour only. No more than six persons in each tour group. Children under 7 yrs. not allowed on tours. Photography not permitted on tour. There are no restaurants nearby. There is a gift shop, but film is not available.

A brochure is available.

Display Automobiles

Bentley, 1960
Cadillac, 1951, 4dr Sedan
Chrysler, 1968, Station Wagon
Ford, 1954, Station Wagon

Lincoln, 1948, Continental
Packard, 1934, Touring Phaeton
Plymouth, 1964, Valiant

Old Idaho Penitentiary

2445 Old Penitentiary Road, Boise, Idaho 83712
(208) 334-2844

The Old Idaho Penitentiary is listed on the National Register of Historic Places and is open for viewing. Self-guided tours provide an inside look at the structures and procedures prevalent in American penal institutions during the last century. Also found on the site are the History of Electricity and Idaho Transportation exhibits.

The Idaho Transportation exhibit is housed in the former prison shirt factory. Artifacts and memorabilia reflect the history of transportation in Idaho. Vehicles displayed include horse-drawn wagons and buggies, fire equipment, a steel-wheel farm tractor, a snowmobile, a railroad boxcar and the following motor vehicles: 1928 Essex, 1955 Buick Super, 1990 Ford Ranger and 1976 Leata — the only car ever produced in Idaho.

DIRECTIONS TO MUSEUM: The Penitentiary is located east of downtown Boise on Old Penitentiary Rd. off of Warm Springs Ave.

ADMISSION COST: Adults $3.00; senior citizens and children $2.00. Under 6 yrs. free.

HOURS OF OPERATION: Open daily noon-5pm Memorial Day through Labor Day. Remainder of year open daily noon-4pm, except closed state holidays.

MUSEUM NOTES: There are no restaurants nearby. The museum has a gift shop and film is available

A brochure is available.

1976 Leata Sedan. *Theorizing that domestic automakers would not offer economy cars, Donald Stinebaugh conceived the Leata in response to the Arab Oil Embargo. Stinebaugh designed an engine for the car, but a Ford engine was eventually chosen. Nineteen cars were produced during 1975 and 1976, as well as three trucks, before production ceased. The fiberglass body covered a chassis and drivetrain comprised of off-the-shelf parts of other auto manufacturers.*

Vintage Wheel Museum

218 Cedar Street, Sandpoint, Idaho 83864
(208) 263-7173

The collection numbers 15 antique and classic cars, most constructed prior to 1930. The museum also has on display sleighs, buggys, logging memorabilia and antiques.

On display are two examples of Stanley Steamers, a 1914 Touring and 1923 Sedan. Steam cars were quick, powerful cars for their day. The Stanley *Wogglebug* held the land speed record in 1906 at 127 mph. With a relatively long history of steam-engine technology at hand, many early car builders opted for steam power. However, refinement of the gasoline engine induced more and more manufacturers to embrace the gasoline engine, leaving steam car builders like Stanley (and electric car builders as well) with declining sales and a bleak future.

DIRECTIONS TO MUSEUM: The museum is located at 3rd St. and Cedar St. in Sandpoint.

HOURS OF OPERATION: Open Monday-Saturday 9:30am-5:30pm, Sunday 11am-5:30pm. Closed Christmas.

ADMISSION COST: Adults $2.50; senior citizens $2.00; high school students $1.00; grade school students 50¢.

MUSEUM NOTES: There is a restaurant nearby. The museum has a gift shop, but film is not available.

A brochure is available.

Display Automobiles

Buick, 1919, Touring Sedan
Cadillac, 1913, Flatbed Truck
Cadillac, 1955, Coupe de Ville
Chrysler, 1926, Sedan
Detroit Electric, 1914
Ford, 1913, Model T Runabout
Ford, 1924, Model T Runabout
Ford, 1924, Model T Touring

Ford, 1929, Model A Pickup Truck
Ford, 1932, Deluxe Roadster
Ford, 1935, Coupe
International, 1907
Rolls-Royce, 1962, Silver Cloud II
Stanley, 1914, Steamer Touring
Stanley, 1923, Steamer Sedan

Bortz Auto Collection

Gurnee Mills, Gurnee, Illinois 60031
Mail Address: P.O. Box 280, Highland Park, Illinois 60035
(708) 855-1889 or 433-7777

Automobile designing is an exercise in coupling esthetics with practicality. At times, design staffs are given a clean sheet with a mandate to explore the styling possibilities with minimal consideration for such things as production and material costs. The result is usually a futuristic, eye-catching wheeled creation. Whole cars sometimes reach the production line based on these exercises, although they may be changed considerably to accommodate the car's moving components. Very often portions of the original design, such as taillights, grilles and dashes, will be included in the design of another car already on the drawing boards.

These "concept" cars are important to the manufacturers since they exercise the talents of their styling departments and allow the manufacturer to gauge public opinion when they are shown in car shows. Marc and Joe Bortz collected several concept and prototype cars (prototypes are closer to production versions), and after displaying the collection on special occasions, subsequently opened a facility for public viewing. The 14 factory dream cars were constructed in the 1950s and 1960s by design teams at Pontiac, Dodge, Chrysler, Buick and others. These are cars that were auto show stars and influenced later automobile designs.

DIRECTIONS TO MUSEUM: The collection is located in Gurnee Mills Mall in Gurnee at intersection of I-94 and Grand Ave. From I-94 northbound take Grand Ave. West exit. From I-94 southbound take Gurnee Mills-Grand Ave. exit.

ADMISSION COST: Adults $2.00; children $1.00.

HOURS OF OPERATION: Open daily 1-6pm.

MUSEUM NOTES: There are restaurants in the shopping center.

Dale's Classic Cars

Route 1, Waltonville Road, Mt. Vernon, Illinois 62864
(618) 244-4118

The collection at Dale's comprises 12 cars and 46 motorcycles. The bulk of the motorcycles are Harley Davidsons, which should make the collection interesting to fans of America's only motorcycle manufacturer.

Of note in the car collection are the Buick Skylarks. Buick introduced the Skylark in 1953 and two examples are found in the collection, although only one is restored. Only 1,690 Skylarks were built in 1953. Skylarks were available only as convertibles and were fully equipped with accessories. Buick debuted a new V-8 engine in 1953 that was the only engine available in Skylarks. Original price for 1953 Skylarks was $4,600. Restored Skylarks are valued in excess of $50,000, placing them among the most prized by collectors of the post-World War II Buicks.

DIRECTIONS TO MUSEUM: From I-57 and I-64 take Exit 95 and travel east to Veterans Memorial Highway. Turn right onto Veterans and follow south then east to Dale's (the road makes a sharp left turn). The building is located on the right behind the Harley Davidson motorcycle shop.

ADMISSION COST: Free.

1953 Buick Roadmaster Skylark. *The Skylark was conceived to commemorate Buick's 50th anniversary. Built on the Roadmaster chassis, the front fenders were without the distinctive Buick "bullet holes." Luxuriously equipped, including leather upholstery, the convertible top was lower than standard and special emblems and trim were attached to uniquely curved sides and doors. Wire wheels replaced the stamped steel wheels found on other models.*

HOURS OF OPERATION: Closed Wednesday & Sunday, otherwise open daily 9am-5pm.

MUSEUM NOTES: There is a restaurant nearby. Film is not available.

A brochure is available.

Display Automobiles

Buick, 1953, Skylark Convertible
Buick, 1954, Skylark Convertible
Cadillac, 1949, Sedan
Cadillac, 1985, Biarritz
Chevrolet, 1969, Chevelle SS
Chevrolet, 1969, Nova

Clobe, 1932
Dodge, 1949, Truck
LaSalle, 1928, Opera Coupe
Packard, 1932, Convertible Coupe
Pontiac, 1966, Bonneville

Grant Hills Antique Auto Museum

Route 20 East, Galena, Illinois 61036
(815) 777-2115

The museum presents 39 cars, some "Best of Show" winners, that range from 1912 to 1956. Also on display is a collection of Illinois license plates and other automotive artifacts, as well as collections of Galena pottery and cast iron banks.

Case was an early manufacturer of cars and the museum has a vintage 1911 example on display. The company claimed an early involvement in auto building when the J.I. Case Threshing Machine Company was involved in the construction of a steam-powered buggy in 1871. However, the company concentrated on the development of gas-engine tractors until 1910 when the Pierce Motor Company was purchased. The former Pierce-Racine marque changed to Case in 1911. The last Case automobiles were built in 1927, after which the company decided to focus on farm machinery rather than battle increasingly intense competition in the automotive market.

DIRECTIONS TO MUSEUM: The museum is located about one mile east of Galena on Rt. 20.

ADMISSION COST: Adults $2.00; senior citizens $1.00; children free.

HOURS OF OPERATION: Open mid-May to mid-October daily 10am-5pm.

MUSEUM NOTES: The museum has a gift shop and there is a restaurant nearby. Film is available.

A brochure is available.

Gray's Ride Through History Museum

1608 E. Main Street, West Frankfort, Illinois 62896
(618) 937-6100 or 937-1770

The museum bears the name of collector and retired U.S. Congressman Ken Gray. Vehicles on display include horse-drawn buggies and wagons, some predating the Civil War, as well as antique and contemporary cars.

Contained in the museum are artifacts and memorabilia of political figures dating from George Washington to George Bush. Also displayed is a doll collection of over 600 dolls dressed in historical costumes. In commemoration of the 200th Anniversary of the Bill of Rights, Mr. Gray erected a 15-foot high, solid aluminum replica of the Statue of Liberty at the museum.

DIRECTIONS TO MUSEUM: From I-57 travel east on Rt. 149 approximately 2 miles to museum.

ADMISSION COST: Adults $1.00; senior citizens and children 50¢.

HOURS OF OPERATION: June-September: Monday-Friday 5-8pm; Saturday and Sunday 2-5pm. Remainder of year: Saturday and Sunday 2-5pm. Closed New Year's Day and Christmas.

MUSEUM NOTES: There is a restaurant nearby. Museum has a gift shop, but film is not available.

A brochure is available.

Display Automobiles

Buick, 1908, Touring
Chevrolet, 1927
Crosley, 1946, 2dr Sedan
Dune Buggy, 1963
Ford, 1915, Model T Speedster

Ford, 1925
Ford, 1966, Convertible
Hudson, 1938, 2dr Sedan
Oldsmobile, 1928, 4dr Sedan
Plymouth, 1981

Hartung's Automotive Museum

3623 W. Lake Street, Glenview, Illinois 60025
(708) 724-4354

The museum presents a wide variety of equipment and artifacts from the area of transportation. Besides the extensive auto collection, there are also several trucks and tractors on display, and over 25 pre-World War II motorcycles. Among the artifacts are collections of license plates, outboard motors, hub caps, emblems, engines, bicycles and more.

The museum's auto collection contains a 1947 Crosley, a small car that Powel Crosley felt America needed. The country, however, spent money on big cars and Crosley closed in 1952. The cars were indeed small, one foot shorter than a later successful small car, the Volkswagen Beetle. Crosleys were powered by a diminutive 44 cubic-inch engine developed during World War II that was built using copper-brazed sheet metal. Corrosion began damaging the engines and a cast-iron version was developed that became a marine engine after the demise of the car. The most popular body style was the station wagon, which became the marques best seller in 1948 with over 23,000 sold.

DIRECTIONS TO MUSEUM: The museum is one-half mile west of the main gate for Glenview Naval Air Station on Lake.

ADMISSION COST: Donation requested.

HOURS OF OPERATION: Hours vary; museum recommends calling ahead.

MUSEUM NOTES: There is a restaurant nearby. Film is not available.

A brochure is available.

Display Automobiles

NOTE: Not listed are many Ford Ts, As and prewar models.

Crosley, 1947, Station Wagon	Ford, 1931, Delivery Truck
Edwards, 1950, Convertible	Ford, 1931, Pickup Truck
Essex, 1932, Terraplane	Ford, 1933, Express Truck
Ford, 1914, Truck	Henney, 1927, Limousine
Ford, 1924, Fuel Truck	Hertz, 1926, Touring
Ford, 1929, Pickup Truck	Lincoln, 1936, Custom Twin
Ford, 1929, Truck	Lincoln, 1941, Continental
Ford, 1930, Pickup Truck	Studebaker, 1922
Ford, 1931, Bus	Veritas, 1950, Convertible

Max Nordeen's Wheels Museum

R.R. 1, Box 65, Alpha, Illinois 61413
(309) 334-2589

The museum claims an inventory of 2,600 items. Collections include cars, farm tractors, world's fair souvenirs, pedal cars, railroad artifacts, watch fobs, Indian relics, Civil War artifacts and purse mirrors. Among the automotive artifacts are collections of hub caps, radiator caps, badges and emblems.

In the museum is a 1926 Velie. The Velie was manufactured from 1909 to 1929 in Moline, Illinois, approximately 35 miles from the museum. The company's founder, Willard Velie, began business as a carriage maker, with a capital boost from his uncle, John Deere. Deere provided further help by offering the car in the Deere catalog and through Deere dealers. The company proved successful with Willard Velie and son Willard, Junior, leading the firm. Tragedy befell the company in late 1928 and early 1929 when the elder Velie died and shortly thereafter his son also died. The company folded and Deere & Company took over the Moline plant.

DIRECTIONS TO MUSEUM: The museum is located north of Woodhull, Illinois. From I-74 exit onto Rt. 17 and travel east towards Woodhull. Turn left onto North Division St. and travel approximately 2 miles to end of road at T intersection. Museum is located to right of intersection.

ADMISSION COST: Adults $2.50; children $1.00.

HOURS OF OPERATION: June, July and August: open Tuesday-Sunday 9am-4pm; closed Monday. May, September and October: open Saturday and Sunday 9am-4pm; closed remainder of week.

MUSEUM NOTES: There is a restaurant nearby. Film is not available.

A brochure is available.

Display Automobiles

Buick, 1941, Special Sedan
Chevrolet, 1963, Corvette
Chevrolet, 1964, Corvair
Chrysler, 1948, Windsor
DeSoto, 1928, 4dr Sedan
Diamond T, 1947, Truck
Dodge, 1934, 4dr Sedan
Dodge, 1948, Club Coupe
LaSalle, 1937, Opera Coupe
Lincoln, 1942, Continental

Lincoln, 1947, Club Coupe
Packard, 1937, Touring
Plymouth, 1930, Business Coupe
Plymouth, 1940, Deluxe Club Coupe
Pontiac, 1934, 2dr Sedan
Studebaker, 1925, 4dr Sedan
Studebaker, 1950, Sprint Car
Studebaker, 1960, Hawk Coupe
Velie, 1926

McDonald's Des Plaines Museum

400 N. Lee Street, Des Plaines, Illinois 60016
(708) 297-5022

The integration of the automobile in American society significantly enhanced an intrinsic characteristic of life in the U.S., freedom to travel. As the car was improved and car usage was more convenient and accessible, businesses catering to the car-traveling populace sprang up. The fast-food restaurant was an outgrowth of the desire to travel quickly with little time spent waiting for food preparation, and a desire for food that could be carried out and eaten while traveling.

McDonald's is the most famous of the fast-food chains. Millions of car travelers have stopped at the Golden Arches, now known worldwide. Dick and Maurice McDonald developed an assembly line approach to serving hamburgers in their San Bernardino, California restaurant. Ray Kroc liked the operation, became the McDonalds franchising agent, then purchased the firm in 1958. Kroc refined and expanded the business into a force in the restaurant industry.

The Golden Arches are an icon to the American motoring public. Where the local drive-in was once predominatly a hangout for teens-with-wheels, McDonalds now serves as eatery, pit stop, meeting place and refuge.

The museum is a reconstruction of a McDonald's restaurant that existed on the site in the mid-1950s. Kitchen equipment, uniforms and signs are either original or accurate reproductions. In the restaurant's basement are artifacts and memorabilia. In the parking lot are four cars of the period, all 1955 models: a Ford Crown Victoria, a Chevrolet Bel Air, a Oldsmobile Super 88 and a Chrysler New Yorker St. Regis hardtop.

DIRECTIONS TO MUSEUM: The museum is on North Lee St. in Des Plaines. Mannheim Rd. in the eastern Chicago suburbs becomes Lee St. in Des Plaines.

ADMISSION COST: Free.

HOURS OF OPERATION: June, July and August open Tuesday-Saturday 10am-4pm; Sunday 1-4pm. May and September open Tuesday, Wednesday, Friday and Saturday 10am-4pm. April and September open Wednesday, Friday and Saturday 10am-4pm. Closed November-March.

MUSEUM NOTES: Food is not served in the McDonald's Museum. There is a restaurant nearby. Film is not available.

Mississippi Valley Historic Auto Club Museum

Front & Cedar Streets, Quincy, Illinois 62301
(217) 224-9210 (for information; museum has no phone)

The collection, previously named the Quinsippi Island Auto Museum, comprises cars and articles owned by members of the Mississippi Valley Historic Auto Club. The number of cars exhibited generally averages 35 cars, but the composition of the collection varies according to availability of member's cars.

Among the cars currently displayed is a car built in not-too-far-away St. Louis, a 1926 Diana. Moon Motor Car Company undertook creation of a separate car company, the Diana Motors Company, to manufacture an upscale car. Attempting to find favor with the increasing number of women drivers, the car was promoted for its easy steering and balloon tires. But financial problems at the parent Moon company resulted in only three model years produced. The Diana was dropped as Moon attempted to regroup by offering a new series of models, all unsuccessful. Moon closed in 1930.

DIRECTIONS TO MUSEUM: Cedar St. is eleven blocks north of the Quincy Memorial Bridge (US 24) across the Mississippi River. Travel west on Cedar St.(towards river) to museum, which is located in All American City Park.

ADMISSION COST: Adults $1.00; children 75¢.

HOURS OF OPERATION: Open on Sunday 11am-5pm from Memorial Day to Labor Day. Call ahead other times.

MUSEUM NOTES: There is a restaurant nearby. Film is not available.

A brochure is available.

Display Automobiles

AMC, 1964, 4dr
Bentley, 1936, 4dr
Bentley, 1956, 4dr
Cadillac, 1966, Convertible
Chevrolet, 1915, Royal Mail
Chevrolet, 1917, V-8 Touring
Chevrolet, 1932, 4dr
Chevrolet, 1960, 2dr Hardtop
Chevrolet, 1963, Corvair
Cord 8/10, 1966, Convertible
Diana, 1926, 4dr
Dodge, 1954, 4dr
Dodge, 1959, 4dr
Ford, 1928, Pickup Truck
Ford, 1929, Model A Coupe
Ford, 1954, 2dr Hardtop
Ford, 1955, 2dr Hardtop
Ford, 1956, 2dr Hardtop
Ford, 1959, 2dr Sedan
Henry J, 1954, 2dr
International, 1918, 2-Ton Truck
Maxwell, 1925, 4dr
MGA
Nash, 1927, Coupe
Overland, 1917, Model 90 Touring
Plymouth, 1949, 4dr
Studebaker, 1931, 4dr
Studebaker, 1963, Avanti
Triumph, 1947, Convertible
Willys-Overland, 1949, Jeepster

Museum of Science and Industry
57th Street and Lake Shore Drive, Chicago, Illinois 60637
(312) 684-1414

The Museum of Science and Industry is segmented into 75 exhibition halls that contain exhibits illustrating scientific principles and industrial concepts. Areas addressed include nutrition, automobile, energy, marine, farm and railroad. Many of the exhibits elicit participation from the visitor.

Some of the more impressive exhibits include the coal mine, the circus, a 16-foot-tall model of the human heart, petroleum and the captured World War II German submarine U-505.

The museum's auto collection is composed primarily of antique and classic vehicles, although some unique cars, such as the record-setting *Spirit of America*, are also on display. Fifteen of the cars were built in 1910 or earlier, some with names still in produc-

1886 Daimler. *Formerly on special loan to the museum was a replica of Gottlieb Daimler's first car. The car was a strengthened horse carriage adapted to accept the engine and drive system. Daimler preferred to build engines and didn't construct another car until 1889.*

1886 Benz. *Formerly on special loan to the museum was a replica of Karl Benz' first car. Benz patented the three-wheel vehicle on January 29, 1886. Power was provided by a single-cylinder, four-stroke engine.*

tion, Benz, Mercedes and Oldsmobile, but other names, Locomobile, Rambler, Brush, Gleason and Orient, are seen only in books and museums.

DIRECTIONS TO MUSEUM: The museum is located just off Lake Shore Dr. on the south side of Chicago in Jackson Park.

ADMISSION COST: Adults $5.00; senior citizens $4.00; children $2.00.

HOURS OF OPERATION: Open Monday-Friday 9:30am-4pm (close at 5:30pm from Memorial Day to Labor Day); Saturday, Sunday and holidays 9:30am-5:30pm. Closed Christmas.

MUSEUM NOTES: There is a cafe in the building. Film is available in the gift shop.

A brochure is available.

Display Automobiles

Alfa Romeo, 1930
Armored Motor Truck, 1898
Aston Martin, 1971
Benz, 1898, Runabout
Bernardi, 1893
Brewster, 1914, Landaulet Town Car
Brush, 1904, Runabout
Brush, 1906, Runabout
Cadillac, 1936, Fleetwood
Duesenberg, 1929, Model J
Ford, 1914, Model T Corning Runabout
Ford, 1919, Model T
Ford, 1929, Model A Mail Truck
Gleason, 1906, Model H
Lincoln, 1948, Continental
Locomobile, 1900, Steamer Runabout
Lola, 1972

Lola, 1978
Marmon, 1911, Model 32
Marmon, 1924
Mercedes, 1913, Roadster
Milburn, 1925, Electric
National, 1913, Roadster
Oldsmobile, 1905, Model B
Orient, 1905
Race Car, 1949, Blue Crown Sparkplug
Race Car, 1963, *Spirit of America*
Rambler, 1902, Model C Runabout
Rolls-Royce, 1929, Phantom I
Rolls-Royce, 1934, Phantom II
Sears, 1910
Simplex, 1911, Touring
Stevens-Duryea, 1904, Model L
Stoddard Dayton, 1907

Volo Auto Museum
27582 W. Highway 120, Volo, Illinois 60073
(815) 385-3644

The museum is located in Old Volo Village, the site for several shops and businesses dealing in crafts, activities and products from the past and present.

The museum has over eighty cars in its collection; most of the cars are for sale, however, so the following list of cars on display may change. There are auctions, shows and gatherings on the grounds. Call the museum for dates and times.

DIRECTIONS TO MUSEUM: The museum is 1/4 mile west of US 12 on Rt. 120.

ADMISSION COST: Adults $2.50; senior citizens $2.00; children $1.50.

HOURS OF OPERATION: Open daily 10am-5pm. Closed Thanksgiving, Christmas Eve and Christmas.

MUSEUM NOTES: A restaurant and a gift shop are located onsite. Film is not available.

A brochure is available.

Display Automobiles

Buick, 1940, Century Convertible
Buick, 1960, LeSabre Convertible
Buick, 1963, Wildcat Convertible
Buick, 1968, Gran Sport
Buick, 1969, Stage I
Buick, 1970, Gran Sport Convertible

Buick, 1970, Stage I Convertible
Buick, 1972, Skylark Convertible
Cadillac, 1935
Cadillac, 1941, 4dr Sedan
Cadillac, 1954, Coupe de Ville
Cadillac, 1960, Convertible

1970 NART. *This luxurious 1970 NART was designed by Luigi Chinetti and constructed at a cost of four million dollars. This is the only NART that was built.*

Cadillac, 1960, Coupe
Cadillac, 1962, Convertible
Cadillac, 1970, Convertible
Cadillac, 1974, Coupe
Chevrolet, 1929, Coupe
Chevrolet, 1937, 2dr Sedan
Chevrolet, 1955, Bel Air
Chevrolet, 1957, 2dr Sedan
Chevrolet, 1957, Bel Air
Chevrolet, 1959, Impala 2dr Hardtop
Chevrolet, 1960, Impala 2dr Hardtop
Chevrolet, 1960, Impala Convertible
Chevrolet, 1961, Impala Convertible
Chevrolet, 1963, Corvette Coupe
Chevrolet, 1964, Chevelle SS
Chevrolet, 1964, SS Impala
Chevrolet, 1965, Corvette Coupe
Chevrolet, 1966, Chevelle SS
Chevrolet, 1967, Corvette Roadster
Chevrolet, 1968, Camaro
Chevrolet, 1968, Camaro SS
Chevrolet, 1968, Camaro Z-28
Chevrolet, 1968, Chevelle Convertible
Chevrolet, 1968, Chevelle SS
Chevrolet, 1969, Camaro Convertible
Chevrolet, 1969, Camaro SS Convertible
Chevrolet, 1969, Chevelle
Chevrolet, 1970, Chevelle, SS
Chevrolet, 1970, Chevelle SS Convertible
Chevrolet, 1971, Corvette Roadster
Chevrolet, 1971, Monte Carlo SS
Chevrolet, 1976, Corvette
Chrysler, 1941, New Yorker Convertible
Cord, 1931, L-29 Cabriolet
Cord, 1931, L-29 Convertible
Cord, 1936, 810 Convertible
Detroit Electric, 1925
Dodge, 1966, Charger

Dodge, 1969, Charger
Dodge, 1969, Coronet
Dodge, 1970, Charger
Dodge, 1971, Charger RT
Ferrari, 1979, 308GTSI
Ford, 1926, Model T
Ford, 1928, Phaeton
Ford, 1939, 2dr Sedan
Ford, 1951, Convertible
Ford, 1956, Fairlane
Ford, 1957, Thunderbird
Ford, 1965, Mustang
Ford, 1965, Mustang Convertible
Ford, 1966, Galaxy Convertible
Ford, 1969, Mustang Mach I
Ford, 1970, Mustang Convertible
Ford, 1971, Mustang
Maxwell, 1912, Roadster
Mercedes, 1906, Roadster
MG, 1953, TD Roadster
NART, 1970, 2dr Coupe
Oldsmobile, 1966, 442
Oldsmobile, 1968, 442 Convertible
Oldsmobile, 1969, Cutlass S Convertible
Oldsmobile, 1970, 442
Oldsmobile, 1970, 442 Convertible
Oldsmobile, 1970, Cutlass
Oldsmobile, 1971, 442 Convertible
Oldsmobile, 1972, Hurst Indy Pace Car
Packard, 1955, 2dr Hardtop
Plymouth, 1968, GTX
Plymouth, 1968, GTX Convertible
Plymouth, 1970, Barracuda Convertible
Plymouth, 1970, Superbird
Pontiac, 1966, GTO
Rolls-Royce, 1967, Coupe
Zimmer, 1987, Quick Silver

Wheels O' Time Museum

Mail Address: 11923 N. Knoxville Avenue, Dunlap, Illinois 61525
(309) 243-9020 or 691-3470

Found in the museum are model trains, steam engines, railroad equipment, including a steam locomotive, cars, and collections of bicycles, cameras, clocks, musical instruments, toys, tools and steam whistles. Many hands-on displays allow the visitor to operate a steam whistle, player piano, siren, model train and antique radio.

Nearby Peoria was home for several auto manufacturers and two examples are displayed. The Duryea brothers constructed cars for a couple years in the late 1880s before going their separate ways. On display is an 1898 Duryea built during the brothers' stint in Peoria. Manufactured over a much longer period in Peoria was the Glide (a 1917 version is displayed). The company did not construct more than 200 cars in any year, nonetheless, the firm built cars for eighteen years, from 1903 to 1920.

DIRECTIONS TO MUSEUM: The museum is north of Peoria on Rt. 88 (Knoxville Ave.) approximately 1 1/2 miles north of intersection with Rt. 6.

ADMISSION COST: Adults $3.00; children $1.00.

HOURS OF OPERATION: Open May-October Wednesday-Sunday noon-5pm.

MUSEUM NOTES: There is a restaurant nearby and a gift shop onsite. Film is not available.

A brochure is available.

Display Automobiles

American LaFrance, 1951, Fire Truck
Arends-Fox, 1931, Fire Truck
Austin Healey, 1961, Roadster
Briscoe, 1924, 4dr Touring
Chevrolet, 1936, Fire Truck
Chevrolet, 1950, Convertible
Chevrolet, 1957, Convertible
Cord, 1930, L-29 Convertible Sedan
DeLorean, 1981
Duryea, 1898
Ford, 1913, Model T Roadster
Ford, 1924, Model T Roadster
Ford, 1929, Roadster
Glide, 1917, 4dr Touring

Lincoln, 1941, Continental Convertible
Lincoln, 1970, Continental Convertible
Mercedes-Benz, 1956, 300SL Roadster
Mercury, 1955, Convertible
Nash, 1957, Metropolitan Sedan
Packard, 1929, Roadster
Packard, 1932, Coupe Roadster
Packard, 1933, Roadster
Packard, 1948, Custom Convertible
Packard, 1956, Caribbean Convertible
Pierce-Arrow, 1933, Sedan
Rolls-Royce, 1933, Sedan
Velie, 1928, Coupe

Auburn-Cord-Duesenberg Museum

1600 South Wayne Street, Auburn, Indiana 46706
(219) 925-1444

This museum is the only automobile museum housed in a former automobile manufacturing facility. The cars of the Auburn-Cord-Duesenberg Museum are displayed in the former showroom and administration building for the Auburn Automobile Company. The building is listed on the National Register of Historic Places. Unused since closure of the company, several offices and work areas have been returned to their appearance of over half a century ago, including engineering drawings and design models made of clay.

Emphasized in the museum are the cars named after the town, Auburn automobiles. Production began in 1903, but lethargic sales resulted in owners Frank and Morris Eckhart losing control of the ailing company to Errett Lobban Cord. Cord revitalized the company into a strong, independent auto maker in the 1920s. Thanks to progressive styling, powerful engines and moderate pricing, Auburns became strong sellers before the Depression. Initially surviving the Depression, Auburn succumbed along with other Cord holdings and 1936 was the last year of production. Over twenty Auburns are on display in the museum.

E.L. Cord was the driving force in the ascendacy of Auburn automobiles in the marketplace, and was also a factor in their demise. After guiding Auburn upward, Cord acquired the Duesenberg Motors Company and began production of the famous car line

1933 Auburn Speedster. *This artist's rendition of the Auburn boattail classic came from the archives of the Auburn-Cord-Duesenberg Museum. Offering exciting styling and high performance at modest cost, the 1933 Auburn Speedsters were offered with either an inline eight-cylinder engine or V-12 engine, both built by Lycoming.*

Two products of E.L. Cord's automotive empire grace the art deco interior of the Auburn-Cord-Duesenberg Museum, a Duesenberg on the left and an Auburn on the right.

that bore his name, the Cord. He continued acquiring companies, but the Depression and suspect business dealings forced him to sell off his empire. Several of the companies continued operation, but production of Auburns, Duesenbergs and Cords was never revived.

Auburn, Indiana, proclaims itself the "Home of the Classics" and each Labor Day hosts the Auburn-Cord-Duesenberg Festival. The highlight of the event is the parade of classic cars through Auburn that shows off over 200 Auburns, Cords and Duesenbergs. The week-long Festival is a city-wide event that caters to the auto enthusiast while providing entertainment for the whole family. Call the museum or Auburn Chamber of Commerce (219-925-2100) for specific dates and events.

DIRECTIONS TO MUSEUM: From I-69 take Exit 129 and travel east on Hwy. 8 (7th St.) into Auburn. Follow signs to museum.

ADMISSION COST: Adults $6.00; senior citizens $4.00; students $4.00; family $15.00.

HOURS OF OPERATION: Open daily 9am-6pm.

MUSEUM NOTES: Film is available in the gift shop. There are restaurants nearby.

A brochure is available.

1932 Duesenberg Model J Speedster. *E.L. Cord, builder of the Auburn-Cord-Duesenberg conglomerate, declared that the Model J Duesenberg was the world's finest automobile. Cost was not a consideration during construction, which limited sales to only the very rich. But the Cord empire expired during the Depression and Duesenbergs were last built in 1937.*

Display Automobiles

Albany, 1908, Surrey
Amphicar, 1967
Aston Martin, 1953, Coupe
Auburn, 1904, Rear Entrance Tonneau
Auburn, 1907, Touring
Auburn, 1910, Roadster
Auburn, 1911, Touring
Auburn, 1912, Salon
Auburn, 1917, Touring
Auburn, 1919, Roadster
Auburn, 1923, Limousine
Auburn, 1926, Roadster
Auburn, 1928, Sport Sedan
Auburn, 1929, Cabin Speedster
Auburn, 1929, Speedster
Auburn, 1930, Cabriolet
Auburn, 1931, Sedan
Auburn, 1932, Sedan
Auburn, 1935, Cabriolet
Auburn, 1935, Speedster (two)
Auburn, 1936, Cabriolet (two)
Auburn, 1936, Convertible Sedan
Austin, 1923, Chummy

Austin, 1934, Delivery Coupe
Autocar, 1903, Runabout
Bentley, 1931, Saloon
Bricklin, 1975, SV1
Buehrig, 1979, Coupe
Bugatti, 1928, T-37-A Grand Prix
Buick, 1953, Skylark Convertible
Cadillac, 1925, Coupe Sedan
Cadillac, 1930, V-16 Imperial Limousine
Cadillac, 1930, V-16 Town Cabriolet
Cadillac, 1939, V-16 Sedan
Cadillac, 1957, Eldorado Brougham
Checker, 1933, Taxicab
Chevrolet, 1938, 2dr Sedan
Chevrolet, 1947, Sedan Delivery Custom
Chevrolet, 1963, Corvette
Chevrolet, 1978, Corvette
Citroen, 1956, Salon
Cord, 1931, L-29 Convertible
Cord, 1936, Sedan
Cord, 1937, Beverly Sedan
Cord, 1937, Convertible Coupe
Cord, 1937, Convertible Phaeton

Cord, 1937, Coupe
Crosley, 1941, Convertible
Crosley, 1952, Station Wagon
Cummins, 1934, Diesel Race Car
DeLorean, 1981, Coupe
DeSoto, 1947, 2dr Sedan
DeTomaso, 1971, Pantera
Dodge, 1944, Army Command Car
Duesenberg, 1925, Model A Sport Touring
Duesenberg, 1926, Model A Sedan
Duesenberg, 1929, Model J Torpedo
   Convertible
Duesenberg, 1929, Model J Towncar
Duesenberg, 1931, Race Car
Duesenberg, 1932, Model J Speedster
Duesenberg, 1966, Sedan
Duryea, 1905
Economy, 1908, MotorBuggy
Elcar, 1932, Princess Coupe
Essex, 1929, Coupe
Ferrari, 1952, Berlineta
Ferrari, 1961, 250GTE
Ferrari, 1970, 365GT
Ford, 1913, Touring
Ford, 1922, Snowcar
Ford, 1927, 4dr Sedan
Ford, 1948, 4dr Sedan
Ford, 1950
Ford, 1951, Victoria
Ford, 1956, Thunderbird
Gasmobile, 1901, Stanhope Phaeton
Haynes, 1918, Roadster
Hupmobile, 1924, Coupe
Hupmobile, 1936, Sedan
Imp, 1913, Cyclecar
Izzer, 1911, Roadster
Jaguar, 1946, Saloon
Jaguar, 1952, XK120

Jaguar, 1963, XK-E
Kiblinger, 1907, Runabout
Kiblinger, 1908, Runabout
Kirsch, 1911, Paddy Wagon
Lincoln, 1933, Dual Cowl Phaeton
Locomobile, 1899
Locomobile, 1919, Limousine
McIntyre, 1909, Autobuggy
Mercedes-Benz, 1936
Mercury, 1939, Barris Custom
MG, 1954, Roadster
MG, 1975, GT
Oldsmobile, 1953, Fiesta Convertible
Packard, 1903
Packard, 1918, Twin Six Touring
Packard, 1929, Coupe
Packard, 1933, Victoria Convertible
Porsche, 1965, 356C
Porsche, 1970, 911S
Premier, 1916, Foursome
Rauch-Lang, 1916, Coach
Regal, 1911, Touring
Rolls-Royce, 1957, Convertible
Sabra, 1965, Roadster
Shelby, 1967, Cobra
Stevens-Duryea, 1913, Touring
Studebaker, 1955, President Speedster
Studebaker, 1963, Lark Sedan
Stutz, 1912, Bearcat
Stutz, 1914, Bearcat
Tasco, 1948, Coupe
Velie, 1918, Touring
Waverly, 1899
Westcott, 1916, Touring
Zimmerman, 1908, Runabout
Zimmerman, 1909, Runabout
Zimmerman, 1910, Runabout

Elwood Haynes Museum

1915 S. Webster, Kokomo, Indiana 46902
(317) 452-3471

The museum's focus is Elwood Haynes, Indiana industrialist. Haynes claimed he built the first car in America, although facts do not substantiate his claim (John Lambert built the first American car in 1891). The car was designed by Haynes and actually built by the Apperson brothers in their Riverside Machine Works shop. In 1898 Haynes and the Appersons formed the Haynes-Apperson Automobile Company.

Production was sporadic at the outset, but by 1900 car production reached one car daily. The Appersons left the company in 1901 and started their own automobile manufacturing company, which failed in 1926. Haynes cars sold successfully until the early 1920s when financial difficulties overcame the company. Haynes cars were last manufactured in 1924. Elwood Haynes died in 1925.

Haynes' spot in industrial history is more prominent for his development of the alloy Stellite. The process is used to produce a hard face on steel that is resistant to high temperatures.

Artifacts and memorabilia from Haynes life are on display at the museum, as well as a 1905 Haynes Model L, 1923 Apperson Jack Rabbit, 1924 Haynes Roadster and 1924 Haynes Touring Car.

DIRECTIONS TO MUSEUM: From US 31 go west on Boulevard St. to Webster St.

ADMISSION COST: Free.

HOURS OF OPERATION: Open Tuesday-Saturday 1-4pm; Sunday 1-5pm. Closed Monday.

MUSEUM NOTES: There is a restaurant nearby. The museum has a gift shop, but film is not available.

A brochure is available.

Indianapolis Motor Speedway
Hall of Fame Museum

4790 W. 16th Street, Indianapolis, Indiana 46222
(317) 248-6747

The Indianapolis Motor Speedway is the most famous race track in the world, and has been recognized as a National Historic Landmark. This is the site for the Indianapolis 500 auto race, an annual sports spectacular that draws the largest single-day crowd for any sporting event in the world, approximately 300,000 spectators attend. Except for intervals during the war years 1917-1918 and 1942-1945, the "500" has been run every year since 1911.

The focus of the car collection is a selection of Indianapolis "500" winners. Also displayed are significant road race cars and sports cars, such as a Maserati "Birdcage", a Ferrari 250LM, a Cooper-Climax, and the Corvette SS. For the Indy race car fan, this is an opportunity to view the evolution of paved-oval race cars from the era of riding mechanics to today's high-tech machinery. Racing-related artifacts are showcased and a movie theater (no charge) presents a history of the Indianapolis 500.

1911 Marmon Wasp. *Ray Harroun drove this Marmon, the* Wasp, *to victory in the 1911 Indianapolis 500 race. The 447.1 cu. in. engine propelled the car to an average speed of 74 mph. During the early years of motor racing, a mechanic rode along to advise the driver of the whereabouts of other cars. Harroun did not want to carry a riding mechanic in his race car, a dangerous situation in the opinion of the other teams. So to view other cars, a mirror was constructed that looked behind the car, the probable first use of a rear-view mirror.*

Several race engines are displayed, including Offenhauser, Miller, Ford and Chevrolet.

The track was constructed in 1909 and racing took place that year and in 1910. Several races were run during each of those years. The track surface in 1909 was crushed stone, but the track deteriorated and was resurfaced with over three million bricks, earning the track the nickname "brickyard." The operators decided that spectators, racers and track management would be best served by a single spectacular race event run on an annual basis, and the "500" was born. Ray Harroun won the first "500" on May 30, 1911, in the Marmon *Wasp* on display in the museum. Harroun drove at an average speed of 74 mph and required 6 hours 42 minutes to finish the race. By comparison, the winners of the last ten races have hovered around an average speed of 160 mph.

In its time, particularly before manufacturers constructed their own test tracks, the track has been the proving ground, both on race day and during test sessions for a myriad of automotive innovations, including improved engine components, brake systems, tires, fuels and suspensions. Early automotive luminaries such as Louis Chevrolet, Henry Ford and the Duesenberg brothers tested and raced at the track. In later times, all major automobile manufacturers have at one time or other put their ideas to the test on the oval. To a race car driver this is the pinnacle, to a race fan this is Mecca.

The month of May is both the best time to visit the Speedway and the worst. If you want to avoid crowds, be aware that opening day of time trials and race weekend (Memorial Day weekend) draw hundreds of thousands of people to the track. But on testing days during the month, the crowds are comparatively sparse, admission to the track is a couple of dollars, seating is free and plentiful, and there is usually plenty of action on the track and in the pits as the teams test their cars. The best vantage point for first-time visitors is the grandstand along pit lane.

Foyt-Gilmore Coyote Indy Car. *One of motor racing's all-time greats, A. J. Foyt, drove the Foyt-Gilmore "14" to a win in the 1977 Indianapolis 500 race, the fourth Indy win for Foyt.*

During racing season, race teams will sometimes use the track to test their race cars. Turns 1 and 2 are visible from the parking lot and the spectator stands nearby are open. No charge for this added attraction.

When the racetrack is not in use, a driving tour of the track is available in Speedway vehicles for $1.00 per person, all ages. Private vehicles are not allowed on the track.

DIRECTIONS TO MUSEUM: The museum is located inside the main building, which is on the race track grounds. Enter the speedway from 16th St. (you travel under the race track). From I-465 exit onto Speedway Ave. eastbound and follow to race track. From downtown Indianapolis follow 16th St. west to race track.

ADMISSION COST: $1.00 if over 15 yrs. old; free if under 16 yrs. old.

HOURS OF OPERATION: Open daily 9am-5pm. Closed Christmas.

MUSEUM NOTES: There are restaurants nearby. Film is available in the gift shop.

A brochure is available.

Display Automobiles

Agajanian-Willard Battery Special, 1963
Alfa Romeo Special, 1948
Bardahl Eagle, 1966

Belanger Special, 1951
Belond Exhaust Special, 1957
Bentley, 1922

Blue Crown Spark Plug Special, 1947
Bowes Seal Fast Special, 1938
Bowes Seal Fast Special, 1961
Boyle Special, 1939
Chevrolet, 1957, Corvette SS
Cole, 1911, 30
Cooper-Climax, 1961
Cord, 1930, L-29
Dean Van Lines Special, 1957
Dean Van Lines Special, 1967
Delage, 1914
Domino's Pizza Special, 1990
Duesenberg, 1914
Ferrari, 1965, 250LM
Ferrari Special, 1952
Fiat, 1912
First National City Travelers Checks, 1978
Ford, 1966, Mark II-B
Fuel Injection Special, 1953
Gilmore, 1977
Gulf-Miller Special, 1941
Italia, 1907
John Zink Special, 1955
Ken-Paul Special, 1960
Leader Card Special, 1962
Lotus-Ford, 1963
Marmon Wasp, 1911
Maserati, 1960, "Birdcage"

Mercedes-Benz, 1927, Type S
Miller Junior, 1925
Miller Special, 1928
Miller-Ford, 1935
Miller-Hartz Special, 1932
Murphy Special, 1922
National, 1912
Noc-Out Hose Clamp Special, 1941
Novi
Patrick Wildcat, 1982
Pennzoil Chaparral, 1980
Premier, 1903
Rislone Special, 1968
Sheraton-Thompson III, 1970
Sheraton-Thompson Special, 1964
Sheraton-Thompson Special, 1967
STP Oil Filter Special, 1973
STP Oil Treatment Special, 1967
STP Oil Treatment Special, 1969
Studebaker Special, 1932
Stutz, 1914
Sunbeam
Sunoco McLaren, 1972
Texaco Star, 1978
Texaco Star, 1983
Thorne Engineering Special, 1946
Wynn's Friction Proofing Special, 1950

S. Ray Miller Foundation Antique Car Museum

2130 Middlebury Street, Elkhart, Indiana 46516
(219) 522-0539

The cars in the museum were collected and restored by S. Ray Miller, Jr. The museum's emphasis is on prestige cars built prior to World War II. Several of the cars have been prize winners in car show competition. In addition to the cars displayed is a collection of radiator auto emblems, the largest in the world, along with other artifacts and memorabilia.

One of the cars on display is a Marmon V-16 Convertible Sedan. Marmons were originally offered as high quality, high priced cars, although more modest models were built later to increase production and revenue. The Convertible Sedans are the most desirable of the Marmons with an estimated current value in excess of $150,000. They were constructed in 1931, 1932 and 1933 and equipped with the Marmon V-16 engine. The advent of the Depression doomed the Marmon Company and production of these fine, luxurious automobiles stopped in 1933. A boost in popularity was achieved in 1911 when the Marmon Wasp won the first Indianapolis 500 race. The car is displayed in the Indianapolis Motor Speedway Hall of Fame Museum.

DIRECTIONS TO MUSEUM: Just off of US 20 and east of intersection of Middlebury St. and Industrial Pkwy.

ADMISSION COST: Adults $3.00; senior citizens and children $2.00.

HOURS OF OPERATION: Open Monday-Friday 1-4pm and on last weekend of month noon-4pm.

MUSEUM NOTES: There are restaurants nearby.

A brochure is available.

1931 Cord L-29 Cabriolet. *The Cord L-29 was the first production car equipped with front-wheel drive, as well as the first with "X" bracing in the frame. Production totaled 5,010 from 1928 to 1932. Power was provided by a Lycoming six-cylinder engine with 298 cubic inch displacement.*

1930 Duesenberg Model J Convertible. *High on any list of classic cars are Duesenbergs, and the Model J tops the list of desirable Duesenbergs. The museum's 1931 convertible was one of approximately 480 Model J Duesenbergs built from 1927 to 1937. At the time, they were the most powerful cars on the road. According to Duesenberg advertising, no greater assessment of a man's stature could be made than, "He drives a Duesenberg."*

Display Automobiles

Auburn, 1935, Speedster
Cadillac, 1931, Fleetwood Roadster
Chevrolet, 1930, Phaeton Touring
Chrysler, 1929, Model 75 Phaeton
Cord, 1931, L-29
Cord, 1937, Phaeton
Dodge, 1924, Touring
Dodge, 1934, Roadster
Duesenberg, 1930, Model J Murphy
  Convertible
Elcar, 1928, Roadster
Erskine, 1927, Touring
Ford, 1903, Runabout
Ford, 1915, Model T
Ford, 1930, Model A Roadster
Ford, 1931, Model A Roadster
Ford, 1936, Phaeton
Ford, 1948, Woody Station Wagon

Graham, 1925, Fire Truck
Kissel, 1920, Tourister
Lincoln, 1948, Continental Cabriolet
Locomobile, 1900
Marmon, 1931, V-16 Convertible Sedan
Nash, 1932, Advanced Victoria
Packard, 1934, Super Eight Phaeton
Pratt-Elkhart, 1911, Touring Car
Reo, 1932, Royale Convertible Coupe
Rolls-Royce, 1928, Phantom I Town Car
Ruxton, 1929, Roadster
Sterling, 1909, Model K
Studebaker, 1931, President Roadster
Studebaker, 1931, Series 54 Roadster
Studebaker, 1932, President St. Regis
  Brougham
Studebaker, 1932, President State Sedan
Stutz, 1931, SV-16, Roadster

Studebaker National Museum
525 S. Main Street, South Bend, Indiana 46601
(219) 284-9714

The Studebaker National Museum serves to document the work of the Studebaker brothers, John, Clem and Henry, and the history of the automobile company that bore their name. The vast collection of Studebaker cars includes the first car built in the South Bend factory, a 1920 Light Six, and the last car built in South Bend, a 1964 Lark Daytona. The collection also includes several wagons built by the Studebakers.

The Studebakers were moguls in the transportation industry before they undertook auto making. During the mid to late 1800s their wagon manufacturing firm was the largest in the world. The company first constructed cars in partnership with the Garford and E-M-F companies. Those firms built the chassis and engines, and Studebaker built the bodies. In 1911 Studebaker was the second largest auto manufacturer in the country, behind Ford. Although the company was responsible for significant highpoints in auto-motive design, such as the post-World War II Loewy/Exner Studebakers and the sporty

1932 Rockne 2dr Sedan. *Attempting to enter the low-priced segment of the market, Studebaker introduced the Rockne car line in the spring of 1932. The car was named after famed Notre Dame football coach Knute Rockne, who died in a plane crash the previous spring. Unlike the coach's success against tough competition, the Rockne car couldn't survive against formidable Ford and Chevrolet, so Studebaker dropped the line in 1933.*

Avanti, and earned significant income during war years, steady decline finally led to construction of the last Studebaker in Hamilton, Canada, in 1966. Ironically, just as the first Studebakers were built using engines manufactured by another company, the last Studebakers were equipped with Chevrolet engines.

DIRECTIONS TO MUSEUM: The museum is located at the intersection of Main St. (US 31) and South St.

ADMISSION COST: Adults $3.50; senior citizens $2.50; children $1.50.

HOURS OF OPERATION: Open Monday-Saturday 9:30am-4:30pm; Sunday noon-4:30pm. Closed Thanksgiving and Christmas.

MUSEUM NOTES: There is a restaurant nearby. Film is available in the gift shop.

A brochure is available.

Display Automobiles

Bendix, 1934, Prototype
E-M-F, 1910
Erskine, 1928
Flanders, 1912
Packard, 1901
Packard, 1955, Patrician
Packard, 1956, Predictor
Packard, 1957, Clipper
Studebaker, 1913, Six
Studebaker, 1917, Big Six
Studebaker, 1917, Special Six
Studebaker, 1919, Big Six
Studebaker, 1920, Light Six
Studebaker, 1920, SLS Series Light Six
Studebaker, 1922, Big Six Touring Car
Studebaker, 1926, Duplex Roadster
Studebaker, 1927, Commander
Studebaker, 1928, Commander
Studebaker, 1929, President
Studebaker, 1931, President Brougham Special
Studebaker, 1932, Rockne 65
Studebaker, 1937, Cab Forward Bus
Studebaker, 1939, Champion
Studebaker, 1939, Champion Coupe
Studebaker, 1939, Commander
Studebaker, 1941, Skyway
Studebaker, 1943, Army Truck
Studebaker, 1943, Weasel
Studebaker, 1946, Truck
Studebaker, 1947, Business Coupe
Studebaker, 1947, Commander
Studebaker, 1948, Champion
Studebaker, 1950, Champion Convertible

Studebaker, 1951, Champion Starlite
Studebaker, 1952, Champion
Studebaker, 1952, Champion Hard Top
Studebaker, 1952, Commander
Studebaker, 1953, Commander Hard Top
Studebaker, 1953, Commander Sedan
Studebaker, 1954, Champion Coupe
Studebaker, 1954, Conestoga Station Wagon
Studebaker, 1955, Commander
Studebaker, 1956, Champion
Studebaker, 1956, Dump Truck
Studebaker, 1956, Flight Hawk
Studebaker, 1956, Pickup
Studebaker, 1956, Sky Hawk
Studebaker, 1957, Golden Hawk
Studebaker, 1958, Fire Truck
Studebaker, 1958, School Bus
Studebaker, 1960, Lark
Studebaker, 1961, Pickup
Studebaker, 1962, GT Hawk
Studebaker, 1962, Lark Dayton
Studebaker, 1962, Pickup
Studebaker, 1963, Avanti
Studebaker, 1963, Lark Regal
Studebaker, 1963, Pickup
Studebaker, 1963, Truck
Studebaker, 1963, Wagonaire
Studebaker, 1964, GT Hawk
Studebaker, 1964, Lark Daytona
Studebaker, 1965, Wagonaire
Studebaker, 1966, Cruiser
U.S. Army, 1985, Hummer

Wayne County Historical Museum

1150 North A Street, Richmond, Indiana 47374
(317) 962-5756

An overview of the lifestyle of inhabitants of Wayne County is the focus of the museum. Artifacts and memorabilia include household goods, clothing, tools and vehicles. A log cabin, general store and various shops are situated on the grounds.

Richmond, Indiana, has been the manufacturing site for 13 automobile builders and the museum has four cars built in Richmond on display, a 1909 Richmond, a 1910 Westcott, a 1918 Davis and a 1920 Pilot. The Davis marque outlived the other three, although 1929 was the last year of manufacture. The Davis, Pilot and Westcott were assembled cars. Major components were purchased from outside vendors and assembled in the company's plant.

DIRECTIONS TO MUSEUM: The museum is located on US 40 (A St.) in Richmond.

ADMISSION COST: Adults $2.50; children $1.00.

HOURS OF OPERATION: Open Tuesday-Friday 9am-4pm; Saturday and Sunday 1-4pm. Closed Monday.

MUSEUM NOTES: There is a restaurant nearby. The museum has a gift shop. Film is not available.

A brochure is available.

Display Automobiles

Baker Electric, 1910, 2dr Sedan
Brush, 1910, Roadster
Crosley, 1939, Convertible
Davis, 1918, Phaeton
Detroit Electric, 1919, 2dr Sedan
Dodge, 1926, Sedan

Ford, 1915, Model T Touring
Maxwell, 1914, Roadster
Pilot, 1920, Touring
Richmond, 1909, Touring
Westcott, 1910, Roadster

Duffy's Collectible Cars

250 Classic Car Court S.W., Cedar Rapids, Iowa 52404
(319) 364-7000

The cars at Duffy's are both for viewing, and for sale. Duffy's is a "collector car store" that specializes in sought-after classic cars.

The vintages of the cars in the collection are primarily from the 1940s, 1950s and 1960s. The bulk of the cars are either convertibles or hardtops. The inventory is constantly changing so call ahead for information on a specific car.

DIRECTIONS TO MUSEUM: From I-380 exit onto 33rd Ave. and travel east. Turn right at J Street S.W. and travel to Classic Car Court S.W.

ADMISSION COST: Adults $2.00; children under 10 yrs. free.

HOURS OF OPERATION: Open Monday-Friday 8:30am-6pm; Saturday 8:30am-4:30pm; closed Sunday.

MUSEUM NOTES: Vending machines are onsite and a restaurant is nearby. Film is available in the gift shop.

A brochure is available.

Display Automobiles

Buick, 1958
Buick, 1966, Electra
Cadillac, 1949
Cadillac, 1956
Cadillac, 1958, Biarritz
Cadillac, 1959, Eldorado Hardtop
Cadillac, 1960, Fleetwood
Cadillac, 1966, Eldorado
Chevrolet, 1950, Bel Air Hardtop
Chevrolet, 1955
Chevrolet, 1955, Bel Air Hardtop
Chevrolet, 1956, Bel Air Hardtop
Chevrolet, 1957, Bel Air
Chevrolet, 1957, Bel Air Convertible
Chevrolet, 1957, Bel Air Hardtop
Chevrolet, 1958, Impala
Chevrolet, 1958, Impala Hardtop
Chevrolet, 1959, Impala
Chevrolet, 1960, Impala
Chevrolet, 1961
Chevrolet, 1962, Impala SS
Chevrolet, 1962, Nova
Chevrolet, 1964, Chevelle SS Hardtop
Chevrolet, 1964, Impala SS Convertible
Chevrolet, 1966, Chevelle SS

Chevrolet, 1966, Impala, SS Convertible
Chevrolet, 1969, Camaro
Chevrolet, 1969, Camaro Z-28
Chevrolet, 1970, Chevelle SS
Chevrolet, 1970, Nova SS
Chevrolet, 1970 1/2, Camaro Z-28
Chevrolet, 1975, Caprice Convertible
Chevrolet, 1982, Corvette
Dodge, 1968, Coronet Hemi
Dodge, 1970, Super Bee
Edsel, 1959, Corsair
Ford, 1928, Truck
Ford, 1929, Model A Panel Delivery
Ford, 1930, Model A
Ford, 1930, Model A Roadster
Ford, 1932, Show Truck
Ford, 1940
Ford, 1954
Ford, 1954, Sunliner Convertible
Ford, 1955, Sunliner Convertible
Ford, 1957, Skyliner
Ford, 1957, Thunderbird
Ford, 1960, Thunderbird
Ford, 1965, Mustang Convertible
Ford, 1966, Mustang GT

Ford, 1969, Mustang Mach I
Ford, 1979, Futura
GMC, 1951, Pickup Truck
Jaguar, 1955, XK-140
Lincoln, 1948, Continental Convertible
Lincoln, 1957, Premier Hardtop
Mercury, 1951
Mercury, 1954, Monterey Hardtop
Mercury, 1956, Montclair Hardtop
Oldsmobile, 1949
Oldsmobile, 1966, 442
Oldsmobile, 1970, Cutlass Convertible
Plymouth, 1948
Pontiac, 1954, Convertible
Pontiac, 1956, Chieftain Hardtop
Pontiac, 1959, Bonneville
Pontiac, 1962, Bonneville
Pontiac, 1967, GTO
Pontiac, 1969, GTO
Studebaker, 1950, Pickup Truck

Olson Linn Museum

Box 124, Villisca, Iowa 50864
(712) 826-7632 or (515) 322-4202

The museum presents antique and classic cars, trucks, buggies and farm machinery.

Among the unique cars in the collection is a 1917 Cole roadster. The Cole Motor Car Company produced an upscale car that rivalled Cadillac, prompting General Motors chairman William Durant to make an offer for the company. But Joseph Cole refused, a decision he probably second-guessed later. In 1919, its best year, Cole built over 6,000 cars, placing it second to Cadillac in the upscale marketplace. Both Cole and Cadillac were powered by a V-8 engine, in fact, both companies bought the engine from the same supplier, the Northway Division of General Motors. Success was fleeting, however, and tough economic times after World War I persuaded Joseph Cole to leave the auto market. Cole automobiles were last built in 1925.

DIRECTIONS TO MUSEUM: The museum is situated on the southeast corner of the square in Villisca.

HOURS OF OPERATION: Open June 1-October 1 Saturday noon-5pm and Sunday 1-5pm.

ADMISSION COST: Adults $1.00; children 50¢.

MUSEUM NOTES: There is a restaurant nearby. Film is not available.

A brochure is available.

Display Automobiles

Allen, 1917, Touring
Buick, 1917, Touring
Buick, 1924, Master 50 4dr Sedan
Buick, 1928, Pickup Truck
Chalmers
Chevrolet, 1929, Truck
Cole, 1917, Cloverleaf Roadster
Diamond T Truck
Dodge, 1924, Roadster
Edsel, 1958, Citation 4dr Sedan
Ford, 1914, Model T Roadster
Ford, 1916, Model T Pickup Truck
Ford, 1917, Model T Roadster
Ford, 1918, Delivery Van
Ford, 1921, Delivery Van
Ford, 1923, Model T Coupe
Ford, 1924, Model T Coupe
Ford, 1926, Model T Coupe
Ford, 1929, Model A 2dr Sedan
Ford, 1929, Model A Coupe
Ford, 1929, Model A Pickup Truck
Ford, 1929, Model AA Truck
GMC, 1930, Truck
Hupmobile, 1930, Coupe
International Truck
Kaiser, 1951, 4dr Sedan
Maxwell, 1910, Roadster
Maxwell, 1924, Coupe
Maxwell Truck
Nash, 1924, 4dr Sedan
Oakland
Overland
Reo, 1920, Truck
Sampson, 1918, Truck
Star, 1924, Touring

Schield International Museum

805 W. Bremer Avenue, Waverly, Iowa 50677
(319) 352-8318

The Schield International Museum is a collection of artifacts and memorabilia gathered by Vern Schield during his travel abroad. In the collection are such items as elephant tusks, a giant clam shell and a Persian rug. Schield donated the collection to Wartburg College, which administers its public viewing.

While there are only two cars on display, a 1912 Ford model T and a 1956 Russian Pobeda, there is also Schield's first Bantam. Built in 1942, Schield constructed the Bantam dragline out of car parts and available machinery. He and his wife operated the machine to gather limestone and supplement their farm income. Mining companies began buying the machines and in 10 years Schield was the largest manufacturer in the world of truck-mounted power cranes and excavators. A testament to the capabilities of individuals who succeed with ingenuity and the supplies at hand.

DIRECTIONS TO MUSEUM: The museum is located on Bremer Ave. (US 218) across from the Wartburg College campus.

HOURS OF OPERATION: Open from Memorial Day to Labor Day Tuesday-Sunday 1-5pm.

ADMISSION COST: Adults $1.00; children 25¢.

MUSEUM NOTES: There is a restaurant nearby. Film is not available.

A brochure is available.

Van Horn's Antique Truck Museum

US 65 North, Mason City, Iowa 50401
(515) 423-0655

The museum specializes in trucks prior to 1930. On display are most of the major manufacturers of trucks in the nation including: Reo, GMC, Mack, Diamond T, GMC, IHC and Ford. Just as the number of auto manufacturers has declined, so have many early truck manufacturers left the marketplace. A visit to Van Horn's offers a look at the machines constructed by the early truck builders.

Also on display are gas pumps, garage tools, signs and other auto and truck artifacts and memorabilia. Of note is a restored 1920 GMC circus truck accompanied by an intricate, large-scale model circus that required 34 years to create.

DIRECTIONS TO MUSEUM: The museum is north of Mason City on US 65 approximately one mile north of Co. Rd. B-20.

MUSEUM NOTES: There is a restaurant nearby and the museum has a gift shop. Film is not available.

ADMISSION COST: Adults $4.00; children (6-12 yrs.) $1.50.

A brochure is available.

HOURS OF OPERATION: Open May 25-September 22 Monday-Saturday 9am-4pm; Sunday 11am-5pm.

1918 Mack Truck. *The pugnacious appearance of early Mack trucks generated the "bulldog" nickname, which was later used in the company's logo and as its hood ornament.*

Display Automobiles

Acme, 1917, Truck
All-American, 1920, Truck
Autocar, 1922, Truck
Avery, 1909, Truck
Bessemer, 1914, Truck
Buick, 1916, Truck
Chase, 1912, Truck
Commerce, 1915, Truck
Diamond T, 1914, Truck
Douglas, 1918, Truck
Ford, , Model T Truck
Fulton, 1918, Truck
Galloway, 1909, Truck
Garford, 1922, Truck
GMC, 1916, Fire Truck
GMC, 1918, Circus Truck
GMC, 1919, Truck
GMC, 1920, Fuel Truck
Graham, 1928, Truck
Graham Bros., 1925, Truck
Hawkeye, 1916, Truck
Hurlburt, 1920, Truck
IHC, 1909, Truck
IHC, 1912, Auto Buggy
IHC, 1925, Truck
Koering, 1930, Dumpster
Mack, 1918, Truck

Mack, 1920, AB Truck
Mack, 1925, AB Military
Master, 1918, Truck
Menomonie Hurryton, 1922, Truck
Nash, 1914, Quad Truck
Nash, 1917, Truck
Nash, 1920, Truck
Old Hickory, 1915, Truck
Oldsmobile, 1919, Truck
Oneida, 1918, Truck
Packard, 1915, Truck
Packet, 1914, Truck
Pierce-Arrow, 1920, Truck
Rapid, 1908, Truck
Reo, 1912, Truck
Reo, 1914, Truck
Reo, 1917, Speed Wagon Truck
Republic, 1916, Truck
Samson, 1920, Truck
Schacht, 1920, Truck
Service, 1925, Truck
Sternberg, 1914, Truck
Stoughton, 1922, Truck
Studebaker, 1930, Wrecker
Traffic, 1923, Truck
Transport, 1918, Truck

Reo Antique Auto Museum

100 N. Harrison, Lindsborg, Kansas 67456
(913) 227-3252

The Reo Antique Auto Museum embodies the private collection of Quintin and Florence Applequist. As the name suggests, the majority of the collection consists of Reo automobiles, although there are several other marques also on display.

The Reo name represents the initials of Ransom E. Olds, a highly successful leader of early American auto manufacturing. He developed the Curved Dash Oldsmobile, which after its introduction in 1901, became the first car produced in quantity in America (over 5500 were built in 1904). In 1904 Olds left the Olds Motor Works after disagreeing with majority owners of the company and formed another firm that bore his initials, the Reo Motor Car Company. Reo quickly captured a significant portion of the market by becoming the third-most prolific car builder in 1907. Reos were marketed successfully until the Depression, when financial problems weakened the firm. In 1936 the last Reo was built and the company channeled all its energy to building trucks (since 1911 the firm had become an established truck manufacturer). R.E. Olds had left the company in the middle 1920s, returned during the early 1930s, and left again after the decision was made to stop car production. He was involved in land development, a lawn mower company and banking during his later years. He died in 1970 at the age of 86.

DIRECTIONS TO MUSEUM: The museum is located at the corner of Bus. US 81 (Harrison) and Lincoln.

ADMISSION COST: Adults $2.00; students $1.00; children under 13 yrs. free.

1929 Reo Flying Cloud Coupe. *The Flying Cloud was introduced in 1927. It was the first car equipped with Lockheed internal-expanding, hydraulic brakes, a design still used today, although largely supplanted by disc brakes. The museum's Flying Cloud is equipped with a compartment to the rear of the passenger door for stowing golf clubs.*

1916 Reo Touring. Before pursuing interests outside Reo, Ransom Olds participated directly in the design of the "Fifth" series, which lasted from 1912 through 1919. The major change was relocation of the transmission gear selector. A 30/35 hp, four-cylinder engine powered the car.

HOURS OF OPERATION: Open Monday-Saturday 9:30am-5pm (10am-3pm during winter); Sunday 1-5pm.

MUSEUM NOTES: There is a restaurant nearby. Film is not available.

A brochure is available.

Display Automobiles

Black, 1908
Cadillac, 1907, Runabout
Chevrolet, 1930, Pickup Truck
Dodge, 1924, Coupe
Ford, 1911, Model T
Ford, 1923, Model T
Ford, 1936, Pickup Truck
Hupmobile, 1922, Touring
Metz, 1916, Raceabout

Plymouth, 1936, Convertible
Reo, 1908
Reo, 1916, Touring
Reo, 1923, Opera Coupe
Reo, 1926, 4dr Sedan
Reo, 1929, Deluxe Coupe
Reo, 1936, 4dr Sedan
Reo, 1948, Truck

Wheels & Spokes

383 Mopar Drive, Hays, Kansas 67601
(913) 628-6477

Wheels & Spokes is the creation of Jerry Juenemann. Starting in 1971, Juenemann has collected an extensive selection of Mopar muscle cars, as well as several antique and classic cars of other marques. The collection also contains the Barris custom car constructed for the movie *Fireball 500* (originally a 1966 Plymouth Barracuda), and the 1969 Plymouth Duster I show car built by Chrysler. As evidenced by the following list of cars on display, this collection should be entertaining to anyone interested in modern era, high performance Chrysler products.

A couple of the cars in the collection are equipped with "hemi" engines, a type of engine identified with post-World War II Chrysler Corporation cars. The engine was a brawny, powerful engine that became the engine of choice for dragsters and "funny cars" in the burgeoning sport of drag racing. With the "muscle car" era reaching a boil, a second-generation hemi engine was made available to Plymouth and Dodge buyers. The engine was available as a special-order "competition" engine in 1964, and in a "street" version in 1966. At the height of the horsepower race, the massive hemi was offered in the lightweight Barracuda and Challenger bodies, a potent, but rare combination that is highly collectible.

DIRECTIONS TO MUSEUM: From I-70 take Exit 159 onto US 183 northbound. Museum is along frontage road just northwest of I-70 and US 183.

ADMISSION COST: Adults & children above 11 yrs. $3.00; under 12 yrs. free.

1958 Plymouth Fury 2dr Hardtop. *Plymouth claimed third in sales for the 1958 model year. The horsepower race was underway and Plymouth offered the Golden Commando engine in the Fury series. With a displacement of 318 cubic inches, 10:1 compression ratio and dual four-barrel carburetors, the engine produced 305 hp.*

HOURS OF OPERATION: Open Monday-Friday 8am-6pm; Saturday 10am-5pm. Closed Sunday and holidays.

MUSEUM NOTES: There are restaurants nearby. Film is not available.

A brochure is available.

Display Automobiles

Cadillac, 1961, Fleetwood
Chevrolet, 1937, Sedan
Chevrolet, 1959, Bel Air
Chrysler, 1962, 300H
Dodge, 1968, Charger
Dodge, 1969, Daytona
Dodge, 1970, Challenger
Dodge, 1970, Challenger T/A
Dodge, 1970, Challenger Trans Am
Dodge, 1970, Daytona
Dodge, 1970, Hemi Charger R/T
Dodge, 1970, R/T
Dodge, 1970, Super Bee
Dodge, 1971, Challenger Pace Car
Dodge, 1971, Charger R/T
Ford, 1929, Model A
Ford, 1937, Coupe

Plymouth, 1955, Belvedere
Plymouth, 1958, Fury
Plymouth, 1959, Sport Fury
Plymouth, 1964, Sport Fury
Plymouth, 1966, Barris Custom Car
Plymouth, 1968, Sport Fury
Plymouth, 1969, Duster Show Car
Plymouth, 1969, Roadrunner
Plymouth, 1970, Barracuda
Plymouth, 1970, GTX
Plymouth, 1970, Roadrunner
Plymouth, 1970, Roadrunner Superbird
Plymouth, 1971, Barracuda
Plymouth, 1974, Barracuda
Pontiac, 1969, GTO Judge
Reo, 1910

Boothbay Railway Village

P.O. Box 123, Boothbay, Maine 04537
(207) 633-4727

Boothbay Railway Village is a complex of 27 exhibit buildings that depict rural life in the early 1900s. A train pulled by a narrow-gauge steam engine transports visitors to sites in the Village, among them a one-room schoolhouse, a doll museum and the auto museum.

A large segment of the cars on display are Fords, and several of them are trucks. Ford did not construct trucks until 1925, although a delivery car/van was offered in 1905 and 1912. However, commercial operators and custom truck builders saw the advantages of the inexpensive, reliable Ford car and modified cars into trucks. Taking advantage of another market, Ford sold the bare Model T chassis starting in 1910 to truck builders. In 1917 Ford offered the Model TT, a stouter version of the Model T chassis. In 1925 the Ford pickup truck was introduced (in 1924 bodies were sold for installation by dealers). With the advent of the Model A series, the truck line was broadened to include the pickup, sedan delivery and panel delivery. From these beginnings, Ford went on to become the manufacturer of the vehicle that annually outsells all other vehicles, the Ford F-150 pickup truck.

DIRECTIONS TO MUSEUM: The Village is on Rt. 27 in Boothbay.

ADMISSION COST: Adults $5.00; children $2.00.

HOURS OF OPERATION: Open daily mid-June to Columbus Day 9:30am-5pm.

MUSEUM NOTES: There is a restaurant nearby and a gift shop onsite. Film is available.

A brochure is available.

Display Automobiles

Black, 1907
Cadillac, 1941, Series 62 Sedan
Chevrolet, 1927, Imperial Landau Sedan
Chevrolet, 1931
Chevrolet, 1948, Woody Station Wagon
Crosley, 1949, Hot Shot Roadster
Dodge, 1926, Truck
Dodge, 1931, DH Sedan
Ford, 1911, Model T Roadster
Ford, 1911, Model T Truck
Ford, 1912, Model T Roadster
Ford, 1914, Model T Pickup Truck
Ford, 1914, Model T Touring
Ford, 1922, Model T Hearse
Ford, 1923, Model T Depot Hack

Ford, 1925, Model T Touring
Ford, 1926, Model T 4dr Sedan
Ford, 1926, Model T Pickup Truck
Ford, 1927, Model T Milk Truck
Ford, 1929, Model AA Truck
Ford, 1930, Model A Deluxe Roadster
Ford, 1930, Model A Roadster
Ford, 1931, Model A Pickup Truck
Ford, 1931, Model A Victoria Coupe
Ford, 1933, Woody Station Wagon
Ford, 1934, Deluxe Roadster
Ford, 1934, Phaeton
Ford, 1936, Roadster
Ford, 1949, Custom 2dr Sedan
Hupmobile, 1932, Model B-216 Cabriolet

International, 1912, Truck
LaSalle, 1939, Sedan
Mack, 1922, Bulldog Truck
Mack, 1927, Truck
Nash, 1962, Metropolitan
Oldsmobile, 1948, Club Sedan
Packard, 1929, Limousine
Packard, 1936, Touring Sedan
Packard, 1941, Limousine
Pierce-Arrow, 1926, Model 80 Roadster

Pontiac, 1931, Sport Coupe
Race Car, 1937, Midget w/Ford V-8
Stanley, 1907, Model EX Steamer
Stanley, 1912, Steamer Touring
Trumbull, 1915, Model 15B Roadster
Volvo, 1935, Carrioca Sedan
Volvo, 1946, Model PV60 Sedan
Willys, 1941, Americar
Willys, 1946, Model CJ-2A Overland Jeep
Willys, 1950, Jeepster

Cole Land Transportation Museum
405 Perry Road, Bangor, Maine 04401
(207) 990-3600

The museum was founded by Galen Cole to collect, preserve and display a cross section of vehicles that characterize transportation in Maine. Offered for viewing are fire trucks, snow plows, railroad equipment, trucks, cars, tractors, snowmobiles, bicycles, wagons and sleighs, as well as related artifacts. The museum possesses one of the most extensive collections of early commercial vehicles in the country.

Among the more massive trucks and cars is a diminutive King Midget, which was advertised as the "World's Lowest Priced Car." First produced in kit form with a Wisconsin single-cylinder engine, King Midgets were manufactured for over twenty years. Approximately 5,000 of the small cars reached owners who were enticed by the car's low price and operating costs — gas mileage approached 60 miles-per-gallon.

DIRECTIONS TO MUSEUM: From I-95 take Exit 45B and turn left at first traffic light. Turn left at Perry Rd. and follow to museum.

ADMISSION COST: Adults $2.00; senior citizens $1.00; under 19 yrs. free.

HOURS OF OPERATION: Open May 1-November 11 daily 9am-5pm.

MUSEUM NOTES: There is a restaurant nearby. The museum has a gift shop, but film is not available.

A brochure is available.

Display Automobiles

Ahrens Fox, 1948, Fire Truck	GMC, 1933, Bus
American LaFrance, 1923, Fire Truck	GMC, 1941, Pickup Truck
American LaFrance, 1931, Fire Truck	GMC, 1941, Truck
Chevrolet, 1936, Wrecker	International, 1936, Oil Truck
Chevrolet, 1941, Log Truck	International, 1926, Cement Mixer
Chevrolet, 1949, Truck	International, 1940, Snow Plow
Chrysler, 1949, New Yorker 4dr Sedan	International, 1944, Fire Truck
Chrysler, 1972, Imperial	King Midget, 1946
Cletrack, 1933, Snow Plow	Lincoln, 1937, Limousine
Diamond Reo, 1970, Tractor	Linn, 1935, Snow Plow
Diamond T, 1958, Tractor	Mack, 1943, Cement Mixer
Divco, 1953, Milk Truck	Mack, 1947, Fire Truck
Dodge, 1962, Truck	Maxim, 1935, Fire Truck
Federal, 1939, Fire Truck	McCann, 1927, Fire Truck
Federal, 1943, Model 29 Tractor	Oldsmobile, 1979, 98
Federal, 1949, Tractor	Oshkosh, 1952, Snow Plow
Ford, 1924, Model T Truck	Packard, 1923, Roadster
Ford, 1940, Truck	Reo, 1923, Truck
Ford, 1956, F600 Truck	Reo, 1927, Speedwagon
Ford, 1960, Fairlane 4dr Sedan	White, 1943, Military Halftrack
FWD, 1931, Truck	Willys, 1945, Jeep

Jay Hill Antique Auto Museum

RFD 2, Box 3450, Jay, Maine 04239
(207) 645-4330

The museum's slogan is "They don't build cars the way they used to! So we show the cars they used to build." If cars built before World War II with the Ford nameplate fit the slogan, then the museum abides by its criteria. The list of cars on display indicates a significant collection of pre-war Fords.

The majority of cars in the collection are Ford Model T's, the car that made Henry Ford the wealthiest man in the U.S., if not the world. The Model T was the fruition of Henry's quest for the simple, inexpensive, but sturdy, car. A component in the success was Ford's use of vanadium steel, a stronger and lighter alloy than the steel then in use in car building. Unavailable in the United States, Ford persuaded a steel-maker in Ohio to undertake the production of vanadium steel, with Ford paying the bill if the experiment failed. The Ford Model N first benefited by its use and the Model T was built with a considerable amount of the steel. Ford's ability to build a lighter car meant less strain on drivetrain parts, greater longevity and better performance.

DIRECTIONS TO MUSEUM: Museum is on Rt.4 north of Jay.

ADMISSION COST: Adults $2.00; children $1.00.

HOURS OF OPERATION: Open Sunday 10am-6pm. Open weekdays by appointment.

MUSEUM NOTES: There are restaurants nearby. Film is not available.

A brochure is available.

Display Automobiles

Cadillac, 1970, Eldorado 2dr Hardtop
Chevrolet, 1938, 4dr Sedan
Chevrolet, 1957, 4dr Hardtop
Chevrolet, 1966, Corvair 4dr Sedan
Chrysler, 1936, 4dr Sedan
Dodge, 1923, Touring
Ford, 1915, Model T Touring
Ford, 1917, Model T Touring
Ford, 1919, Model T Touring
Ford, 1920, Model T Touring
Ford, 1922, Model T Skidder
Ford, 1922, Model T Touring
Ford, 1923, Model T Roadster
Ford, 1923, Model T Touring
Ford, 1924, Model T Touring
Ford, 1925, Model T Touring
Ford, 1926, Model T 4dr Sedan
Ford, 1927, Model T Snowmobile
Ford, 1928, Model A Coupe
Ford, 1928, Model A Truck
Ford, 1930, Model A Roadster
Ford, 1930, Model A Woody Station Wagon
Ford, 1932, Model B Truck
Ford, 1934, Truck
Ford, 1936, 4dr Sedan
Ford, 1939, Coupe
Ford, 1947, Fire Truck
Ford, 1963, Galaxie 500 Hardtop
Plymouth, 1938, 4dr Sedan
Plymouth, 1948, 4dr Sedan
Plymouth, 1971, Scamp Coupe
Volkswagen, 1970, Convertible

Owls Head Transportation Museum

P.O. Box 277, Rt. 73, Owls Head, Maine 04854
(207) 594-4418

The Owls Head Transportation Museum takes pride in having "one of the finest collections of antique automobiles, aircraft and engines on the Eastern Seaboard." Most of the artifacts date from the turn of the century. On weekends various cars, tractors, planes and engines are operated on the museum grounds. Throughout the summer the museum stages special events that bring together collectors who exhibit their antique cars, planes and other machinery. Contact the museum for a current calendar of events.

The broad-based collection comprises approximately 60 cars and trucks, most of which are pre-World War II models. Several examples of upscale marques such as Mercedes-Benz, Stutz, Rolls-Royce, Pierce-Arrow and Packard are displayed. Among the cars are Ford models ranging from a 1907 Model K Touring to a 1955 Crown Victoria. Most of the Fords were built before World War II providing the visitor an overview of early Ford lineage.

Henry Ford is best known for his inexpensive Model T, so the $2,500 original price of the Model K may be surprising. Ford was partners with Alexander Malcomson when Ford Motor Company was conceived. Malcomson desired an upscale car and the six-cylinder Model K was the result. High priced and dissimilar to other models in the line, Ford disliked the car because it didn't fit his manufacturing philosophy. Ford's dream

1903 Mercedes Simplex. *Mercedes was built by Daimler Motorengesellschaft. The car's name transpired as a result of a Daimler director stating he would purchase 36 of the new cars if they were named after his daughter, Mercedes.*

1928 Mercedes-Benz Model S Cabriolet. *From 1923 to 1929, Ferdinand Porsche served as designer at Daimler, culminating with his work on the Mercedes S, SS and SSK series. Fewer than 400 were sold. The museum's Cabriolet is powered by a supercharged, 6.8 liter, six-cylinder engine.*

was building one model, as rapidly as possible, at one facility. Ford bought out Malcomson, expanded his manufacturing so he could build his own major components, dropped the current models (including the Model K), and launched the Model T. The Model T, with various body styles, was the only Ford model for nineteen years.

DIRECTIONS TO MUSEUM: The museum is located two miles south of Rockland on Rt. 73 at the Knox County Airport. Follow signs.

ADMISSION COST: Adults $4.00; senior citizens $3.50; children $2.50.

HOURS OF OPERATION: Open May through October daily 10am-5pm. Call museum for winter hours of operation. Closed New Year's Day, Thanksgiving and Christmas.

MUSEUM NOTES: Film is available in the gift shop. Several restaurants are located nearby and refreshments are offered during special events.

A brochure is available.

Display Automobiles

Alfa Romeo, 1931, Gran Sport
Autocar, 1906, Touring
Benz, 1914, Touring
Black, 1906, Motor Buggy
Buick, 1910, Truck
Buick, 1919, Roadster
Cadillac, 1907, Model K Runabout

Chevrolet, 1932, Roadster
Chevrolet, 1955, Bel Air 2dr Sedan
Citroen, 1925, Torpedo
Delaunay Belleville, 1905, Cape Top Tourer
Erskine, 1929, Model 52 Sport Coupe
Essex, 1929, Super Six Boattail Roadster
Fiat, 1912, Type 53A

1905 Panhard et Levassor. *Panhard was the originator of the once-typical drive system that comprised a front-mounted engine coupled through a drive train to rear-driving wheels. The configuration was quickly copied world-wide, then refined over decades of use, although front-wheel-drive systems are now favored by some carmakers. The museum's Panhard et Levassor was built in France as a chassis and engine, then shipped to New York where the touring body was added.*

Ford, 1907, Model K Touring
Ford, 1908, Model S Runabout
Ford, 1916, Speedster
Ford, 1917, Model T Fire Truck
Ford, 1925, Model T Station Wagon
Ford, 1926, Model T Snowmobile
Ford, 1928, Racer
Ford, 1929, Roadster
Ford, 1929, Truck
Ford, 1931, Special Coupe
Ford, 1932, Roadster
Ford, 1935, Coupe
Ford, 1936, Phaeton
Ford, 1937, Phaeton
Ford, 1940, Station Wagon
Ford, 1947, Convertible
Ford, 1955, Crown Victoria 2dr Sedan
Holsman, 1902, Highwheeler
International Harvestor, 1911, Truck
Leon Bollee, 1898, Tricar
Marion, 1910, Model 10

Mercedes, 1903, Simplex
Mercedes-Benz, 1928, Model S Cabriolet
Mercedes-Benz, 1937, 540K Cabriolet
Mercedes-Benz, 1955, 300SL
Mercer, 1914, Raceabout
MG, 1946, TC Roadster
Oldsmobile, 1902, Curved Dash Runabout
Overland, 1908, Runabout
Packard, 1929, 640 Phaeton
Packard, 1929, 640 Roadster
Packard, 1939, Super Eight Town Car
Panhard et Levassor, 1905, Tourer
Peugeot, 1913, Bebe
Peugeot, 1914, Phaeton
Pierce-Arrow, 1923, Model 33 Roadster
Pierce-Arrow, 1926, Model 80 Touring
Prescott, 1903, Steam Car
Race Car, 1925
Renault, 1926, Model 45 Tourer
Rolls-Royce, 1913, Silver Ghost
Rolls-Royce, 1929, Phantom 1 Tourer

1947 Ford Club Convertible. *Automakers didn't make major changes after World War II, so the 1947 Fords were similar to the 1946 models, which were simply a restyling of the 1942 models. The 1948 models were more of the same and Ford continued to trail corporate rivals General Motors and Chrysler. Management changes (Henry Ford died in 1947) and the introduction of significantly improved 1949 models boosted Ford's outlook for the 1950s.*

Sears, 1908, High Wheeler
Stanley, 1904, Steamer Runabout
Stanley, 1907, Model EX Steamer Roadster
Stanley, 1908, Model K Steamer

Stevens-Duryea, 1913, Touring
Stutz, 1916, Bearcat
Stutz, 1932, Bearcat Speedster
Woods, 1912, Brougham

Seal Cove Auto Museum

Seal Cove, Maine
(207) 244-9242

The museum's collection comprises cars manufactured from 1899 to 1934. Of the over 100 antique cars displayed, special emphasis is placed on cars from 1905 to 1917, the "Brass Era."

In the collection is an 1899 de Dion-Bouton. Built in France, de Dion-Bouton was one of the earliest car builders, starting production of steam-powered vehicles in the late 1880s. The firm changed to gasoline engines and became a major engine manufacturer for other car builders. De Dion-Bouton successfully manufactured commercial vehicles, but an attempt to set up manufacturing in the United States failed. Car sales began to slide in the 1920s and production was halted in 1932.

DIRECTIONS TO MUSEUM: From Ellsworth take Rt. 3 towards Mt. Desert Island. After bridge onto island, bear right onto Rt. 102 towards Southwest Harbor. After passing through the town of Somesville and just past fire department, turn right onto Petty Marsh Rd. Follow Petty Marsh Rd. approximately 5.8 miles to museum, a large blue building set back from road on right.

ADMISSION COST: Adults $5.00; children $2.00.

HOURS OF OPERATION: Open June-September daily 10am-5pm.

MUSEUM NOTES: There is a restaurant nearby. Film is not available.

A brochure is available.

Stanley Museum

P.O. Box 280, Kingfield, Maine 04947
(207) 265-2729

The Stanley Museum was organized to memorialize two Maine natives, Francis E. and Frelan Ozro Stanley. The brothers built what was probably the most famous steam-driven automobile in history, the Stanley Steamer.

The Stanleys built their first car in 1897, built their first production car in 1899 and sold the business that same year to John Walker and Amzi Barber. The Stanleys were retained as engineers, but Walker (who started Locomobile) and Barber parted ways, so the Stanleys started another company, the Stanley Motor Carriage Company.

In 1902 the new company introduced its first car, the last was built in 1927. In between, the Stanleys and the firm's later owners attempted to find buyers for the Stanley Steamers. But problems prevented the mass appeal needed to keep the company afloat. The steam-driven cars, although powerful enough in the earlier years (the Stanley *Wogglebug* held the world speed record of 127.66 mph in 1906), possessed a fatal flaw, the ability to start quickly. Steam cars required a startup period to build steam pressure before driving away, a distinct disadvantage when self-starters replaced the crank on gas-engined cars. At the turn of the century, sales of steam cars were nearly even with their gas-burning brethren, but ten years later steamer sales were virtually gone. The Stanleys retired from the company in 1917. Subsequent management attempted to keep the company afloat, but the public knew what it wanted, and it wasn't steam.

Three Stanley automobiles are on display in the museum, a 1905 Model CX, a 1910 Model 705 and a 1916 Model 725, as well as artifacts related to steam cars.

DIRECTIONS TO MUSEUM: Follow signs in Kingfield to museum.

ADMISSION COST: Adults $1.00; children 50¢.

HOURS OF OPERATION: Open Tuesday-Sunday 1-4pm. Closed in April and November. Closed Christmas.

MUSEUM NOTES: There are restaurants nearby. The museum has a gift shop, but film is not available.

A brochure is available.

Wells Auto Museum
Route 1, P.O. Box 496, Wells, Maine 04090
(207) 646-9064 or 646-5054

The Wells Auto Museum includes a broad-based collection of approximately 80 vehicles, as well as collections of motorcycles, bicycles, nickelodeons, arcade games, toys, tools and memorabilia.

Along with the more familier marques are several rare, less well-known names, such as United States, Grout, Red Bug, Crestmobile, Atlas and Templar. Many of the marques in the museum went out of production long ago, the result of any of a number of reasons that force a business to close.

In spite of bad decisions, some auto firms did survive, exemplified by the Chrysler Airflow displayed by the museum. Chrysler's engineering department built a car that was at the forefront of technology — features included unit-body construction, faired-in headlights, improved seating — but the wind-tunnel-tested aerodynamic shape of the Airflow, also built under the DeSoto marque, proved unpalatable to the marketplace. Chrysler dropped from one of the leading manufacturers to mid-pack. Fortunately for the corporation, the conventionally designed Dodges and Plymouths remained respectable sellers. The Chrysler and DeSoto Airflows were produced only three years, 1934 through 1937. Chrysler misjudged the marketplace and paid for it; many other car manufacturers didn't get a second chance.

DIRECTIONS TO MUSEUM: From I-95 take Exit 2 onto Rt. 109 and travel east to Wells. Turn right onto US 1 and travel one mile south to museum.

ADMISSION COST: Adults $3.00; children (6-12 yrs.) $2.00.

HOURS OF OPERATION: Open daily mid-June through September 10am-5pm.

Open weekends 10am-5pm from Memorial weekend through Columbus weekend. Closed during winter.

MUSEUM NOTES: There are restaurants nearby and the museum has a gift shop. Film is available.

A brochure is available.

Display Automobiles

Atlas, 1908, Touring
Auburn, 1928, Model 88 Boattail Speedster
Austin-Healey, 1963, Sprite
Baker, 1908, Electric Touring
Bantam, 1939, Roadster
Bentley, 1954, 4dr Sedan
Bombardier, 1940, Snowmobile
Brush, 1910, Roadster
Buick, 1909, Model 17 Touring
Buick, 1911, Truck

Buick, 1916, Touring
Cadillac, 1905, Roadster
Cadillac, 1949, Fleetwood 4dr Sedan
Chase, 1910, Touring
Chevrolet, 1928, Truck/Calliope
Chevrolet, 1934, Convertible Coupe
Chrylser, 1941, Town & Country
Chrysler, 1934, Model CU Airflow
Chrysler, 1938, Royal Convertible Sedan
Chrysler, 1968, Imperial

Crestmobile, 1900, Roadster
Crosley, 1951, Super Sport Roadster
DeSoto, 1947, 4dr Sedan
Dodge, 1941, Command Car
EMF, 1908, Touring
Ford, 1906, Model N
Ford, 1911, Model T Depot Hack
Ford, 1923, Model T Snowmobile
Ford, 1930, Model A Roadster
Ford, 1936, Convertible Sedan
Franklin, 1905, Touring
Franklin, 1927, Touring
Grout, 1905, Steamer
Henry J, 1953
Hupmobile, 1912, Roadster
Hupmobile, 1925, Sedan
International, 1908, Autobuggy
Knox, 1902, Roadster
Lagonda, 1935, M45 Touring
LaSalle, 1940, Model 52 Convertible Sedan
Lincoln, 1937, Zephyr 2dr Sedan
Maxwell, 1910, Model AB Roadster
Metz, 1911, Roadster
Oldsmobile, 1904, Curved Dash
Oldsmobile, 1905
Orient, 1901, Buckboard
Overland, 1917, Cloverleaf Touring

Packard, 1941, Model 160 Convertible Coupe
Pathfinder, 1912, Armored Roadster
Pierce-Arrow, 1918, Roadster
Pierce-Arrow, 1926, Model 80 Roadster
Rambler, 1905, Roadster
Red Bug, 1920, Electric
Renault, 1908
Reo, 1911, Truck
Riley, 1953, 2dr Sedan
Rolls-Royce, 1924, Pall Mall Tourer
Schact, 1907, Touring
Seagraves, 1937, Fire Truck
Sears, 1909, Autobuggy
Stanley, 1904, Model CX Steamer
Stanley, 1907, Gentleman's Speedy
   Steamer Roadster
Stanley, 1909, Model E2 Steamer
Studebaker, 1963, Avanti
Studebaker, 1963, Lark Convertible
Stutz, 1918, Bearcat
Templar, 1920, Touring
Thomas, 1901
United States, 1900, Runabout
White, 1907, Touring
Willys, 1949, Jeepster
Willys-Knight, 1929, Roadster
Winton, 1902, Tonneau

Edaville Railroad

P.O. Box 7, Rt. 58, Carver, Massachusetts 02366
(508) 866-4526

The Edaville Railroad is a crafts village and family fun park that focuses on life in the early 1900s. The ground was originally a part of a large cranberry plantation. The steam locomotive and railroad equipment that formerly worked on the plantation now provide rides for visitors. Rides on a trolley, fire engine, and carousel are also offered, as well as, crafts, a petting zoo, and New England artifacts.

Three antique cars are found at Edaville, a 1917 Ford Model T Roadster, a 1931 La-Salle Sedan and a 1954 Citreon. The park also has a 1922 International truck and three fire engines from the 1920s and 1930s.

DIRECTIONS TO MUSEUM: From I-495 take Exit 2 onto Rt. 58. Travel north and follow Rt. 58 to Edaville Railroad. From US 44 take Rt. 58 south and follow through Carver to Edaville Railroad.

ADMISSION COST: Adults $12.50; senior citizens $8.50; children (3-12 yrs.) $7.50. Price includes all rides and attractions.

HOURS OF OPERATION: May: Weekends and holidays noon-5pm. First Saturday in June through Labor Day open daily 10am-5:30pm. After Labor Day through 4th Sunday in October open Monday-Friday 10am-3pm; Saturday, Sunday and holidays 10am-5:30pm. First Friday through first Sunday after New Year's Day open Monday-Friday 4-9pm; Saturday and Sunday 2-9pm. Closed Thanksgiving and Christmas. Open New Year's Day.

MUSEUM NOTES: There is a restaurant onsite. Film is not available.

A brochure is available.

Heritage Plantation of Sandwich
Pine and Grove Streets, Sandwich, Massachusetts 02563
(508) 888-3300

The Heritage Plantation of Sandwich is located on 76 acres near the town of Sandwich on Massachusetts' Cape Cod. The Plantation encompasses an auto collection, a military museum, an arts and crafts museum, a 1912 carousel, an 1800 windmill and a Shaker Round Barn.

The auto collection has 29 different marques on display including a Pope-Hartford. The car was built by the Pope Manufacturing Company in their Hartford, Connecticut, factory. Colonel Albert Pope was the founder of the company, which Pope built into a bicycle manufacturing empire in the late 1800s. Pope attempted to transform the company into an automobile company and manufactured cars under the names Columbia, Hartford, Robinson, Toledo, Tribune and Waverley. The venture was unsuccessful and after divesting and subsequent bankruptcy, the Pope-Hartford was the last car built by Pope. Colonel Pope died in 1909, the company floundered and car production ceased in 1914.

DIRECTIONS TO MUSEUM: From US 6 take Exit 2 to Rt. 130. Follow Rt.130 north to Grove St., just past pond. Follow Grove St. and signs to museum.

ADMISSION COST: Adults $7.00; senior citizens $6.00; children (6-18 yrs.) $3.50.

HOURS OF OPERATION: Open daily 10am-5pm from Mother's Day through October.

MUSEUM NOTES: There is a restaurant nearby. The museum has a gift shop and film is available.

A brochure is available.

Display Automobiles

Auburn, 1932, Boattail
Brewster, 1916, Landaulet
Cadillac, 1910, Roadster
Cadillac, 1930, Convertible Coupe
Cord, 1937, 812 Phaeton
Duesenberg, 1930, Model J Derham Tourster
Ford, 1913, Model T Roadster
Ford, 1915, Model T Couplet
Ford, 1931, Model T Phaeton
Franklin, 1925, Runabout
Knox, 1910, Model R Touring
LaSalle, 1927, Sport Phaeton
Lincoln, 1927, Sport Touring
Mercer, 1912, Type 35 Raceabout
Milburn, 1915, Light Electric
Oldsmobile, 1904, Model T Runabout
Oldsmobile, 1912, Autocrat Roadster

Packard, 1912, Model 1-48 Victoria
Packard, 1933, Model 1002 Victoria
Peerless, 1910, Model 27 Roadster
Pierce-Arrow, 1919, Model 48 Touring
Pope-Hartford, 1913, Model 35 Roadster
Reo, 1909, Model D Touring
Rickenbacker, 1925, Model 8 Coupe
Rolls-Royce, 1922, Silver Ghost Pall
    Mall Phaeton
Sears, 1910, Model P Surrey
Simplex, 1916, Model 5 Touring
Stanley, 1911, Model 62 Steamer Runabout
Stevens-Duryea, 1903, Runabout
Stutz, 1915, Bearcat
Waltham-Orient, 1908, Buckboard
White Steam, 1909, Model M
Winton, 1899, Motor Carriage

Museum of Transportation

Larz Anderson Park, 15 Newton St., Brookline, Massachusetts 02146
(617) 522-6140

The Museum of Transportation is housed in a late nineteenth century carriage house originally owned by Larz Anderson. Designed to replicate a European castle, the building is listed in the National Register of Historic Places.

The Andersons offered their auto collection for public viewing in the carriage house in 1927. The Anderson collection is believed to be the oldest, single-owner assemblage in the country and now forms the nucleus of the museum collection.

Autombiles posssessed by the museum as well as on loan are displayed using an underlying theme. In past years, themes focused on "muscle cars," sports cars, future cars and convertibles. Artifacts and memoribilia reflect lifestyles of the period. Call the museum for information on the current theme and cars on display.

The museum emphasizes the importance of the automobile in American life. Interactive displays and special activities are provided for young and old. Among the displays is a

1906 CGV. *The French firm CGV was started by Charron, Girardot and Voigt. All three were formerly affiliated with Panhard, which influenced the design of their car. The marque was renamed Charron in 1906 and lasted until 1929.*

visitor-operated 1920s gas pump and a 1925 Model T Ford that is open for "driving." On weekends, children can design cars and receive a photograph of their creation. Adult-oriented events include car meets, vintage car shows and rallies on the weekends. Call the museum for event information.

DIRECTIONS TO MUSEUM: Eastbound on Rt. 9. Four traffic lights past Chestnut Hill Mall turn right onto Lee St. Turn left onto Newton St. and follow to museum on left.

Northbound on US 1 (VFW Pkwy.). At circle intersection with Rt. 203 follow US 1 north to next circle intersection. Follow 3/4 around circle and turn onto Pond St./Newton St. Going past Jamaica Pond means the circle was passed. Follow Newton St. to museum on right.

Southbound on US 1 (Storrow Dr./Brookline Ave./Jamaica Way). Go past Jamaica Pond and at circle intersection follow 1/4 around and turn onto Pond St./Newton St. Follow Newton St. to museum on right.

From I-93 take Exit 12 onto Rt. 203 westbound. Follow to circle intersection with US 1. Follow US 1 north to next circle intersection at Jamaica Pond. Follow 3/4 around circle and turn onto Pond St./Newton St. Going past Jamaica Pond means the circle was passed. Follow Newton St. to museum on right.

ADMISSION COST: Adults $4.00; senior citizens and children $2.00.

HOURS OF OPERATION: During summer open Wednesday-Sunday 10am-5pm including holidays. Call museum for winter hours of operation.

MUSEUM NOTES: Automobiles are exhibited on a theme basis that is changed periodically. Call museum for description of current exhibit theme. There are no restaurants nearby. There is a gift shop, but film is not available.

A brochure is available.

Display Automobiles

NOTE: The following cars are on permanent display.

Bailey, 1908, Electric Runabout
CGV, 1906
Panhard, 1911

Rochet Schneider, 1900
Winton, 1901

Alfred P. Sloan Museum

1221 E. Kearsley Street, Flint, Michigan 48503
(313) 760-1169

The museum is a multi-faceted facility that encompasses subjects related to health sciences, geology, anthropology, local history, dolls and automobiles. But of particular interest to automobile enthusiasts are the artifacts and memorabilia related to Alfred Sloan and the automotive history pertinent to Flint, Michigan, home of General Motors.

Alfred P. Sloan took over the controls of General Motors in 1923 and guided the corporation into the position of largest auto maker in the world. Sloan instituted an organizantional framework that benefitted General Motors and averted competition between the various car divisions. Virtually any car buyer could find a car to match his budget from the marques built by General Motors. It was Sloan's hope that people with meager budgets would purchase a Chevrolet, and as their finances improved, buy progressively expensive General Motors cars, until hopefully, they purchased a Cadillac.

Sloan is also credited with the annual change in models. Sloan wanted the car owner to feel that the new model was better than his current auto, whether real or perceived. The least expensive method to create noticeable changes is by altering the bodywork through styling. Sloan was the first to see the economic benefits of styling for the mass-produced automobile. He hired Harley Earl in 1930 to head the new General Motors "Arts and Colour" department. Sloan wanted General Motors styling to entice buyers, then entice them again the next year. The strategy worked because of the massive size of General Motors. Smaller companies couldn't afford the machinery or manpower to change annually, nor did they have the advertising muscle to convince buyers that change was good.

DIRECTIONS TO MUSEUM: From I-475 take Exit 8A onto Longway Blvd. and travel east. Turn right at Forest St. and follow signs to museum parking lot.

1910 Buick Bug. The two Buick Bugs driven by Bob Burman and Louis Chevrolet were the dominant racers of their day. They won half the races they entered in two seasons of racing. Each weighed 2,600 pounds and was powered by a huge 622 cubic-inch displacement four-cylinder engine. The tubes over the cowl are part of the cooling system.

ADMISSION COST: Adults $3.00; senior citizens $2.50; children $2.00.

HOURS OF OPERATION: Open Tuesday-Friday 10am-5pm; Saturday and Sunday noon-5pm. During July and August open Monday 10am-5pm. Closed major holidays.

MUSEUM NOTES: There are restaurants nearby. Film is not available in the gift shop.

A brochure is available.

Display Automobiles

Buick, 1904
Buick, 1905, Model C
Buick, 1908, Model 10
Buick, 1910, Model 10
Buick, 1910, Racer
Buick, 1910, Truck
Buick, 1920, Model K
Buick, 1925, Opera Coupe
Buick, 1932, Model 86
Buick, 1950, Station Wagon
General Motors, 1954, P-4003 *Wildcat II*
General Motors, 1956, Centurian Sedan
Buick, 1985, Le Sabre
Chevrolet, 1913, Classic Six
Chevrolet, 1915, Baby Grand

Chevrolet, 1932
General Motors, 1962, Corvair *Super Spyder*
Chevrolet, 1962, Impala
Chevrolet, 1975, Chevette
Dort, 1922
Flint, 1902, Roadster
Flint, 1925
Little, 1911
Marr, 1914, Cycle Car
Monroe, 1915
Paterson, 1919
General Motors, 1956, XP-43 *Firebird II*
Randolph, 1910, Truck
Whiting, 1911

Automotive Hall of Fame
3225 Cook Road, Midland, Michigan 48640
(517) 631-5760

The Automotive Hall of Fame honors the men and women who have made significant contributions in the automotive industry. The organization also fosters and promotes programs that further educational and career opportunities in the automotive field.

Each honoree in the Hall of Fame is represented by a display that chronicles their life and achievements. Recipients of the award must be deceased or retired and have had a dramatic impact on the development of the automobile or on the automotive industry. To date, nearly one hundred people have been selected. A walk through the display area provides an opportunity to learn more about the designers, racers, journalists, manufacturers, inventors, educators and others who impacted the automobile industry and American society.

The Hall of Fame also awards the Distinguished Service Citation. Since 1940 there have been approximately 300 individuals awarded citations for their work in the automobile industry. Each recipient's contribution is outlined on a plaque.

DIRECTIONS TO MUSEUM: From US 10 exit onto Eastman Rd. and travel to Saginaw Rd. Turn right onto Saginaw Rd. and follow to Cook Rd. Turn left onto Cook Rd. and follow Cook Rd. to Northwest Institute. The Hall of Fame is located on Cook Rd. on the Institute grounds.

ADMISSION COST: Free.

HOURS OF OPERATION: Open Monday-Friday 9am-4pm. Closed major holidays.

MUSEUM NOTES: There are no vehicles on display. There is a restaurant nearby.

A brochure is available.

Detroit Historical Museum

5401 Woodward Avenue, Detroit, Michigan 48213
(313) 833-1805

The Detroit Historical Museum documents the history of Detroit from the early 1700s to the present. Artifacts are displayed as part of recreated Detroit streets.

Only a portion of the large automobile collection is exhibited. Among the noteworthy cars in the collection are two Stout Scarabs (1930s aerodynamic styling), four Scripps-Booths (Bi-Autogo, Da Vinci Pup, cyclecar and roadster), a 1934 Chrysler Airflow, a 1964 Chrysler Turbine car and a 1963 Ford Mustang prototype.

The Scripps-Booth Bi-Autogo is particularly interesting. It was designed and built by James Scripps-Booth in 1913. The vehicle was supported by two wheels similar to a motorcycle with two lever-operated outrigger wheels to provide stability when stopped. A V-8 engine powered the two-ton cyclecar. Engine cooling was provided by water circulated through cooper tubing woven across the engine and hood. The Bi-Autogo was never put into production.

DIRECTIONS TO MUSEUM: The museum is located at the intersection of Woodward Ave. and Kirby Ave., which is between Warren Ave. and I-94.

ADMISSION COST: Donation requested.

HOURS OF OPERATION: Open Wednesday-Saturday 9:30am-5pm. Closed major holidays.

MUSEUM NOTES: There is a restaurant nearby. Film is not available.

A brochure is available.

Domino's Classic Car Collection

44 Frank Lloyd Wright Drive, Ann Arbor, Michigan 48106
(313) 995-4258

The Domino's Collection is housed at Domino's Farms, a multi-faceted park that encompasses a prarie house, a petting farm, the Detroit Tigers Museum, and the Domino's Center for Architecture & Design, which spotlights the career of Frank Lloyd Wright.

The cars on display provide a wide-angle look at the world of automobiles — ranging from the basic transportation provided by a Ford Model T to the sophistication of an Indy race car, from the inexpensive VW Beetle to the Bugatti Royale Berline de Voyage (estimated current value $14 million). Most of the cars on display predate World War II.

DIRECTIONS TO MUSEUM: From US 23 take Exit 41 to Plymouth Rd. then travel east one mile to Earhart Rd. Turn left onto Earhart Rd. and follow signs.

ADMISSION COST: Adults $6.00; senior citizens $4.00; children $4.00.

HOURS OF OPERATION: Open Monday-Saturday 10am-5pm; Sunday noon-5pm.

During winter closed Monday and Tuesday. Closed major holidays.

MUSEUM NOTES: There are vending machines and a cafe onsite. There is a restaurant nearby. Film is available in the gift shop.

A brochure is available.

Display Automobiles

American, 1906, Truck
BMW, 1931, Dixi Cabriolet
Bugatti, 1931, Royale Berline de Voyage
Buick, 1942, Roadmaster
Cadillac, 1939, Station Wagon
Chevrolet, 1957, Bel Air Convertible
Chevrolet, 1957, Truck
DeLorean, 1981
Dodge, 1948, Coupe
Duesenberg, 1929, Model J Murphy Cabriolet
Duesenberg, 1934, Model SJ LaGrande Dual
  Cowl Phaeton
Ford, 1920, Model T

Hispano-Suiza, 1930, Town Car
Indy Race Car, 1984
Lincoln, 1941, Continental Convertible
Maserati, 1949, Pinin Farina Coupe
Packard, 1936, Super 8
Rolls-Royce, 1909, Silver Ghost
Rolls-Royce, 1922, Woody
Roth, 1959, *Custom Outlaw*
Roth, 1962, *Surfite Yellow*
Tatra, 1951
Volkswagen, 1960, Beetle
Volvo, 1971, 1800E

Gilmore-Classic Car Club Museum

6865 Hickory Road, Hickory Corners, Michigan 49060
(616) 671-5089

The museum is affiliated with the Classic Car Club of America, which was organized in 1952 and currently counts over 5,000 members. The club coined the term "classic car" and defined a classic car as a fine or unusual foreign or domestic motor car built from 1925 through 1948, with fine design, high engineering standards and superior workmanship. The museum contains an interesting mix of classic, antique and later model cars.

High on the list of classic cars are those cars built by Packard, of which several are on display. The company was an outgrowth of the electrical company owned by the Packard brothers, James and William. In 1900 the concerns were separated and Packard Electric Company continued on as a successful electrical supplier to the automotive market. In 1903 the Packard brothers left the Packard Motor Company to concentrate on their electrical business. Packard captured a significant portion of the upscale market and sold over 50,000 cars in 1928. Packard, unlike many independent car makers, survived the Depression and prospered in the late 1930s, building over 83,000 cars in 1936. After World War II, the company lost stride by leaving the luxury car market, which Cadillac filled, then acquiring the troubled Studebaker company. The momentum was lost and the company ceased production of Packards in 1958 while the company struggled to produce Studebakers for the greater low-priced market, ultimately failing.

1937 Cadillac Convertible Sedan. *Seeking to cut costs, Cadillac changed from the overhead-valve V-16 used in 1937 and introduced a flat-head V-16 in 1938. In 1937 hydraulic brakes were installed for the first time, as well as a pressure cap on the radiator and a front stabilizer bar.*

1930 Packard Speedster. *The Packard Speedsters were lower and narrower than other Packards. A high performance version (125 hp) of the big eight-cylinder engine (384.8 cu. in.) was installed, with additional power available (145 hp) from an optional engine. Typical of engines of the era, the engine's 5-inch stroke was very long in comparison to the 3-inch bore.*

DIRECTIONS TO MUSEUM: From I-94 take Exit 80 to Sprinkle Rd. Travel north on Sprinkle Rd. five miles and turn right onto Gull Rd. (M-43). Follow Gull Rd. to village of Richland, then turn left at traffic light and follow Rt. M-43. Follow Rt. M-43 six miles to Hickory Rd. and follow to museum.

ADMISSION COST: Adults $6.00; senior citizens $5.00; children under 12 yr. free.

HOURS OF OPERATION: Open mid-May through mid-October daily 9am-5pm.

MUSEUM NOTES: There is a restaurant nearby. A gift shop is located in the museum and film is available.

A brochure is available.

Display Automobiles

AEC, 1950, London Double-Deck Bus
Alfa Romeo, 1957, Giulietta Spyder
    Convertible
AMX-3, 1969, Bizzarini
Auburn, 1932, Boattail Speedster
Auburn, 1936, Convertible Sedan
Autocar, 1904, Runabout
Barley, 1922, Touring
Brush, 1909, Runabout
Bugatti, 1927, Model 43A Roadster
Buick, 1911, Model 32 Roadster
Buick, 1963, Riviera
Cadillac, 1903, Runabout
Cadillac, 1910, Model 30 Touring
Cadillac, 1937, Convertible Sedan
Cadillac, 1940, Town Car
Cadillac, 1956, Eldorado Seville

Cadillac, 1958, Eldorado Brougham
Cadillac, 1959, Limousine
Cadillac, 1965, Limousine
Cadillac, 1966, Fleetwood Brougham
Checker, 1922, Taxi Cab
Checker, 1936, Taxi Cab
Checker, 1982, Taxi Cab
Chevrolet, 1928, Fire Truck
Chevrolet, 1946, Fire Truck
Chevrolet, 1954, Ambulance
Chevrolet, 1966, Corvette
Chevrolet, 1969, Corvair
Chevrolet, 1975, Cosworth Vega
Chrysler, 1931, Convertible Coupe
Chrysler, 1935, Airflow Coupe
Chrysler, 1948, Town & Country Convertible
Chrysler, 1960, 300 2dr Hardtop

1910 Lozier Touring. *The museum's 1910 Lozier Touring was one of 528 constructed that model year. Born out of the Lozier Motor Company, manufacturer of marine engines, the company set out to compete with the upscale manufacturers Packard, Cadillac and Mercedes. They were among the best built, most expensive cars of the time. Mismanagement coupled with ownership changes resulted in closure in 1918.*

Chrysler, 1963, 300 2dr Hardtop
Chrysler, 1966, 300 2dr Hardtop
Citroen, 1972, Mascrat
Columbia, 1903, Electric Runabout
Cord, 1930, L-29 Convertible Sedan
Cord, 1937, Beverly Sedan
Daimler, 1939, Sedanca Coupe
Datsun, 1970, Model 810
Delahaye, 1939, Convertible Coupe
DeLorean, 1982, 2dr Sedan
Dodge, 1962, Dart 440
Dodge, 1969, Daytona
Duesenberg, 1929, Dual Cowl Phaeton
Edsel, 1958, 4dr Sedan
EMF, 1909, Roadster
Excalibur, 1965, SS Roadster
Ford, 1903, Model A
Ford, 1906, Model N Roadster
Ford, 1910, Model T Touring
Ford, 1931, Model A Convertible Sedan
Ford, 1932, Pickup Truck
Ford, 1934, Panel Truck
Ford, 1946, Woody Sportsman Convertible
Ford, 1948, Woody Station Wagon
Ford, 1950, 4dr Sedan
Ford, 1965, Mustang
Ford-Gilmore, 1927, Electric Sedan
Franklin, 1905, Roadster
Handley-Knight, 1922, Touring
Holsman, 1909, Runabout

Hudson, 1923, Phaeton
Hupmobile, 1910, Runabout
Jaguar, 1971, XK-E 2 + 2
Jeep, 1941
Juvenile, 1907, Electric Runabout
LaSalle, 1933
Lincoln, 1929, Sport Touring
Lincoln, 1940, Zephyr Continental Convertible
Lincoln, 1956, Continental
Lincoln, 1971, Continental
Locomobile, 1899, Steam Runabout
Lozier, 1910, Touring
Mars Renault, 1968, Electric Sedan
Mercedes-Benz, 1956, 300SL
Mercedes-Benz, 1972, Limousine
Mercer, 1917, Runabout
MG, 1953, TD Roadster
MG, 1962, A Roadster
Michigan, 1903, Runabout
Oldsmobile, 1904, Runabout
Packard, 1905, Model N Touring
Packard, 1908, Model 30 Runabout
Packard, 1910, Model 18 Touring
Packard, 1917, Touring
Packard, 1930, Phaeton
Packard, 1930, Speedster Sedan
Packard, 1934, 4dr Sedan
Packard, 1934, LeBaron Convertible Coupe
Packard, 1936, Victoria Convertible
Packard, 1937, Coupe

Packard, 1938, Victoria Convertible
Packard, 1939
Packard, 1939, Coupe
Packard, 1939, Victoria Convertible
Packard, 1948, Station Sedan
Packard, 1951, Sedan
Packard, 1956, 2dr Hardtop
Pierce-Arrow, 1920, Model 48 Touring
Pierce-Arrow, 1925, Model 80 Roadster
Plymouth, 1974, Road Runner
Pontiac, 1984, Fiero Indy Pace Car
Rauch & Lang, 1914, Electric Coupe
Roamer, 1917, Touring
Roamer, 1920, Roadster
Roamer, 1920, Town Car Landaulet
Rolls-Royce, 1910, Silver Ghost Touring
Rolls-Royce, 1913, Touring
Rolls-Royce, 1929, Phantom I Phaeton
Rolls-Royce, 1929, Touring
Rolls-Royce, 1930, Sedanca De Ville Town Car
Rolls-Royce, 1930, Victoria
Rolls-Royce, 1932, Victoria Coupe
Rolls-Royce, 1933, Phantom II Coupe
Rolls-Royce, 1936, Tourer
Rolls-Royce, 1938, Phantom III Limousine
Rolls-Royce, 1963, Silver Cloud III
Stanley, 1908, Steamer Runabout
Stanley, 1911, Steamer Touring
Stanley, 1913, Steamer Mountain Wagon
Stearns-Knight, 1927, Opera Coupe
Stevens-Duryea, 1903
Stutz, 1920, Bulldog Touring
Tucker, 1948, 4dr Sedan
Waltham, 1905, Orient Buckboard
White, 1903, Steam Touring
White, 1925, Park Bus
Wills Sainte Claire, 1926, 4dr Phaeton
Woods Mobilette, 1915, Roadster

Henry Ford Museum & Greenfield Village

20900 Oakwood Boulevard, P.O. Box 1970, Dearborn, Michigan 48121
(313) 271-1620

Displayed at the Henry Ford Museum & Greenfield Village are Americana dating from the 1600s to the present. Special emphasis is placed on the relationship between industrial technology and American history as reflected in the collections of automobiles, locomotives and aircraft. Changes in transportation, agriculture, industry, leisure, entertainment and domestic living are traceable in the collections and exhibits. Glass blowing, printing, weaving and pottery are among the crafts demonstrated.

More than 80 historic structures make up Greenfield Village, many of which were moved to the sight by Henry Ford. Visitors can walk through or view the Menlo Park laboratory complex where Thomas Edison produced more than 400 inventions; the bicycle shop where the Wright brothers designed and built their first airplane; the house

The evolution of the automobile and its industry is illustrated by a procession of cars on this multi-level, serpentine roadway, beginning with early bikes and carriages and ending with a 1981 Ford Escort and 1983 Honda Accord.

1902 Ford 999. *In 1902 Barney Oldfield drove Henry Ford's 999 to victory over the Winton* Bullet, *the first auto racing victory for Oldfield, and in fact, his first driving attempt. The victory boosted the careers of both Ford and Oldfield. The huge 1153 cubic inch engine propelled the car around a one-mile track in less than a minute, a record. In 1904 Henry Ford drove the car to a land speed record of 91.37 mph. The car was named after a fast train of the day.*

where Noah Webster wrote his American dictionary; the birthplace and boyhood farm of tire pioneer Harvey Firestone; and the farmhouse where Henry Ford was born and raised.

The portion of the museum devoted to the automobile is entitled "The Automobile in American Life." The area is segmented into themes addressing the evolution of the automobile, its significance in the American culture, the joy of driving, the impact on travel, designing the auto, and the marketing of the auto. The broad collection of autos should be interesting to any enthusiast, but the exhibit will appeal to virtually everyone because of the displays outlining the effect of the car on American lives.

Highlights in the exhibit include: a twin-row presentation of significant cars and related changes in technology; an overview of the process, tools and concept cars used in automotive design; displays that chronicle the changes in traveling by auto, from early tent camps to modern motels; the advertising, promotion, stunts and gimmicks used to market cars; and the changing landscape, from drive-in theaters and restaurants, to service stations and Burma Shave signs.

Approximately 100 cars comprise a collection that encompasses an 1865 Roper steam carriage, a rare and expensive 1931 Bugatti Royale — six were built, each currently valued in multiple millions, the 15-millionth Ford Model T built, the Harley Earl-designed 1938 Buick "Y-Job" concept car, and Henry Ford's *999* race car, which was built by Ford and driven by Barney Oldfield and Ford to speed records.

In the 1950s and 1960s people headed in droves to drive-in theaters, a new recreational activity that combined two American passions, movies and cars. Audiences covered the spectrum of young America from newly licensed teenagers to budget-minded families, from rowdy pranksters to back-seat lovers. Parked beneath the museum's drive-in theater sign is a 1949 Mercury that was customized by Barris.

DIRECTIONS TO MUSEUM: From eastbound I-94 exit onto northbound Southfield (M-39); go three miles to northbound Oakwood then go two miles.

From westbound I-94 exit onto northbound Oakwood then go three miles.

From northbound I-75 exit onto northbound Southfield (M-39); go eight miles to northbound Oakwood then go two miles.

From eastbound I-96 exit onto southbound Southfield (M-39); go west on Michigan Avenue then turn left onto Oakwood and go 1/2 mile.

ADMISSION COST: Adults $11.50; senior citizens $10.50; children (5-12 yrs.) $5.75. Tickets are separate but priced the same for either Henry Ford Museum or Greenfield Village. Combination tickets for admission available at reduced cost.

HOURS OF OPERATION: Open daily 9am-5pm. Some structures closed January 2-March 16. Closed Thanksgiving and Christmas.

MUSEUM NOTES: Restaurants are located on the grounds. Film is available in the gift shop. Contact museum for special events and exhibits.

A brochure is available.

Display Automobiles

Apperson, 1916, Touring
Auburn, 1930, Convertible Sedan
Autocar, 1900
Baker, 1901, Electric Runabout
Benz, 1894, Velo
Benz, 1903, Parsifal

Brewster, 1915, Landaulet Town Car
Bugatti, 1931, Royale Type 41 Cabriolet
Buick, 1909, Model 10 Touring
Buick, 1938, "Y-Job" Concept Car
Buick, 1950, Roadmaster Sedan
Buick, 1963, Riviera

Cadillac, 1903, Runabout
Cadillac, 1912, Touring
Cadillac, 1915, Touring
Cadillac, 1959, Eldorado Convertible
Chevrolet, 1923, Coupe
Chevrolet, 1929, Sedan
Chevrolet, 1955, Bel Air Hardtop
Chevrolet, 1955, Corvette
Chevrolet, 1956, Convertible
Chevrolet, 1960, Corvair 4dr Sedan
Chrysler, 1924
Chrysler, 1932, Custom Imperial Landau Sedan
Chrysler, 1940, Crown Imperial Phaeton
Chrysler, 1950, New Yorker Sedan
Chrysler, 1964, Ghia Turbine
Cord, 1937, 812 Convertible
Crosley, 1951, Hot Shot
DeDion-Bouton, 1900, Motorette
DeSoto, 1934, Airflow 4dr Sedan
Detroit Electric, 1914, Brougham
Duesenberg, 1931, Rollston Convertible
    Victoria
Duryea, 1896
Edsel, 1958
Essex, 1924, Coach
Ford, 1902, *999* Race Car
Ford, 1903, Model A Runabout
Ford, 1906, Model N
Ford, 1914, Model T Touring
Ford, 1927, Model T
Ford, 1930, Model A Phaeton
Ford, 1932, Cabriolet
Ford, 1932, Hot Rod Coupe
Ford, 1935, Touring
Ford, 1939, Convertible
Ford, 1949, Sedan
Ford, 1953, *X100* Concept Car
Ford, 1953, Sunliner Convertible
Ford, 1956, Thunderbird
Ford, 1962, Mustang I
Ford, 1964, Mustang Convertible
Ford, 1981, Escort
General Motors, 1951, *LeSabre* Experimental
    Car
General Motors, 1958, *Firebird III* Concept Car
Graham Brothers, 1928, Nomad House Car

Honda, 1983, Accord
Hupmobile, 1911, Coupe
Kaiser, 1949, Traveller Sedan
LaSalle, 1927, Roadster
Lincoln, 1929, Dietrich Victoria
    Convertible
Lincoln, 1936, Zephyr Sedan
Lincoln, 1939, *Sunshine Special*
Lincoln, 1941, Continental Cabriolet
Lincoln, 1950, Parade Limousine
Lincoln, 1956, Continental
Locomobile, 1899, Steam Runabout
Mercer, 1916, Touring
Mercury, 1939, Sedan
Mercury, 1949, Customized Convertible
MG, 1949, TC Roadster
Nash, 1926, 4dr Sedan
Nash, 1950, Rambler 2dr Convertible
Northern, 1904
Oldsmobile, 1903, Curved Dash Runabout
Overland, 1918, Touring
Packard, 1903, *Old Pacific* Runabout
Packard, 1904, Model L Touring
Packard, 1916, Camp Truck
Packard, 1929, Speedster
Plymouth, 1933, Coupe
Pontiac, 1965, GTO 2dr Hardtop
Pope-Hartford, 1904, Tonneau
Rambler, 1904, Canopy Tonneau
Rolls-Royce, 1926
Roper, 1865, Steam Carriage
Saxon, 1916
Sears, 1909, Autobuggy
Selden, 1907, Motor Buggy
Studebaker, 1951
Studebaker, 1963, Avanti
Stutz, 1923, Bearcat Roadster
Toyota, 1966, Corona Sedan
Tucker, 1948, 4dr Sedan
Volkswagen, 1949, Sedan
Volkswagen, 1959, Westphalia Camper
White, 1921, Camp Truck
Wills St. Claire, 1926, Roadster
Willys, 1942, Jeep
Winton, 1900

Motorsports Hall of Fame

P.O. Box 194, Novi, Michigan 48376
(313) 349-7223

NOTE: The Motorsports Hall of Fame is moving to the Novi Expo Center and will re-open in fall 1992.

The Motorsports Hall of Fame honors noteworthy competitors in all venues of motor-sports, from boat racing to airplane racing, but the emphasis lies with auto racing. Established in 1985, the Hall of Fame inducted its first eight honorees in 1989. The exploits of the motorsport legends that have been selected are documented. Cars and artifacts associated with the honorees are also displayed. On permanent display are Art Arfons *Green Monster* land speed record car and the hydroplane *Miss US 1*. Exhibits are changed periodically.

To any fan of Indy car racing from the 1940s to the 1960s, the name Novi is immediately identified with a race car of that era. Known for its power and distinctive sound among the Offys, the Novi Special is displayed at the Hall of Fame.

DIRECTIONS TO MUSEUM: The Hall of Fame is located in the Novi Expo Center, which is just off the Novi Rd. exit along I-96.

ADMISSION COST: To be announced later in 1992.

HOURS OF OPERATION: To be announced later in 1992.

MUSEUM NOTES: There are restaurants nearby.

Poll Museum of Transportation

13045 New Holland Street, Holland, Michigan
Mailing Address: 1715 104th Avenue, Zeeland, Michigan 49464
(616) 399-1955 or 772-6188

The museum contains a collection of 40 vehicles ranging from 1902 to 1966 model years. Predominately comprised of automobiles, there are also early fire trucks and pickup trucks. Several classic cars are displayed including a 1921 Pierce-Arrow, 1929 Marmon and 1931 Packard. Also exhibited are collections of model trains, bicycles, bells and toys.

One of the more unique cars on display is a 1965 Amphicar. As the name implies, the car could be driven on a road or in water. The rear-mounted engine powered the rear wheels or, if selected by the driver, two propellers. The front wheels acted as rudders when the car traversed water. Top road speed was around 65 mph while top speed in water was 7 knots. Approximately 800 were built in Berlin, Germany, from 1961 to 1968. Faced with more stringent auto and marine regulations and an unprofitable balance sheet, the company folded in 1968.

Also on the premises is the 1st Michigan Museum of Military History, which contains military artifacts and memorabilia of Michigan residents. Admission to the Poll Museum provides entrance to the military museum as well.

DIRECTIONS TO MUSEUM: The museum is located on US 31 approximately four miles north of Holland at 13045 New Holland St.

ADMISSION COST: Adults $2.00; children (10-12 yrs.) 50¢.

HOURS OF OPERATION: Open May 1-October 1 daily 9am-5pm.

MUSEUM NOTES: There is a restaurant nearby and the museum has a gift shop. Film is not available.

A brochure is available.

Display Automobiles

Ahrens-Fox, 1924, Fire Truck
American LaFrance, 1920, Fire Truck
American LaFrance, 1949, Fire Truck
Amphicar, 1966
BMW Isetta, 1957
Buick, 1910, Roadster
Buick, 1911, Roadster
Case, 1911, Touring
Chevrolet, 1963, Corvair Convertible
Chrysler, 1930, Coupe

Chrysler, 1948, Convertible
Crosley, 1942, Convertible
Dayton, 1902, Touring
Ford, 1915, Fire Truck
Ford, 1923, Touring
Ford, 1929, Sport Coupe
Holsman, 1902, Pickup Truck
Hudson, 1912, Touring
Hudson, 1916, Convertible Coupe
Hudson, 1917, Limousine

International, 1909, Pickup Truck
Kelsey, 1911, Roadster
Lincoln, 1957, Continental
Marmon, 1929, Roadster
Maxwell, 1909, Roadster
Mitchell, 1934, Roadster
Morgan, 1934, Roadster
Oakland, 1911, Roadster
Oldsmobile, 1902
Overland, 1911, Speedster

Overland, 1913, Touring
Packard, 1931, Touring
Packard, 1940, Convertible
Pierce-Arrow, 1921, Roadster
Pratt-Elkhart, 1911
Rauch-Lang, 1915, Electric
Regal, 1913, Underslung
Seagrave, 1939, Fire Truck
Studebaker, 1953, Coupe

R.E. Olds Transportation Museum

240 Museum Drive, Lansing, Michigan 48933
(517) 372-0422

The museum's purpose is to collect, preserve, study and exhibit objects that illustrate the development of transportation in the greater Lansing area, with emphasis on the automobile and its impact on the community and the nation.

The focus of the museum is the achievements of Ransom Eli Olds, a pioneer in automotive history. Olds first significant car was the Curved Dash runabout, conceived in Detroit, but built in Lansing. It was America's first quantity-built car with over 5,000 built in 1904 — the most popular car until the advent of the Ford Model T. Olds left the company in 1904 after disagreeing with corporate directors and formed the Reo Motor Car Company. Reo proved highly successful and Olds left the company in the mid-20's to pursue other business interests. After Ransom Olds departed, Oldsmobile was later integrated into General Motors and remains today as a major automobile manufacturer.

The museum has over twenty Oldsmobiles on display, including the first-year 1897 Olds, as well as ten Reo autos, which provides the visitor with an opportunity to view

1904 Oldsmobile Curved Dash Runabout. *In 1904 Oldsmobile built 5,500 Curved Dash runabouts, and built even more the next year. The Curved Dash was the most popular car in the country until Ford built the Model T. During its six-year lifespan, the Curved Dash sold for $650.*

the evolution of these auto makers. Also on display is a collection of 33 Oldsmobile engines dating from 1932 to present, plus a 707 cubic inch, six-cylinder engine used in some 1910 and 1911 Oldsmobiles.

DIRECTIONS TO MUSEUM: From I-496 exit onto Larch and travel north to Michigan. Turn left onto Michigan and travel to Museum Dr. on left.

ADMISSION COST: Adults $2.50; senior citizens and children $1.50.

HOURS OF OPERATION: Open Monday-Saturday 10am-5pm. Closed New Year's Day, Easter, Thanksgiving and Christmas.

MUSEUM NOTES: There is a restaurant nearby. A gift shop is onsite, but film is not available.

A brochure is available.

Display Automobiles

Jet Engineering, 1984, Indy Car
Oldsmobile, 1897
Oldsmobile, 1901, Curved Dash Runabout
Oldsmobile, 1904, Curved Dash Runabout
Oldsmobile, 1905, Runabout
Oldsmobile, 1921, Touring
Oldsmobile, 1926, Sedan
Oldsmobile, 1932, Sedan
Oldsmobile, 1937, Model F-37 Sedan
Oldsmobile, 1940, Series 70 Coupe
Oldsmobile, 1949, Indy Pace Car Convertible
Oldsmobile, 1951, Model 88 4dr Sedan
Oldsmobile, 1955, Model 98 4dr Sedan
Oldsmobile, 1961, Model 88 Sedan
Oldsmobile, 1966, Toronado
Oldsmobile, 1968, Hurst Cutlass
Oldsmobile, 1969, Hurst Cutlass

Oldsmobile, 1972, Cutlass Coupe
Oldsmobile, 1972, Hurst Cutlass
Oldsmobile, 1977, Toronado
Oldsmobile, 1979, Coupe
Oldsmobile, 1979, Hurst Cutlass
Oldsmobile, 1985, Indy Pace Car Convertible
Reo, 1906, Model B Runabout
Reo, 1909, Touring
Reo, 1909, 2-cylinder Touring
Reo, 1910, Touring
Reo, 1919, Model F Truck
Reo, 1923, Speedwagon Truck
Reo, 1927, Wolverine Coupe
Reo, 1929, Flying Cloud Sedan
Reo, 1931, Royale Sedan
Reo, 1937, Flying Cloud 2dr Sedan
Star, 1926, 2dr Coach

Ypsilanti Antique Auto, Truck & Fire Museum
110 W. Cross, Ypsilanti, Michigan 48105
(313) 483-0042

The vehicles, artifacts and memorabilia were collected by Tom Conway and are housed in an 1898 fire house.

The centerpiece of the collection is the replica of a service station from an era when service brought in customers. Exhibited are products that were offered in a service station of the day, which provides an interesting view of what operation and ownership of a 1920s or 1930s car entailed. The service station artifacts include a rare twin-reservoir gas pump, neon signs and a collection of over 300 pump globes (a lighted, glass adornment that sat atop the gas pump) bearing familiar names like Texaco and Sinclair, and the forgotten names of Red Hat and White Eagle.

Among the cars in the collection is an award-winning 1933 Plymouth Cabriolet. Plymouth restyled the body and introduced a six-cylinder engine for all models in 1933. The engine displacement was actually less than the former four-cylinder engine, but horsepower increased by five horsepower. The flathead-design engine wasn't removed from service until 1960 in Plymouths, and was found in Dodge Power-Wagons until the late 1960s.

DIRECTIONS TO MUSEUM: The museum is located on Cross Street, which is three blocks north of Michigan Ave. (US 12), between N. Huron and Washington.

ADMISSION COST: Free.

HOURS OF OPERATION: Hours flexible; call ahead.

MUSEUM NOTES: There are restaurants nearby. Film is not available.

Display Automobiles

Cadillac, 1955, Series 60 4dr Sedan
Chevrolet, 1932, Pickup Truck
Chevrolet, 1948, Station Wagon
Ford, 1914, Model T Fire Truck
Ford, 1925, Model T Pickup Truck
Ford, 1928, Model TT Fire Truck
Ford, 1930, Model A Deluxe Coupe
Ford, 1932, Cabriolet
Ford, 1937, Club Cabriolet
Ford, 1940, Standard Station Wagon

Ford, 1947, Business Coupe
Ford, 1966, Mustang
Ford, 1979, Daytona Prototype
Ford, 1979, Ranchero
Graham Brothers, 1927, Delivery Truck
Mercury, 1960, Comet
Packard, 1940, Super 8 Touring
Packard, 1948, 4dr Sedan
Plymouth, 1933, Cabriolet
Willys, 1950, Jeepster

Autos of Yesteryear

US 63N, Rolla, Missouri 65401
(314) 364-1810

Autos of Yesteryear is a portion of the Memoryville U.S.A. complex. Contained in Memoryville are stores representative of town life during the early twentieth century. Exhibited are artifacts from a machine shop, barber shop, hotel, general store, blacksmith shop, dress shop and other businesses. An art gallery is located in the gift shop.

In the car collection is a 1902 Holsman, an early highwheeler built in Chicago. Holsman was very successful and built cars until 1910. Failure to change the design when highwheelers became less desirable resulted in closure. The museum's Holsman has the original rope drive, a mechanism that was changed on later models to chain drive when wet weather proved that a rope was inadequate.

An auto restoration shop is attached to the Memoryville building through a concourse. Windows permit visitors to view the shop and restoration projects.

DIRECTIONS TO MUSEUM: Memoryville/Autos of Yesteryear is located on east side of US 63 just north of intersection with I-44.

ADMISSION COST: Adults $2.75; children (6-12 yrs.) $1.25.

HOURS OF OPERATION: Autos of Yesteryear open all year. Portions of Memoryville closed during winter. Open Monday-Friday 8am-6pm; Saturday and Sunday 9am-5pm. Closed New Year's Day, Thanksgiving and Christmas.

MUSEUM NOTES: There is a restaurant nearby. Memoryville has a gift shop, but film is not available.

A brochure is available.

Display Automobiles

Buick, 1910
DeLorean, 1984
Dodge, 1915, Touring
Essex, 1931, 2dr Coupe
Ford, 1914, Model T Touring
Ford, 1926, Model T 4dr Sedan
Ford, 1936, 2dr Coupe
Ford, 1939, Deluxe 4dr Sedan
Holsman, 1902, Runabout
Kissel, 1929, White Eagle 4dr Sedan
LaSalle, 1932

Maxwell, 1908
Overland, 1917, Touring
Overland, 1924, 4dr Sedan
Packard, 1932, 4dr Sedan
Paige, 1917
Pierce-Arrow, 1925, 2dr Sedan
Pontiac, 1926, 2dr Sedan
Rolls-Royce
Stanley, 1917, Steamer Touring
Stutz, 1926, 4dr Sedan
Terraplane, 1933, 4dr Sedan

Kelsey's Antique Cars

Highway 54E, Camdenton, Missouri 65020
(314) 346-2506

The collection includes several noteworthy cars including an 1899 Mobile Steamer, 1906 Stanley Steamer Gentleman's Speedy Roadster, 1914 Stutz Bearcat, 1931 Cadillac V-16 and 1933 V-12 Auburn Boattail Roadster.

The Mobile and Stanley marques share similar early histories. In 1899 the Stanley brothers sold their business to John Walker and Amzi Barber. They formed the Locomobile Company, then quarreled and separated. Barber retained all capital assets, leaving Walker with only the rights to produce the old Stanley-designed cars. Walker named his new firm the Mobile Company and built Mobile steam cars until 1903. Walker realized he couldn't compete with the Locomobile, the White steamers and the revived Stanley and sold the factory to Maxwell.

DIRECTIONS TO MUSEUM: Kelsey's is located on east US 54 in Camdenton.

HOURS OF OPERATION: Open May-October daily 8am-6pm.

ADMISSION COST: Adults $2.50; children $1.00.

MUSEUM NOTES: There are no restaurants nearby. Film is not available.

National Museum of Transport

3015 Barrett Station Road, St. Louis, Missouri 63122
(314) 965-7998

The museum presents an extensive collection of railroad equipment, trucks, automobiles, buses, carriages and aircraft. The collection of railroad locomotives and rolling stock is one of the largest in the country. Adjacent to the grounds are the oldest tunnels west of the Mississippi.

Among the cars in the collection is one of the oldest St. Louis-built automobiles existing. The car was built by the St. Louis Motor Carriage Company, which was organized 1891 and became the first successful automobile manufacturer, albeit short lived, west of the Mississippi. Production reached 300 cars in 1905, then seeking a larger manufacturing facility, the company moved to Peoria, Illinois. But the anticipated sales did not materialize and the company went bankrupt in 1907.

DIRECTIONS TO MUSEUM: From I-270 southbound, exit at Big Bend Rd. and travel west to Barrett Station Rd. Follow signs to museum. From I-270 northbound, exit at Dougherty Ferry Rd. and travel west to Barrett Station Rd. Follow signs to museum.

ADMISSION COST: Adults $3.00; senior citizens $1.50; children (5-12 yrs.) $1.50.

HOURS OF OPERATION: Open daily 9am-5pm. Closed New Year's Day, Thanksgiving and Christmas.

1906 Ford Model N. *The Model N was Henry Ford's first indication that his "everyman" dream car might appeal to buyers. Ford sold five times more Model Ns than any other model in 1907, while turning a substantial profit. Ford became the number one automaker in 1906. In 1908 Ford introduced the milestone Model T.*

1956 Citreon 2CV.
*Much like the original
Volkswagon, the
French-built Citreon
2CV was designed to
provide no-frills, func-
tional transportation.
Introduced in 1948, a
diminutive 325 cc (later
enlarged to 602 cc)
two-cylinder, air-cooled
engine powers the car
through a front-wheel-
drive system. A canvas,
roll-back top covers a
spartan interior. The
seats consist of canvas
hung on a tube frame.
The 2CV remained in
production into the
1980s.*

MUSEUM NOTES: There is a cafe onsite   **A brochure is available.**
and a restaurant nearby. The museum has
a gift shop, but film is not available.

Display Automobiles

Austin, 1935, Taxi   Falcon-Knight, 1927, Roadster
Austin, 1949, Taxi   Ford, 1915, Model T
Cadillac, 1921   Isetta, 1956
Cadillac, 1941, Fleetwood   Jaguar, 1935, SS
Chrysler, 1964, Turbine   LaSalle, 1935
Di Dia, 1964, Custom Car   Rolls-Royce, 1929
Dodge, 1950, Sedan   St. Louis, 1901

Patee House Museum

12th and Penn Streets, Box 1022, St. Joseph, Missouri 64502
(816) 232-8206

Patee House opened in 1858 as a luxurious, 140-room hotel. Now a National Historical Landmark, the hotel served as headquarters for the Pony Express and as a women's college before conversion to a garment factory in the late 1800s. Displayed in the building and on surrounding grounds are artifacts reflecting life in St. Joseph and the West from the Civil War through the early twentieth century. Also on the grounds is the home of Jesse James where he was slain by Bob Ford.

One of the cars in the museum, the Flint, represents the closing portion of the saga of William Durant, one of auto history's great wheeler-dealers. The 1927 Flint was the last of a brief four-year production run under the corporate umbrella of Durant. After acquiring Buick in 1904, Durant created General Motors in 1908, lost control, regained it, then was forced out for good. Durant attempted to recreate another auto giant, producing the Durant, Star, Locomobile and Flint, but due to inept managership and the stock market crash, Durant again lost his ownership of an auto company. He filed for bankruptcy in 1936 and ceased to influence the auto market.

DIRECTIONS TO MUSEUM: From US 36 exit onto 10th St. Travel north on 10th St. to Penn St., turn right and travel to museum at 12th St.

ADMISSION COST: Adults $2.00; children $1.00.

HOURS OF OPERATION: Open April-October daily 10am-4pm (until 5pm during summer). Open weekends January, February, March and November 1-5pm.

MUSEUM NOTES: There is a restaurant nearby. The museum has a gift shop. Film is not available.

A brochure is available.

Display Automobiles

American LaFrance, 1922, Fire Truck
Federal, 1918, Beer Truck
Flint, 1927
Ford, 1921, Model T Pickup Truck

Franklin, 1929, Touring
GMC, 1943, Truck
Race Car, 1921

Oscar's Dreamland

4002 Story Road, Billings, Montana 59102
(406) 656-0966 or 656-9476

Oscar Cooke's "dream" of passing on to following generations a sense of early life on the Montana plains is realized in Dreamland. Antique buildings and artifacts depict homesteading days at the turn of the century. Early structures include the first schoolhouse in Yellowstone County, the church with the oldest steeple in Billings, general store, blacksmith shop, barber shop, jail, fire station, auto garage, train depot and family home.

Among the machinery are an auto and truck collection, 300 gas tractors, 40 steam traction engines, 100 threshers, a steam-powered saw, a wooden oil well rig, the tallest air motor windmill, the largest revovling clock, antique hand tools, a 120-ton Corlis steam engine, and horse-drawn equipment.

The auto and truck collection comprises approximately 30 restored vehicles and includes several Ford Model Ts and As, a 1917 Metz, a 1906 Sears, several Chevrolets and Buicks, and World War I trucks. Most of the vehicles were built in the 1910s and 1920s.

DIRECTIONS TO MUSEUM: From east on I-90 take Exit 446 and travel west on frontage road on south side of freeway to Dreamland. From west on I-90 take Exit 437 and travel east on frontage road on south side of freeway to Dreamland.

ADMISSION COST: Over 16 yrs. $5.00; 12-16 yrs. $2.50; 6-12 yrs. $1.50.

HOURS OF OPERATION: Open May 1-September 31 daily 9am-6pm. Remainder of year call ahead.

MUSEUM NOTES: There is a concession stand onsite and a restaurant nearby. Dreamland has a gift shop, but film is not available.

A brochure is available.

Towe Ford Museum

1106 Main Street, Deer Lodge, Montana 59722
(406) 846-3111

The Towe Ford Museum is the result of efforts by Edward Towe. The Montana businessman and rancher transformed his interest in Ford automobiles into the world's most complete collection of cars built by Ford. The collection is split between two locations, Deer Lodge, Montana, and Sacramento, California (also found in this book). Both locations provide a comprehensive viewing of antique and classic Fords.

Among the cars in the collection is a 1903 Ford Model A Runabout. The Model A was the first production car of the Ford Motor Company. It was the first car to wear the now distinctive Ford emblem and the first production car engine with vertical cylinders. But Ford did not build the production engines. All mechanical components were built by the Dodge brothers. The body was built by the Wilson Carriage Company.

The Ford Motor Company was organized with very little capitol, so several investors were needed to achieve the goal of car builder. The company didn't have the resources to build a facility capable of building a complete car (virtually all car builders of the era

1924 Ford Model T Touring. *Prices for Model Ts reached their low point from late 1924 to early 1926. A Roadster sold for $260 while a Touring was priced at $290. Ford sold over two million cars in 1924.*

1930 Ford Model A. *The 1930 Model A was the third model year of the second A series (the first A series started in 1903). Changes included stainless steel trim and smaller diameter wheels, 19 inches, with larger tires. Ford sold over 120,000 roadsters during 1930, placing them behind two-door sedans and coupes in popularity.*

subcontracted construction), so a deal was struck with the Dodge brothers who were building components for Ransom Olds at the time. For a stake in the Ford Motor Company, the Dodge brothers delivered chassis, engines, transmission and rear axles. Success for Ford spelled success for the Dodge brothers and in 1914 they started producing their own line of cars. An acrimonious court battle ensued when Henry Ford would not buy back shares held by the Dodge brothers or pay dividends. So for a couple of years the Ford Motor Company actually brought in revenue that went into the pockets of a rival manufacturer.

DIRECTIONS TO MUSEUM: From I-90 take Exit 184 or 187 to Deer Lodge. Museum is on south end of Main St.

ADMISSION COST: Adults $5.00; senior citizens $4.50; children $2.00.

HOURS OF OPERATION: June-August: open daily 8am-9pm. September, October, April and May: open daily 8:30am-5:30pm. November-May: open Monday-Friday 9am-4pm, Saturday and Sunday 10:30am-5pm.

MUSEUM NOTES: A restaurant is nearby. Towe has a gift shop and film is available.

A brochure is available.

1903 Ford Model A Runabout. *This was the first production car built by the Ford Motor Company and was priced at $850. An 8 hp engine could propel the car to a top speed of 30 mph. The transmission provided two forward speeds and reverse.*

Display Automobiles

American LaFrance, 1929, Fire Truck
Auburn, 1932, Cabriolet
DeSoto, 1932, Roadster
Edsel, 1958, Sedan
Edsel, 1959, Ranger
Ford, 1903, Model A Runabout
Ford, 1905, Model C Runabout
Ford, 1906, Model N Runabout
Ford, 1907, Model K-640 Roadster
Ford, 1908, Model S Runabout
Ford, 1909, Model T Tourster
Ford, 1910, Model T Touring
Ford, 1911, Model T Torpedo Runabout
Ford, 1911, Model T Town Car
Ford, 1911, Model T Touring Car
Ford, 1913, Model T Depot Hack
Ford, 1913, Model T Runabout

Ford, 1914, Model T Runabout
Ford, 1914, Model T Speedster
Ford, 1914, Model T Touring
Ford, 1915, Model T Runabout
Ford, 1915, Model T Town Car
Ford, 1916, Model T Touring
Ford, 1917, Model T Touring
Ford, 1918, Model T Touring
Ford, 1920, Model T Touring
Ford, 1921, Model T Roadster
Ford, 1924, Model T Touring
Ford, 1926, Model T Coupe
Ford, 1926, Model T Sedan
Ford, 1927, Model T Touring
Ford, 1928, Model A Roadster
Ford, 1928, Model A Snowmobile
Ford, 1928, Model AR Phaeton

1907 Ford Model K 6-40 Roadster. *The Model K cost $2,800 in 1907. Ford did not produce another car in the Ford line, not including Lincoln, as expensive as the Model K until the introduction of the Thunderbird in 1955. A six-cylinder, 405-cubic-inch, 40-hp engine powered the Model K.*

Ford, 1929, Model A Coupe
Ford, 1929, Model A Roadster
Ford, 1929, Model A Special Coupe
Ford, 1929, Model A Station Wagon
Ford, 1929, Model A Town Sedan
Ford, 1929, Model T
Ford, 1930, Model A Deluxe Roadster
Ford, 1930, Model A Phaeton
Ford, 1930, Model A Pickup Truck
Ford, 1931, Model A Deluxe Phaeton
Ford, 1931, Model A Pickup Truck
Ford, 1931, Model A-400 Convertible Sedan
Ford, 1932, Deluxe Phaeton
Ford, 1932, Model B Pickup Truck
Ford, 1932, Sports Coupe
Ford, 1933, Station Wagon
Ford, 1933, Truck
Ford, 1934, Deluxe Roadster
Ford, 1936, Phaeton
Ford, 1936, Truck
Ford, 1937, Pickup Truck
Ford, 1937, Roadster

Ford, 1939, Coupe
Ford, 1940, 2dr Sedan
Ford, 1941, Pickup Truck
Ford, 1941, Station Wagon
Ford, 1942, Jeep
Ford, 1947, 2dr Sedan
Ford, 1951, 4dr Sedan
Ford, 1951, Crestliner 2dr Sedan
Ford, 1953, 2dr Sedan
Ford, 1955, Ambulance
Ford, 1955, Crown Victoria
Ford, 1955, Thunderbird
Ford, 1956, Thunderbird
Ford, 1958, 4dr Sedan
Ford, 1959, 4dr Sedan
Ford, 1961, Thunderbird
Ford, 1963, Falcon Convertible
Ford, 1963, Galaxie
Ford, 1963, Thunderbird
Ford, 1964, Galaxie 500
Ford, 1966, Mustang
Ford, 1966, Thunderbird

Ford, 1970, Galaxie 500
Ford, 1978, Thunderbird
Lincoln, 1922, Camper
Lincoln, 1922, Sedan
Lincoln, 1923, 4dr Sedan
Lincoln, 1925, Coupe
Lincoln, 1925, Dual Windshield Phaeton
Lincoln, 1936, Zephyr Sedan
Lincoln, 1937, Zephyr Landaulet Limousine
Lincoln, 1937, Zephyr Sedan

Lincoln, 1939, Zephyr Coupe
Lincoln, 1946, Continental
Lincoln, 1947, Continental
Lincoln, 1950, Cosmopolitan Sedan
Lincoln, 1955, Capri Coupe
Lincoln, 1957, Premiere
Lincoln, 1959, Premiere
Mercury, 1950, 4dr Sedan
Mercury, 1951, 4dr Sedan
Mercury, 1963, Comet

Chevyland U.S.A.

Rt. 2, Box 11, Elm Creek, Nebraska 68836
(308) 856-4208

NOTE: Chevyland U.S.A. is for sale at time of publication, but remains open. Call ahead for current status.

The collection reflects its name. With the exception of a couple of years, an example of each Chevrolet model year from 1914 to 1975 is found in the collection. Most of the later models are sport models — Corvettes, Super Sports, Nomads, Bel Airs and Impalas. Roadsters, coupes and tourers make up most of the early models.

One of the more interesting Chevrolet body styles on display is the Nomad. Seeking to attract buyers looking for a sporty station wagon equally functional at the hardware store and the country club, Chevrolet introduced the Nomad in 1955. Stylish lines, upscale interiors and V-8 power appealed to approximately 6,000 buyers annually. Excluding the Corvette, the Nomad was the most expensive model in the Chevrolet line. The 1955, 1956 and 1957 Nomads are particularly prized by collectors.

DIRECTIONS TO MUSEUM: From I-80 take Exit 257 onto US 183. Travel north on US 183 to first intersection (approximately 200 yards from freeway). Turn right at intersection and follow road approximately one mile to Chevyland on the right.

ADMISSION COST: Adults $4.00; children (12-16 yrs.) $2.00.

HOURS OF OPERATION: Open daily during summer 8am-5pm. See NOTE above.

MUSEUM NOTES: There is a restaurant nearby. Chevyland has a gift shop, but film is not available.

1947 Chevrolet Fleetline 2dr Sedan. Chevrolet sold over 680,000 cars in 1947, more than any other automaker. The styling was basically unchanged from the pre-war design. The wood adorning the sides of the museum's car was not a Chevrolet option, but was offered by Engineered Enterprises for installation by dealers.

Hastings Museum

1330 N. Burlington Avenue, Hastings, Nebraska 68901
(402) 461-2399

The Hastings Museum is a multi-faceted museum that presents exhibits in the areas of history and science with particular emphasis on natural history, geology, Native American history, pioneer history and Americana. The J.M. McDonald Planetarium adjoins the museum.

The autos on display were manufactured prior to World War I. A marque in the collection that had little impact from a long term view, but was significant at the time, was the Sears automobile. Sears perceived that cars were not faddish and offered a car in their catalog. The first version was built by contract in Evansville, Indiana. Anticipating long-term production, Sears built their own plant in Chicago, but mail-order cars were not profit makers and the plant closed in 1912. Sears attempted again in 1952 and 1953 to market a car, the Allstate, which was a rebranded Henry J, with similar results.

DIRECTIONS TO MUSEUM: From I-80 take Exit 312 and travel south on US 281 to Hastings. Museum is on US 281 at 14th St.

ADMISSION COST: Adults $4.00; senior citizens $3.50; children (6-15 yrs.) $2.00.

HOURS OF OPERATION: Open Monday-Saturday 9am-5pm, Sunday and holidays 1-5pm. Closed New Year's Day, Thanksgiving and Christmas. Close at noon on Christmas Eve.

MUSEUM NOTES: There is a restaurant nearby. The museum has a gift shop, but film is not available.

A brochure is available.

Display Automobiles

Brush, 1911, Model E26 Roadster
Buick, 1910, Model F Touring
Cadillac, 1905, Runabout
International Harvester, 1912, Model A
   Auto Wagon
Maxwell, 1918, Truck
Rauch & Lang, 1912, Model B26 Town Car
Reo, 1906, Runabout
Sears, 1909

Sawyer's Sandhills Museum
440 Valentine Street, Valentine, Nebraska 69201
(402) 376-3293

The Sandhills Museum contains a variety of artifacts that includes firearms, dishes, pianos, lamps, dishes, music boxes, farm machinery, automobiles and a two-headed, five-legged calf.

Of the 18 cars exhibited, most were built before 1920, and a couple are rarely seen on display. The Jeffery was built in 1914, the first year of the marque's three-year lifespan. The car was originally named the Rambler. After the death of Thomas Jeffery, the company's founder, Charles Jeffery renamed the car to commemorate his deceased father. Jeffery decided automaking was not his lifelong aspiration and retired in 1916 at the age of 40. The company was purchased by Charles Nash, who revived the Rambler name in 1950.

DIRECTIONS TO MUSEUM: The museum is four blocks west of Main St. on US 20.

ADMISSION COST: Adults $2.00; children (6-12 yrs.) $1.00.

HOURS OF OPERATION: Open Memorial Day-Labor Day daily 9am-6pm. Remainder of year by appointment.

MUSEUM NOTES: There is a restaurant nearby. Film is not available.

A brochure is available.

Display Automobiles

American La France, 1919, Fire Truck
Austro-Daimler, 1912, Touring
Buick, 1909, Model F Touring
Cadillac, 1907, Model K Roadster
Chalmers, 1911, Model 30 Touring
Chevrolet, 1927, Coupe
Flanders, 1910, Model 20 Touring
Flint, 1924, Model E55 Touring
Ford, 1924, Model T Coupe
Imperial, 1913, Touring
Jeffery, 1914, Touring
Lloyd, 1957, Coupe
Locomobile, 1901
Maxwell, 1909, Model A Roadster
Mercedes-Benz, 1967, 250 4dr Sedan
Paterson, 1916, Touring
Rattler, 190?, Homemade
Whippet, 1927, Roadster

Stuhr Museum

3133 W. Highway 34, Grand Island, Nebraska 68801
(308) 381-5316

The Stuhr Museum offers a view of prairie life through recreation of a prairie railroad town and displays of artifacts and memorabilia from the 1800s and early 1900s. Approximately sixty buildings reflect all aspects of life for Nebraska prairie dwellers during the last decades of the nineteenth century. Two steam locomotives and related railroad equipment and artifacts are displayed in the railyard. Artifacts and memorabilia depicting life on the prairie, as well as Native American and Old West items, reside in the main museum building.

Adjoining the prairie community site is a building housing over 200 pieces of antique farm machinery and cars. The bulk of the collection consists of early steam engines, tractors, and horse- and tractor-drawn farm implements. The auto collection is small, but several interesting cars are displayed, Overland, American, Velie and Pullman. Of course, the Ford Model T was the car of choice for most of America and the museum has three, a roadster, a coupe and a truck. The low-cost ruggedness of the "T", coupled with ease-of-repair, was particularly attractive to rural car owners.

Note that main museum building is open all-year-round, but other buildings, including auto building, are only open May 1 through October 15.

DIRECTIONS TO MUSEUM: From I-80 take exit 312 onto US 34/281. Travel north on US 34/281 approximately four miles to museum.

ADMISSION COST: May 1-October 15: adults $6.00; children (7-16 yrs.) $3.50. October 16-April 30: adults $4.00; children (7-16 yrs.) $2.00.

HOURS OF OPERATION: May-October 15: open daily 9am-5pm; close at 5:30 during July and August. October 16-April 30: open Monday-Saturday 9am-5pm; Sunday 1-5pm.

MUSEUM NOTES: Main museum building is open all-year-round, but other buildings, including auto building, are only open May 1 through October 15. Food is available onsite May-October 15 and there is a restaurant nearby. There is a gift shop, but film is not available.

A brochure is available.

Display Automobiles

American, 1903
Chevrolet, 1940, 4dr Sedan
Chevrolet, 1960, Corvair 4dr Sedan
Ford, 1914, Model T Roadster
Ford, 1922, Model T Coupe
Ford, 1922, Model T Truck

Ford, 1929, Model A 2dr Sedan
Hudson, 1923, 2dr Sedan
Overland, 1913
Pullman, 1916, Touring
Velie, 1922

Imperial Palace Auto Collection

3535 S. Las Vegas Boulevard, Las Vegas, Nevada 89109
(702) 731-3311

The Imperial Palace Auto Collection is one of the world's largest, privately owned automobile museums in the world. There are more than 700 vehicles in the collection, with approximately 200 on display. The remainder are on tour, loaned to other museums or in storage.

The collection celebrated its tenth anniversary in December 1991. Recently, the Duesenberg Room was opened and now houses the largest collection of Model J Duesenbergs in the world. On display are approximately 25 of the classic cars ranging from 1929 to 1937. Past owners include James Cagney, Billy Rose, Max Baer, Paul Whiteman and Phillip K. Wrigley. The Model J is the most sought-after of Duesenbergs, and any Model J is worth at least $250,000, with some considerably more.

Many of the cars here are distinctive due to their past owners. Cars of politicos include Eisenhower, Truman, Kennedy, Johnson, Hoover, Hitler, Mussolini, Hirohito and Czar Nicholas. Entertainers and public figures include Cagney, McQueen, Liberace, Presley, Fields, Caruso, Benny and Hughes. Most of these cars were customized to suit the owner. One of the more bizarre modifications, but characteristic of the owner's eccentric nature, was the installation of a purification system in the 1954 Chrysler owned by Howard Hughes. The modification cost more than the car.

1948 Tucker 4dr Sedan. *This Tucker is one of only 51 built. Conceived by the innovative Preston Tucker, production was aborted in 1948 when Tucker was indicted by the government for fraud. Tucker was acquitted in 1950, but with the company in disarray, the program was not revived.*

1948 Chrysler Town and Country. *Media stars have been known to "personalize" their automobiles, and Leo Carillo (Pancho of the Cisco Kid series) chose to customize his Chrysler Town and Country by attaching a steer's head to the hood.*

DIRECTIONS TO MUSEUM: The collection is located in the parking facility adjacent to the Imperial Palace hotel.

ADMISSION COST: Adults $6.95; senior citizens $3.00; children $3.00. Under 5 yrs. free.

HOURS OF OPERATION: Open daily 9:30am-11:30pm.

MUSEUM NOTES: There is a restaurant nearby and a gift shop onsite. Film is available.

A brochure is available.

Display Automobiles

NOTE: This is a partial list.

Alfa Romeo, 1939
Buick, 1908, Truck
Buick, 1933, Limousine
Cadillac, 1929
Cadillac, 1930
Cadillac, 1930, V-16
Cadillac, 1938, V-16 Touring
Cadillac, 1964, Limousine
Cadillac, 1976, Eldorado
Chrysler, 1948, Town & Country

Chrysler, 1952, Imperial Convertible
Chrysler, 1954
Chrysler, 1966, Imperial
Cord, 1937
Delage, 1928, Limousine
DeLorean, 1981
Dodge, 1924, Depot Hack
Duesenberg, 1937, Model J
Ford, 1914, Model T Pie Wagon
Ford, 1917, Model T Gasoline Truck

Ford, 1924, Model T Depot Hack
Ford, 1924, Model T Fire Truck
Ford, 1929, Model AA Dump Truck
Ford, 1929, Model AA Truck
Ford, 1931, Truck
Ford, 1932, Woody Wagon
Ford, 1946, Pickup Truck
Haynes-Apperson, 1897
Hudson, 1920
LaNef, 1898
Lincoln, 1950, 4dr Cosmopolitan
Lincoln, 1962, Continental
Little Giant, 1912, Truck
Maxwell, 1910
McFarlan, 1926
Mercedes, 1909

Mercedes-Benz, 1939, 770K
Packard, 1935, Limousine
Packard, 1939
Packard, 1939
Packard, 1939, V-12
Pierce-Arrow, 1904, Omni-Bus
Plymouth, 1932
Rapid, 1905, Bus
Rolls-Royce, 1914, Silver Ghost
Rolls-Royce, 1966
Seagulls, 1913, Fire Truck
Stanley, 1913, Bus
Tucker, 1947
UNIC, 1908, Taxi
Yellow Cab, 1923, Taxi
Zimmer, 1981, Golden Spirit

Liberace Museum

1775 E. Tropicana Avenue, Las Vegas, Nevada 89119
(702) 798-5595

Liberace brought glitz, glamour and showmanship to the craft of piano playing. The museum offers the accouterments that Liberace used on stage, as well as a collection of rare pianos.

Liberace extended his flamboyance on stage to his automobiles. Several of Liberace's show cars reside in the museum. No other museum displays a red, white and blue Rolls-Royce, a pink Volkswagen, a Rolls-Royce with mirror tiles or a custom Duesenberg covered with rhinestones. This is customizing carried to garish extreme.

DIRECTIONS TO MUSEUM: The museum is at the corners of Tropicana Ave. and Spencer St.

ADMISSION COST: Adults $6.50; senior citizens $4.50; students $3.50; children (6-12 yrs.) $2.00.

HOURS OF OPERATION: Open Monday-Saturday 10am-5pm; Sunday 1-5pm.

Closed New Year's Day, Thanksgiving and Christmas.

MUSEUM NOTES: There are restaurants nearby. The museum has a gift shop, but film is not available.

A brochure is available.

Display Automobiles

English Taxi Cab, 1957
Ford, 1931, Model A
Bradley GT
Duesenberg

Rolls-Royce, 1954
Rolls-Royce
Volkswagen

National Automobile Museum
10 Lake Street South, Reno, Nevada 89501
(702) 333-9300

William "Bill" Harrah created the collection that now resides in the National Automobile Museum. Before his death in 1978, Harrah accumulated one of the largest, best-known auto collections in the world. A significant portion is now exhibited in the museum under the auspices of the Harrah Foundation.

The collection comprises over 200 cars, some important because of their impact on the auto industry, some noteworthy because of their accomplishments and some distinctive because of their owner. Among "impact" cars are a Panhard et Levassor, Olds Curved Dash, Chrysler Airflow and Ford Model T. Cars performing notable accomplishments include the 1907 Thomas Flyer that won the "Great Race" from New York to Paris, the McLaren race cars that dominated Can Am races, and Don Garlits famous *Wynnscharger*. Several cars were owned or associated with Hollywood stars John Wayne (Corvette), Mary Pickford (Ford), James Dean (Mercury), Al Jolson (Cadillac), Lana Turner (Chrysler), Frank Sinatra (Ghia) and Jack Benny (Maxwell).

1907 Thomas Flyer. *George Schuster and Montague Roberts won the 1908 New York-to-Paris race in this Thomas Flyer. The car was essentially in stock condition and completed the grueling trip across the United States, Asia and Europe in 169 days.*

1938 Packard 1607 Convertible Coupe. *Collectors highly value the 1938 Packard Convertible Coupes. They were available only as 1607 models, which were powered by the big V-12 engine (473 cubic inches) and stopped by vacuum-boosted hydraulic brakes.*

The automobile has inspired all sorts of designers, artists and craftsmen to exercise their mental and tactile talents towards creating innovatively designed cars. Such exercises resulted in the museum's 1938 Phantom Corsair, a Batmobile look-a-like, the 1934 Dymaxion that's equipped with periscopes rather than a rear-view mirror, and Ed "Big Daddy" Roth's 1960s classic *Beatnik Bandit*.

The cars are exhibited in contemporary street settings. Also found are hands-on displays, artifacts, a confectioner's shop and an interpretive audio system that presents facts and stories.

DIRECTIONS TO MUSEUM: From I-80 take Exit 13 onto Virginia St. and travel south on Virginia. Turn left onto Mill St. and travel two blocks to museum at intersection with Lake St. Free parking on east side of building.

ADMISSION COST: Adults $7.50; senior citizens $6.50; children (6-18 yrs.) $2.50.

HOURS OF OPERATION: Open daily 9:30am-5:30pm. Closed Thanksgiving and Christmas.

1933 Cadillac Series 452C All-Weather Phaeton. *The Series 452C models were the top of the line for Cadillac in 1933 and the museum's was previously owned by Al Jolson. The body was built by Fleetwood while an overhead-valve V-16 provided 165 horsepower.*

MUSEUM NOTES: A restaurant and gift shop are onsite. There are restaurants nearby. Film is available.

A brochure is available.

Display Automobiles

Adams-Farwell, 1906, Convertible Runabout
Airomobile, 1937, Sedan
Allstate, 1952, Sedan
American LaFrance, 1917
Auburn, 1933, Custom Speedster
Austin/American, 1933, Roadster
Auto Red Bug, 1928, Roadster
Baker Electric, 1912, Coupe
Battery Box, 1973, Electric Streamliner
Black, 1909, Motor Buggy

Briggs & Stratton, 1920, Flyer Buckboard
Briscoe, 1915, Cloverleaf Roadster
Brooks, 1924, Steamer Sedan
Brush, 1908, Runabout
Buick, 1914, Touring
Buick, 1937, Special 4dr Sedan
Buick, 1954, Skylark
Cadillac, 1903, Model A Runabout
Cadillac, 1907, Model M Side Entrance
   Tonneau

Cadillac, 1913, Roadster
Cadillac, 1933, Series 452C All-Weather
    Phaeton
Cadillac, 1957, Eldorado Brougham
Cadillac, 1973, Eldorado Coupe
Cameron, 1903, Runabout
Capitol, 1902, Steam Chariot
Chevrolet, 1917, Model D-5 Touring
Chevrolet, 1923, Model M Coupe
Chevrolet, 1926, Superior Deluxe Depot
Chevrolet, 1928, Pickup Truck
Chevrolet, 1933, Master Phaeton
Chevrolet, 1941, Special Deluxe Town Sedan
Chevrolet, 1953, Corvette
Chevrolet, 1960, Corvair
Chevrolet, 1969, Corvair
Chevrolet, 1975, Cosworth Vega
Chevrolet, 1977, Monza GT Race Car
Chrysler, 1924, Model B Phaeton
Chrysler, 1934, Airflow
Chrysler, 1941, Newport Dual Cowl Phaeton
Chrysler, 1956, 300B Coupe
Citroen, 1965, 2CV Saloon
Cole, 1917, Tourcoupe
Cord, 1936, 810 Westchester Sedan
Cord, 1936, Limousine
Cord, 1937, 812 Beverly Sedan
Cretors, 1913, Popcorn Wagon
Crosley, 1941, Convertible Coupe
Cunningham, 1919, Model V-3 Touring
Dedion-Bouton, 1901, Model A Motorette
DeLorean, 1981
DeSoto, 1936, Taxicab
Detroit Electric, 1914, Gentleman's Roadster
Dodge, 1915, Touring
Dodge, 1922, Custom Victoria
Dodge, 1963, Polara Convertible
Dodge, 1982, Pace Car
Dodge, 1984, Caravan
Duesenberg, 1925, Roadster
Duryea, 1903, 3-wheeled Phaeton
Dutcher, 1974, Steam Sedan
Dymaxion, 1934
Edsel, 1958, Citation 4dr Hardtop
Essex, 1929, Challenger Speedabout
Faulkner, 1935, Midget Race Car
Ferrari, 1955, Grand Prix Race Car
Fiat, 1914, Model 56 Touring
Fiat, 1961, Model 600 Berlinetta
FKE 1, 1977, Enduro Road Racer
Flying Caduceus, 1960, Land Speed Car

Ford, 1903, Model A Tonneau
Ford, 1909, Model T Touring
Ford, 1911, Model T Runabout
Ford, 1915, Model T Town Car
Ford, 1921, Model T Kampkar
Ford, 1926, Model T Runabout
Ford, 1926, Model TT Pump Truck
Ford, 1928, Model A Sport Coupe
Ford, 1929, Model A, Cabriolet
Ford, 1929, Model A Mail Truck
Ford, 1929, Model A Pickup Truck
Ford, 1931, Model A-400 Convertible Sedan
Ford, 1931, Model A Deluxe 4dr Sedan
Ford, 1932, Model B Deluxe Roadster
Ford, 1939, Custom Convertible Coupe
Ford, 1955, Thunderbird
Ford, 1957, Skyliner
Ford, 1962, Thunderbird Hardtop
Ford, 1964, Custom Daytona Coupe
Ford, 1965, Mustang Fastback 2 + 2
Franklin, 1903, Light Roadster
Franklin, 1908, Model G Brougham
Franklin, 1910, Model D Touring
Franklin, 1911, Averell Special
Franklin, 1917, Series 9A Sedan
Franklin, 1925, Series 11A Sport Runabout
Franklin, 1930, Series 145 Pursuit
Franklin, 1933, Series 17B Club Brougham
Frayer-Miller, 1908, Model B Touring
Frazer, 1951, Manhattan Convertible Sedan
Frontmobile, 1918, Touring Sedan
Garlits, 1974, *Wynnscharger* Dragster
Ghia, 1961, L.6.4. Hardtop
Herda/Knapp/Milodon, 1962, Land Speed Car
Hispano-Suiza, 1937, Type J-12 Berline
Holmes, 1921, Series 4 Sedan
Hudson, 1929, Sport Phaeton
Hudson, 1936, Deluxe Eight Sedan
Hudson, 1953, Super Jet Sedan
Imp, 1914, Cycle Car
International, 1910, Model F Roadster
International, 1912, Panel Express
Iso Rivolta, 1969, 4dr Sedan
Jaguar, 1949, XK-120 Roadster
Jeep, 1991
Jerrari, 1977, Custom 4wd
Jordan, 1926, Playboy
Julian, 1925, Sport Coupe
K-R-I-T, 1913, Touring
Kaiser, 1947, K-100 Special 2dr Sedan
Kaiser-Darrin, 1954, 161 Sports Car

Knox, 1904, Touring
Kurtis, 1955, Indy Race Car
Leon Bollee, 1897, Voiturette
Lincoln, 1927, Model L-134B Coaching Brougham
Lincoln, 1932, Model KA Murray Sedan
Lincoln, 1941, Continental Coupe
Lincoln, 1948, Continental Cabriolet
Lincoln, 1954, Capri Custom Coupe
Lincoln, 1956, Continental
Lincoln, 1962, Continental Convertible
Lincoln, 1972, Continental
Lippard-Stewart, 1914, Express
Locomobile, 1899, Steamer
Lotus-Ford, 1965, Indy Race Car
Marmon, 1923, Coupe
Marquette, 1930, Sport Roadster
Maxwell, 1911, Runabout
Maxwell, 1923, Touring
McFarlan, 1925, Town Car
McLaren, 1972, Can Am Race Car
McLaren-Drake, 1975, Indy Race Car
Mercedes-Benz, 1936, Type 500K Special Roadster
Mercedes-Benz, 1939, Type 230 Cabriolet "B"
Mercedes-Benz, 1956, 300SL Sports Coupe
Mercer, 1913, Raceabout
Mercury, 1939, Town Sedan
Mercury, 1949, Coupe
Metz, 1913, Roadster
MG, 1949, TC Roadster
Monroe, 1917, M-3 Roadster
Morgan, 1934, Super Sports
Oldsmobile, 1902, Model R Runabout
Oldsmobile, 1910, Limited Touring
Oldsmobile, 1966, Toronado
Overland, 1927, Whippet
Packard, 1900, Model B Runabout
Packard, 1920, Twin 6 3-35 Limousine
Packard, 1938, Model 1607 Convertible Coupe
Packard, 1942, Super 8 Convertible Victoria
Packard, 1952, Mayfair 250 Sports Hardtop
Panhard et Levassor, 1892, Voiturette
Peugeot, 1913, Bebe Torpedo
Phantom Corsair, 1938, Experimental Car
Philion, 1892, Steamer Road Carriage
Pierce-Arrow, 1913, Model 66-A-1 Touring

Plymouth, 1929, Model Q Roadster
Plymouth, 1939, Deluxe Convertible Coupe
Plymouth, 1966, Belvedere Satellite 2dr Hardtop
Plymouth, 1970, Road Runner Superbird
Pontiac, 1926, Model 6-27 Coach
Pontiac, 1957, Star Chief 2dr Sedan
Pope-Hartford, 1911, Model W Touring
Porsche, 1950, 356 Coupe
Porsche, 1977, 935 Coupe
Prudhomme, 1975, Drag Car
Rambler, 1912, Model 73-400 Cross-Country
Rambler, 1965, Marlin
Renault, 1904, Racing Voiturette
Reo, 1937, Pickup Truck
Rolls-Royce, 1910, Silver Ghost Tourer
Rolls-Royce, 1927, Phantom Cabriolet Deville
Rolls-Royce/Springfield, 1923, Silver Ghost Tourer
Roth, 1961, *Beatnik Bandit*
Scimitar, 1959, Sedan
Selden, 1912, Model 47-A Roadster
Sheridan, 1921, Model B-41 Touring
Stanley, 1913, Model 810 Steamer Mountain Wagon
Stanley, 1926, Model 262 Steamer Sedan
Steam-Powered Auto, 1977, *Steaming Demon* Racer
Stearns, 1910, Model 30-60 Limousine
Studebaker, 1924, Model EK Big-Six Sedan
Studebaker, 1933, Model 56 Sedan
Studebaker, 1953, Champion Starliner Hardtop Convertible
Studebaker, 1962, Gran Turismo Hardtop Coupe
Studebaker, 1966, Wagonaire
Stutz, 1913, Series B Bearcat
Talbot, 1925, Type Z10
Thomas, 1907, Racer
Tucker, 1948, 4dr Sedan
Volkswagen, 1947, Limousine
White, 1909, Steamer Touring
White, 1910, Touring
Wills St. Claire, 1922, Model A-68 Roadster
Wills St. Claire, 1924, Model B-68 Gray Goose Special
Winton, 1899, Phaeton

Grand Manor Antique & Classic Car Museum

P.O. Box 158, Glen, New Hampshire 03838
(603) 356-9366

The museum's collection consists of cars manufactured from 1910 to 1970. Although a wide variety of manufacturers and styles is on display, there is a significant selection of high-performance cars including a Ford hot-rod coupe, a Thunderbird, a Corvette, an Avanti and a Plymouth Hemi-Cuda.

Among the classic cars are three award-winning cars, a Packard 1926 Phaeton, an Auburn 1931 Convertible Sedan and a Cadillac 1930 Roadster.

Car owners have often felt that their cars possess personality, good or bad depending on the situation. But the 1958 Plymouth Fury in the museum embodies the notion of "car from hell" because the car was the evil force in the Stephen King movie *Christine*. An otherwise forgettable car to car buyers will be unforgettable to at least one generation of moviegoers.

DIRECTIONS TO MUSEUM: On US 302 and Rt. 16 in Glen.

ADMISSION COST: Adults $5.00; children (6-12 yrs.) $3.00.

1957 Chevrolet Convertible. *The 1957 Bel Air Convertible is one of the more highly valued post-war Chevrolet models. Now a modern-day classic, a little over 47,000 Bel Air Convertibles were built.*

The 1933 Packard Victoria (foreground) and 1926 Packard Phaeton exemplify upscale class and style in their era. The Victoria is prized among collectors and often valued in six figures.

HOURS OF OPERATION: Open June-September daily 9:30am-5pm. Open weekends 9:30am-5pm in May and October.

MUSEUM NOTES: Cars in collection are on loan and constantly changing. There are restaurants nearby. The museum has a gift shop, but film is not available.

A brochure is available.

Display Automobiles

A.C., 1958, Ace Roadster
Auburn, 1931, Convertible Sedan
Cadillac, 1959, Fleetwood
Cadillac, 1930, Roadster
Chevrolet, 1957, Bel Air Convertible
Chevrolet, 1960, Impala Hardtop
Chevrolet, 1964, Corvette
Chevrolet, 1969, Camaro SS
Dodge, 1950, Wayfarer Convertible
Dodge, 1955, Sedan
Edsel, 1959, Ranger
Ford, 1922, Model T Centerdoor Sedan
Ford, 1924, Model T Roadster
Ford, 1929, Model A Snowmobile
Ford, 1933, Hot Rod Coupe
Ford, 1933, Woody
Ford, 1936, Sedan
Ford, 1957, Fairlane 500
Ford, 1957, Thunderbird
Ford, 1963, Galaxie Hardtop
Ford, 1967, Shelby Mustang GT500
    Coupe

Ford, 1968, Shelby Mustang GT500
    Convertible
Jaguar, 1973, XK-E
MG, 1948, TC Roadster
Nash, 1957, Metropolitan
Oldsmobile, 1940, Hot Rod
Oldsmobile, 1952, Sedan
Oldsmobile, 1969, 442 Convertible
Packard, 1926, Phaeton
Packard, 1933, Victoria Convertible
Packard, 1947, Clipper
Pierce-Arrow, 1918, Phaeton
Plymouth, 1958, Fury *Christine*
Plymouth, 1969, GTX Convertible
Plymouth, 1970, Hemi-Cuda
Pontiac, 1940, Sports Coupe
Pontiac, 1953, Chieftain Convertible
Pontiac, 1964, GTO Hardtop
Stanley, 1909, Steamer Touring
Studebaker, 1950, Champion Convertible
Studebaker, 1963, Avanti
Triumph, 1958, TR-3A

Space Farms Zoo and Museum

218 Route 519, Beemerville, New Jersey 07461
(201) 875-5800

Space Farms is a zoo that features North American wildlife as well as other exotic animals, birds and reptiles. The museum displays various vehicles including cars and motorcycles.

Among the cars displayed is an example of a Kaiser-Darrin. Dutch Darrin was designer for the Kaiser-Frazer company and created the fiberglass-bodied sports car based on a Henry J chassis. The car was powered by a Continental engine and used a unique door mechanism that slides the door forward into the fender. Only 435 were sold during 1946. Struggling Kaiser-Frazer ceased production to concentrate on more profitable lines. Darrin thought the car was sellable, purchased fifty bodies from Kaiser-Frazer and installed Cadillac engines. The car was sold through 1958, but no more were produced.

DIRECTIONS TO MUSEUM: Space Farms is located in Beemerville, which is on County Road 519 between the towns of Branchville and Plumbsock.

ADMISSION COST: Adults $7.50; children $3.50.

HOURS OF OPERATION: Open May-October daily 9am-6pm.

MUSEUM NOTES: Fast food is available onsite. There is a gift shop and film is available.

A brochure is available.

Display Automobiles

Buick, 1906, Roadster	Ford, 1931, Model A Roadster
Buick, 1910, Touring	Ford, 1932, Model B Coach
Buick, 1911, Truck	Ford, 1937, 4dr Sedan
Buick, 1931, 4dr Sedan	International, 1907, Auto Buggy
Cadillac, 1937, 2dr Sedan	International, 1910, Pickup Truck
Chevrolet, 1917, Model 490	Jewett, 1925, Sedan
Chevrolet, 1928, Pickup Truck	Kaiser-Darrin, 1954, Roadster
Chevrolet, 1932, Deluxe 2dr Sedan	Kissel, 1931, 4dr Sedan
Chrysler, 1927, 2dr Sedan	Lincoln, 1946, 4dr Sedan
Dodge, 1914, Touring	Marmon, 1928, Roosevelt
Dodge, 1924, 4dr Sedan	Orient, 1903
Dort, 1924, Touring	Overland, 1917
Ford, 1909, Model T Touring	Packard, 1937, Coupe
Ford, 1911, Torpedo Runabout	Pierce-Arrow, 1931, 4dr Sedan
Ford, 1919, Model T Roadster	Pontiac, 1929, Cabriolet
Ford, 1922, Model T Snowmobile	Premier, 1918, Touring
Ford, 1925, Model T Truck	Reo, 1914
Ford, 1927, Model T 2dr Sedan	Studebaker, 1925
Ford, 1929, Pickup Truck	White, 1914, Touring
Ford, 1930, Model A Coupe	Willys-Knight, 1931, Victorian Coupe
Ford, 1931, 2dr Sedan	

Auto Memories
County Rt. 38, Arkville, New York 12406
(914) 586-3300

Auto Memories offers a variety of antique and classic cars, as well as gas station equipment, motorcycles, farm equipment, toys, antique water pumps and antique gas engines.

The collection consists of several classic marques, such as Cord, Packard, Mercedes, plus examples of Corvette, Thunderbird, Jaguar, Lincoln and Cadillac. Also displayed are examples of extinct marques Maxwell, Kaiser, Hudson and Overland.

DIRECTIONS TO MUSEUM: Arkville is located on Rt. 28 in Catskills. Traveling west on Rt. 28 turn right before railroad tracks onto County Rt. 38, then turn right at museum sign. Traveling east on Rt. 28 turn left after railroad tracks onto County Rt. 38, then turn right at museum sign.

ADMISSION COST: Adults $3.00; senior citizens $3.00; children under 12 yrs. free.

HOURS OF OPERATION: During June open weekends 10:30am-4:30pm; July through Labor Day open daily 10:30am-4:30pm; after Labor Day open weekends 10:30am-4:30pm to Columbus Day.

MUSEUM NOTES: There is a restaurant nearby. Auto Memories has a gift shop. Film is not available.

Display Automobiles

NOTE: This is a partial list.

Buick, 1932, Rumble Seat Coupe
Cadillac, 1959, 4dr Hardtop
Chevrolet, 1929, 4dr Sedan
Chevrolet, 1954, Corvette
Chevrolet, 1962, Corvette
Chevrolet, 1965, Corvette
Chevrolet, 1967, Camaro Convertible
Cord, 1936
Ford, 1915, Model T
Ford, 1922, Model T
Ford, 1932, Model B
Ford, 1936, 2dr Coupe
Ford, 1949, 2dr Sedan
Ford, 1956, Thunderbird

Ford, 1962, Thunderbird
Ford, 1964, Station Wagon
Hudson, 1939, Coupe
Jaguar, 1954
Jeep, 1949, Jeepster
Kaiser, 1951, 4dr
Lincoln, 1959, Continental Convertible
Lincoln, 1965, 4dr Convertible
Maxwell, 1907
Mercedes, 1937, Convertible
Mercury, 1954, Sun Valley Coupe
Overland, 1923, 4dr Sedan
Packard, 1939, V-12 Rumble Seat Convertible
Pontiac, 1958, Chieftain Convertible

BMW Gallery

320 Park Avenue, New York, New York 10022
(212) 319-0088

The BMW Gallery is BMW of North America's corporate showroom. A variety of current, vintage and racing cars and motorcycles are usually on display along with other auto related exhibits.

BMW (Bayerische Motoren Werke) was created when two aircraft engine manufacturers merged in 1916. In 1929 BMW began building cars as well as manufacturing aircraft engines and motorcycles. World War II severely crippled the company, as did a financial crisis in the late 1950s. A program of continuous development combined with understated styling resulted in an ardent customer base and prosperity during the 1970s and 1980s.

DIRECTIONS TO MUSEUM: The BMW Gallery is located on the southwest corner of Park Ave. and 51st St., across from St. Bartholomew's Church.

ADMISSION COST: Free.

HOURS OF OPERATION: Open Monday-Friday 10am-6pm and Saturday noon-6pm. Closed Sunday.

MUSEUM NOTES: There are restaurants nearby. Film is not available.

A brochure is available.

Collectors Cars Museum

56 W. Merrick Road, Freeport, New York 11520
(516) 378-6666

Collectors Cars is a museum, auto sales organization and restoration shop. The company has approximately fifty cars on display, all of which are for sale. Since the cars on display are always changing, no list of permanently displayed cars was available. The inventory is composed of fine antique and classic cars, which should make a visit enjoyable and interesting.

DIRECTIONS TO MUSEUM: The museum is approximately one mile west of Meadowbrook Pkwy. on Merrick Rd.

ADMISSION COST: Free.

HOURS OF OPERATION: Open Monday-Wednesday 9am-6pm, Thursday-Friday 9am-8pm, Saturday 9am-6pm, Sunday 9am-5pm.

MUSEUM NOTES: There are restaurants nearby. Film is not available.

A brochure is available.

Himes Museum of Motor Racing Nostalgia

15 O'Neil Avenue, Bayshore, New York 11706
(516) 666-4912

Martin Himes, a former short-track racer, is the owner of the Himes Museum of Motor Racing Nostalgia. It is through his efforts and zeal that a significant quantity of racing artifacts and memorabilia are preserved.,

Virtually anything qualifies for inclusion in Himes' collection, from complete race cars to driver's gloves, from photographs to helmets. There is even the toll booth from Islip Speedway, and jars of dirt from various race tracks. Among the noteworthy race cars is a Kurtis-Kraft midget once driven by Mario Andretti. Himes' collection is a "find" for any race fan.

DIRECTIONS TO MUSEUM: From Sunrise Hwy. go south on Brook Ave. Turn left onto Redington then right onto O'Neil Ave.

MUSEUM NOTES: There is a restaurant nearby and a gift shop. Film is not available.

ADMISSION COST: Donation appreciated.

A brochure is available.

HOURS OF OPERATION: Open daily 9am-9pm. Call ahead for holiday hours.

Display Automobiles

Allen , 1953, Midget
Chevrolet, 1937, Race Car
Crosley, 1948, Tow Truck
Dodge, 1933, Coupe
Ford, 1937, Race Car
Ford, 1948, Truck
Ford, 1956, Race Car
Hillegass, 1947, Midget
Hillegass, 1948, Midget
Houseman , 1937, 3/4 Midget
Karl , 1959, 3/4 Midget

Kohler , 1947, Midget
Kurtis-Kraft, 1947, Midget
Kurtis-Kraft, 1947, Sprint Car
Muller, 1963, 3/4 Midget
Offyette , 1950, 1/4 Midget
Owens , 1950, 3/4 Midget
Plymouth, 1938, Race Car
Savona , 1959, 3/4 Midget
Seltman, 1965, 1/4 Midget
Zirenski , 1959, 3/4 Midget

Old Rhinebeck Aerodrome

Stone Church Road, Rhinebeck, New York 12572
(914) 758-8610

The Old Rhinebeck Aerodrome provides both theatrical and historical entertainment. During the week antique aircraft, cars, motorcycles and engines are on display, and on weekends an airshow is presented.

The Sunday air show is the centerpoint for a melodramatic play complete with heroes, heroines and villains. Set in World War I, the costumes, buildings and machinery reflect the last era of chivalry in the air. The play is entertaining for all ages while airplane enthusiasts will enjoy watching the early aircraft performing above the grass airfield. Antique cars and motorcycles are driven before and as part of the show. Saturday's airshow presents airplanes from the Pioneer and Lindbergh eras.

While the facility is aviation oriented, the auto collection does have several interesting marques: Rolls-Royce, Hudson, Morgan, Metz and Pierce. Coinciding with the theme of the Aerodrome, most of the cars were built during or prior to World War I.

DIRECTIONS TO MUSEUM: The Aerodrome is located north of Rhinebeck on US 9, then follow Stone Church Rd. The Aerodrome is also accessible off of Route 199 between US 9 and the Taconic Pkwy.

ADMISSION COST: Weekend airshows: Adults $9.00; children (6-10 yrs.) $4.00. Weekdays: Adults $4.00; children (6-10 yrs.) $2.00.

HOURS OF OPERATION: Open daily May 15 through October 10am-5pm. Weekend airshows 2:30pm (approximately 1 1/2 hrs. duration).

MUSEUM NOTES: The Aerodrome offers "fast food" and there are restaurants in nearby towns. Film is available in the gift shop.

A brochure is available.

Display Automobiles

Austin, 1931, Model 7
Baker, 1911, Electric
Brush, 1907
Buick, 1920, Roadster
Buick, 1922, Touring
Cadillac, 1959, 2dr
Cadillac, 1959, 4dr
Cadillac, 1959, Convertible
Cadillac, 1959, Limousine
Cleveland, 1920, Speedster
Columbia, 1917, Ambulance
Ford, 1914, Touring
Ford, 1919, Speedster
Franklin, 1928, 4dr Sedan
Grout Steamer

Hudson, 1917, Super 6 Sedan
Hupmobile, 1912
Maxwell, 1910
Metz, 1911
Morgan, 1936
Overland, 1920, Speedster
Packard, 1911, Moving Van
Pierce, 1904, Stanhope
Renault, 1909, Touring
Rolls-Royce, 1932, Boattail
Saxon, 1914, Roadster
Scripps-Booth, 1914, Touring
Sears, 1908
Studebaker, 1916, Touring
Willys, 1917, Touring

Wilson Historical Museum

645 Lake Street, Wilson, New York 14172
(716) 751-9886

Artifacts and memorabilia are displayed that document the history of Wilson. The museum is housed in three buildings with the main museum situated in an early 1900s railroad depot. The car collection is contained in the Argue Memorial Building.

The museum's 1904 Covert was built in nearby Lockport by the Covert Motor Vehicle Company. Car production began in 1902 with a chainless drive system — most early cars were equipped with a drive chain. A Covert auto was the only car to finish an endurance run from Buffalo to St. Louis in 1904. Car sales ceased in 1908 when the company decided to concentrate on the manufacture of drive components.

DIRECTIONS TO MUSEUM: Wilson is situated on Lake Ontario, on Rt. 425, northeast of Niagara Falls.

ADMISSION COST: Free.

HOURS OF OPERATION: Open Sunday 2-4pm.

MUSEUM NOTES: There is a restaurant nearby. A gift shop is onsite, but film is not available.

Display Automobiles

Cadillac, 1959, Series 62 DeVille Convertible
Chevrolet, 1928, Truck
Chevrolet, 1968, Corvair 2dr Hardtop
Chrysler, 1946, Imperial Limousine
Citicar, 1975, Electric
Covert, 1904
Ford, 1919, Model T Truck
Ford, 1941, WWII Sound Truck
Lincoln, 1957, Continental Sedan
Metz, 1909
Pontiac, 1967, Tempest Convertible
Reo, 1927
Studebaker, 1963, Avanti
Volvo, 1967, 1800X 2dr Coupe
Willys-Overland, 1953, Jeep

Backing Up Classics

4545 Highway 29, Harrisburg, North Carolina 28075
(704) 788-9494

Backing Up Classics is located just north of Charlotte Motor Speedway, an institution on the NASCAR racing schedule.

The cars line a "memory lane" that includes several high-performance cars, including an Indianapolis 500 race car and stock cars driven by Richard Petty and Fred Lorenzen. Among the high-performance production cars are 1960s "muscle cars" and a 1981 De-Lorean. Several customized cars and hot rods reflect the car crazes of the 1950s and 1960s.

DIRECTIONS TO MUSEUM: The museum is located on US 29 in Harrisburg, which is northeast of Charlotte.

ADMISSION COST: Adults $3.75; senior citizens $2.90; students $2.90; children under 12 yrs. $1.50.

HOURS OF OPERATION: Open Monday-Saturday 9am-5pm; Sunday noon-5pm. Closed Thanksgiving and Christmas.

MUSEUM NOTES: There is a restaurant nearby. The museum has a gift shop, but film is not available.

A brochure is available.

Display Automobiles

AMC, 1978, Matador
American Bantam, 1939, Convertible
Buick, 1939

Buick, 1967, Special
Cadillac, 1939
Cadillac, 1960, Convertible

1930 Ford Coupe. *A favorite car of hot rodders was the Ford coupe. Originally popular because of its flathead V-8 engine, a wide variety of engines and drive trains have been installed. This example sports a chopped top and a Chevrolet V-8 engine.*

1950 Ford 2dr Sedan. *Customizing cars took off in the 1950s, catering to the car owner who wanted something different than the factory offering. This Ford has been modified by the addition of side pipes, a custom grille insert, spotlights, electric door locks and a recessed, electric radio antenna.*

Cadillac, 1960, Convertible
Chevrolet, 1923, Touring
Chevrolet, 1956, Nomad
Chevrolet, 1957, Corvette
Chevrolet, 1957, Fuel Injected
Chevrolet, 1957, Pickup Truck
Chevrolet, 1957, Race Car
Chevrolet, 1967, Camaro
Chevrolet, 1967, Chevelle
Chevrolet, 1968, Chevelle
Chrysler, 1961, New Yorker
Chrysler, 1965
DeLorean, 1981
Dodge, 1950, Convertible
Dodge, 1969, Hemi
Ford, 1926, Model T
Ford, 1929, Model A Truck
Ford, 1930, Hot Rod

Ford, 1934, Race Car
Ford, 1948, Highway Patrol Car
Ford, 1949, Highway Patrol Car
Ford, 1950, Pickup Truck
Ford, 1951, Victoria
Ford, 1951, Woody Wagon
Ford, 1963, "Lorenzen" Race Car
Graham, 1939
Mercury, 1973, Cougar
Nash, 1960, Metropolitan
Peel, 1962
Pontiac, 1967, Le Mans
Pontiac, 1968, GTO
Pontiac, 1989, "Petty" Race Car
Race Car-Midget
Race Car-Sportsman
Vanguard, 1977, Citicar
Willys, 1953, Jeep

C. Grier Beam Truck Museum

P.O. Box 238, 117 N. Mountain St., Cherryville, North Carolina 28021
(704) 435-1346 or 435-3072

The museum serves to preserve the histories of the trucking industry and Carolina Freight Corporation. C. Grier Beam began Beam Trucking with one truck in the early 1930s, then in 1937 incorporated as Carolina Freight Corporation. The original headquarters, a converted service station, was restored and is now part of the museum. Trucking industry and Carolina Freight artifacts and memorabilia are displayed along with several trucks dating from 1928.

Some trucks in the collection were built by Mack. The "bulldog" appearance of early Mack trucks resulted in the company adopting the canine as its corporate logo and as a hood ornament. Mack was founded in 1909.

DIRECTIONS TO MUSEUM: The museum is located in downtown Cherryville.

ADMISSION COST: Free.

HOURS OF OPERATION: Open Thursday 1-5pm, Friday 10am-5pm and Saturday 10am-3pm.

MUSEUM NOTES: There is a restaurant nearby. The museum has a gift shop and film is available.

A brochure is available.

Display Trucks

Chevrolet, 1926	Mack, 1947
Chevrolet, 1931 (two)	Mack, 1950
Chevrolet, 1932	Mack, 1958
Ford, 1933	Mack, 1962 (two)
International, 1935	White, 1947
Mack, 1945	White, 1962

Greensboro Historical Museum

130 Summit Avenue, Greensboro, North Carolina 27401
(919) 373-2043

The museum presents artifacts that reflect the history of Greensboro, Guilford County and the surrounding region. Emphasized are the lives of two people, Dolley Madison and William Sidney Porter, better known by his pen name, O. Henry. Both were natives of the area. On the grounds are several restored log houses and early structures.

As opposed to the integration of the automobile in modern day lives, the impact the auto had on people was still considerable in the early 1900s. Acquiring a car was a major accomplishment (now most families own two or more cars). Possessing a car meant freedom to travel when and where one desired, and improved employment, housing and vacation options (30-mile commuting, out-of-the-way suburbs and 1,500-mile vacations are commonplace today). Recognizing the impact of the automobile on the lives on North Carolinians, the museum has four automobiles on display, a 1904 Reo, a 1906 Cadillac, a 1916 Ford Model T Touring and a 1926 Ford Model T Sedan.

DIRECTIONS TO MUSEUM: From I-85 exit onto S. Elm St. and follow Elm St. north to Bellemeade. Turn right on Bellemeade and follow to Summit Ave. and museum. From I-40 exit onto Wendover Ave. and follow through town to Summit Ave. Turn right onto Summit Ave. and follow to museum.

ADMISSION COST: Free.

HOURS OF OPERATION: Open Tuesday-Saturday 10am-5pm; Sunday 2-5pm. Closed Monday and major holidays.

MUSEUM NOTES: A restaurant is nearby. There is a gift shop, but film is not available.

A brochure is available.

North Carolina Transportation Museum

411 S. Salisbury Avenue, P.O. Box 165, Spencer, North Carolina 28159
(704) 636-2889

The museum is located at the Spencer Shops, which was the largest steam locomotive servicing facility of the Southern Railway. At one time, over 2,500 people worked here. The advent of diesel locomotives relegated Spencer Shops to a lesser role and eventual closure. Visitors can view the roundhouse, shop, and other structures on the grounds, as well as railroad equipment, artifacts and mementos reflecting the history of Spencer Shops and railroading. A train ride behind a steam locomotive or early diesel locomotive is offered several times during the day (call museum for schedule).

Although the site primarily reflects railroad history, the museum also displays several automobiles and artifacts in the Bumper to Bumper exhibit area. A few vehicles are dis-

1949 Packard Super 4dr Sedan. *While the sales of over 104,000 cars was substantial for Packard on its 50th anniversary, it was also the precipice of a steep decline to only 13,000 sales in 1956. Failing to see the changing American buying attitude and unable financially to undertake the annual changes sought by buyers, Packard's prominence quickly eroded. Packard and Studebaker merged in 1954 in an attempt to strengthen both companies, then Curtiss-Wright bought Studebaker-Packard. Except for sporadic success, the decline continued. The Packard nameplate was last applied in 1958 and Studebaker production ceased in 1966.*

1922 Buick Touring. *Buicks in 1922 were equipped with either an overhead valve, 40-horsepower, four-cylinder engine or an overhead valve, 60-horsepower, six-cylinder engine. The least expensive Buick, a roadster, cost $935, while the expensive seven-passenger sedan cost $2,635. Buick built a little over 106,000 of its 1922 models.*

played in the main building while the bulk of the collection is located in a display area in an adjacent building (follow signs).

DIRECTIONS TO MUSEUM: From I-85 take Exit 79 to Andrew St. Follow Andrew St. west to Salisbury Ave. (US 29). Turn left onto Salisbury Ave. and follow to museum.

ADMISSION COST: Museum is free. Train ride: adults $3.50; senior citizens and children $2.50.

HOURS OF OPERATION: April-October: open Monday-Saturday 9am-5pm; Sunday 1-5pm. November-March: open Tuesday-Saturday 10am-4pm; Sunday 1-5pm; closed Monday. Closed major holidays.

MUSEUM NOTES: A restaurant is located nearby. There is a gift shop, but film is not available.

A brochure is available.

Display Automobiles

Buick, 1922, Touring
Buick, 1922, Touring
Buick, 1965, Riviera
Chevrolet, 1927, 2dr Coach
Chevrolet, 1941, Special 2dr Sedan
Chevrolet, 1956, Bel Air Convertible
Ford, 1913, Model T Depot Hack
Ford, 1935, Convertible

Ford, 1935, Deluxe Phaeton
Hupmobile, 1912
Lincoln, 1921, Roadster
Oldsmobile, 1904, Curved Dash
Packard, 1949, Super 4dr Sedan
Plymouth, 1970, Superbird
Studebaker, 1963, Avanti

Richard Petty Museum

P.O. Box 86, Rt. 4, Branson Mill Road, Randleman, North Carolina 27317
(919) 495-1143

The museum chronicles the racing achievements of two members of the Petty family, Lee and his famous son, Richard. Walls loaded with trophies are exhibited along with artifacts and memorabilia collected from over forty years of involvement in motorsports. The museum is situated on the grounds of the Petty home and racing shop.

Lee Petty entered stock car racing during the emergence of NASCAR and was crowned champion of the sanctioning body's racing series in 1954, 1958 and 1959. Richard's driving skills coupled with the expertise of the Petty family team propelled Richard to a career that has overshadowed all his competitors and set marks that may not be surpassed. Richard Petty captured the NASCAR crown seven times and won 200 races. Petty's driving career will end in 1992, leaving behind over thirty years of accomplishments and thrills for his fans' memories.

On display are three of the "43" race cars driven by Richard Petty, a 1926 Ford Model T owned by Lee Petty, a Plymouth Superbird and a 1985 Ford Thunderbird Winston Cup race car.

DIRECTIONS TO MUSEUM: From US 220 take Business 220 to Level Cross. Continue east at intersection with Randleman Rd. Museum is on left approximately 1/2 mile from Randleman Rd.

ADMISSION COST: Adults $3.00; children $1.50; under 6 yrs. free.

HOURS OF OPERATION: Open Monday-Saturday 9am-5pm. Closed Sunday. Closed Thanksgiving and Christmas.

MUSEUM NOTES: There are no restaurants nearby. The museum has a gift shop.

A brochure is available.

1974 Dodge Charger. *Richard Petty has driven either Dodges or Plymouths through most of his racing career. His Daytona 500 wins in 1964, 1966, 1971, 1973 and 1974 were in a Dodge or Plymouth, as well as two wins at Charlotte in Dodges and two wins at Darlington in Plymouths.*

Canton Classic Car Museum

555 Market Avenue S.W., Canton, Ohio 44702
(216) 455-3603

The Canton Classic Car Museum focuses on automobiles built during the 1920s and 1930s, with emphasis on the upscale marques, such as Cadillac, Lincoln, Packard, Pierce-Arrow and Rolls-Royce. Several seldom seen cars are present as well — Benham, McFarlan, Holmes, Lea Francis and King Midget. The museum is located in a building that housed an early Ford-Lincoln dealership. Artifacts and memorabilia reflect auto travel from the 1920s to the 1950s.

There are five cars in the collection bearing the Lincoln nameplate. Veiled under the pretext of saving the bankrupt Lincoln Motor Company, Henry Ford appeared to be rescuing the Lelands, the shareholders and the workers. But Ford shrewdly bought the company and assets for half of their value, and with some irony, then owned the company of the man who had been instrumental in Henry's departure from the Henry Ford Company in 1902. As in the first situation, Henry Leland and Henry Ford could not work together, but this time it was Leland who left. The company was converted to the Ford style of car production, a traumatic occurrence for the Lincoln workers, and Edsel Ford added the styling needed to transform the marque into a respectable seller. The Lincoln division begat the Mercury, which was created to fill the mid-priced market, and Lincolns later evolved into the highly successful Continental series. Calvin Coolidge choose a Lincoln for presidential use, a practice continued by subsequent presidents.

DIRECTIONS TO MUSEUM: From I-77 exit onto Tuscarawas St. and travel east to Market Ave. Turn right onto Market Ave. and follow for five blocks to museum.

ADMISSION COST: Adults $3.00; senior citizens $2.50; children $2.00.

HOURS OF OPERATION: Open daily 10am-5pm. Closed major holidays.

1932 Lincoln KB Touring. *A selling point during the 1930s was the number of engine cylinders. Lincoln enhanced its image in 1932 with the introduction of its massive V-12 engine in the KB models. The engine produced 150 horsepower from 447.9 cubic inches. Car weight was approximately 5,700 pounds, of which 1,000 pounds was engine weight.*

MUSEUM NOTES: There is a restaurant nearby. The museum has a gift shop, but film is not available.

A brochure is available.

Display Automobiles

Benham, 1914, Roadster
Cadillac, 1938, Convertible Sedan
Cadillac, 1958, Eldorado Biarritz Convertible
Cadillac, 1959, Eldorado Biarritz Convertible
Chevrolet, 1940, Pickup Truck
Chevrolet, 1963, Corvette
Ford, 1911, Model T Roadster
Ford, 1926, Model T Speedster
Ford, 1956, Thunderbird
Franklin, 1922, Model 9-B Roadster
Holmes, 1922, Series 4 Coupe
King Midget, 1956, Convertible
Kissel, 1929, White Eagle Speedster
Lea Francis, 1928, Coupe
Lincoln, 1931, Model K Judkins Berline
Lincoln, 1932, Model KB Touring
Lincoln, 1933, Model KB Victoria Coupe
Lincoln, 1936, Model K Convertible Coupe

Lincoln, 1939, Model K Lebaron Sedan
Marmon, 1931, Victoria Coupe
McFarlan, 1919, Model 138 Boattail Speedster
Packard, 1920, Limousine
Packard, 1921, Victoria
Packard, 1928, Touring
Packard, 1937, Flower Car
Packard, 1937, Hearse
Packard, 1937, Invalid Sedan
Packard, 1946, Clipper Sedan
Pierce-Arrow, 1916, Model 66 Touring
Pierce-Arrow, 1921, Model 48, Tow Truck
Plymouth, 1970, Super Bird
Racer, 1937, Midget Racer
Rolls-Royce, 1929, Phantom I Derby Phaeton
Rolls-Royce, 1937, Phantom III Town Car
Studebaker, 1937, President Police Car

Carillon Historical Park

2001 S. Patterson Boulevard, Dayton, Ohio 45409
(513) 293-3638

Carillon Historical Park presents a wide variety of artifacts and memorabilia that reflect the history of Dayton and the surrounding area. Whole buildings have been moved to the site and restored, as well as an 1870 covered bridge, a railroad yard tower, and a canal lock, which was moved to the park and placed in the original canal bed.

Dayton was the manufacturing site for several auto manufacturers, including Maxwell, Stoddard-Dayton, Speedwell and Courier. Examples of these four makes are on display, as well as a 1981 Chevrolet S10 pickup truck, the first to roll off the production line from the Dayton plant.

Also on the park grounds is a replica of the Deeds Barn. Edward A. Deeds was a prominent Dayton resident who, along with his wife, founded the park. It was in Deeds Barn that Charles Kettering invented the electric self-starter for automobile engines. A replica of the barn is situated in the park. Inside the barn is a 1912 Cadillac — Cadillacs were the first cars equipped with the self-starter. Kettering was the founder of Dayton Engineering Laboratories (Delco) and later served as president of General Motors.

DIRECTIONS TO MUSEUM: From I-75 take Exit 51 and travel east on Moses Blvd. to Stewart St. Turn right and follow Stewart, then turn right onto Patterson Blvd. Follow Patterson to park.

The museum's circa 1924 service station formerly stood at Brown and Warren Streets in Dayton. To operate a mechanical gas pump, the attendant actuated a lever on the pump's side to fill the glass reservoir on top with gas. The reservoir was marked in gallons. After pumping the desired quantity into the reservoir, the valve in the hose was opened to allow the gas in the reservoir to flow into the car's tank. The glass globe on top of the reservoir identified the gasoline brand.

ADMISSION COST: Free.

HOURS OF OPERATION: Open Tuesday-Saturday 10am-6pm; Sunday 1-6pm. Closed Monday unless Monday is holiday, then open Monday 1-6pm.

MUSEUM NOTES: There is a restaurant nearby. Film is not available in gift shop.

A brochure is available.

Display Automobiles

Cadillac, 1912, Touring
Chevrolet, 1981, S10 Pickup Truck
Courier, 1910, Roadster
Custer, 1921

Maxwell, 1923, Touring
Speedwell, 1910, Touring
Stoddard-Dayton, 1908, Touring
Xenia, 1914, Cycle Car

Frederick C. Crawford Auto-Aviation Museum

10825 East Boulevard, Cleveland, Ohio 44106
(216) 721-5722

The Crawford Museum has evolved over the last fifty years into a major transportation museum. The museum focuses on automotive artifacts and memorabilia with over 120 automobiles on display, as well as motorcycles, bicycles and airplanes.

The collection is named after Frederick C. Crawford, who was the moving force behind the collection from it's start in 1937 by Thompson Products, Inc., a major supplier to the automotive market and later renamed TRW. Known as the *Thompson Auto Album*, the collection was passed on to the Western Reserve Historical Society from the company at the urging of Crawford on his retirement.

In the collection are several Winton automobiles. The firm founded by Alexander Winton was a significant auto manufacturer in the early era, and in 1899 was the largest American manufacturer of gasoline-engine powered cars. At the turn of the century, Wintons often made headlines. In 1903 a Winton was the first automobile to cross the country. Alexander Winton drove *Bullet No. 1* to a speed record of 70.31 mph, then Barney Oldfield drove *Bullet No. 2* to a record 83.7 mph (both cars are on display). Wintons were built until 1923, when Alexander Winton asked the stockholders if they would back his new engine manufacturing company and cease car production, or keep the car firm operating. The decision was to stop car production and finance engine manufacturing.

1930 Packard Dual Cowl Phaeton. *Collectors value the Dual Cowl Phaeton the highest of the Packard models. Originally selling for approximately $4,800, this lengthy (145-inch wheelbase), heavyweight (4845 pounds) carried only four people, but in the highest style of its day.*

1932 Cadillac V-8 Sport Phaeton. *The body was built by Fisher, a division of General Motors. President of Cadillac was Lawrence Fisher, one of the seven Fisher brothers whose auto body company had been purchased by General Motors. Cadillac featured a ride-control system in 1932. The driver could change valve action in the shock absorbers thereby altering the car's ride.*

The collection is broad based with examples of very basic cars, such as a Ford Model T and a Honda Civic, as well as upscale makes such as Mercedes, Rolls-Royce and Pierce-Arrow. The bulk of the collection predates 1941. Auto and travel related artifacts and memorabilia are also on display.

DIRECTIONS TO MUSEUM: From I-90 exit onto Martin Luther King Dr. and travel south. At circle turn right onto East Blvd. Turn left at East 108th St. then right onto Magnolia Dr.

ADMISSION COST: Adults $4.00; senior citizens $2.00; children $2.00.

HOURS OF OPERATION: Open Tuesday-Saturday 10am-5pm; Sunday noon-5pm. Closed major holidays.

MUSEUM NOTES: There is a gift shop and a restaurant is nearby. Film is not available.

A brochure is available.

Display Automobiles

Alco, 1913, Berline Limousine
AMC, 1966, AMX
American Gas, 1902, Runabout
Aston Martin, 1981, Lagonda
Auburn, 1935, Cabriolet

Austro-Daimler, 1913, Cloverleaf Roadster
Baker, 1902, Runabout
Baker, 1904, Newport
Baker, 1915, Roadster
Baker Electric, 1906, Imperial

1935 Chrysler Imperial Airflow Sedan. *Chrysler sold almost 3,000 of its Imperial version of the Airflow. Base price was $1,475. Sagging sales through 1936 forced Chrysler to drop the Airflow, an exercise in engineering and aerodynamics that didn't attract style-conscious buyers.*

Bentley, 1935, Drophead Coupe
Benz, 1897-98
Bobsey, 1975, Sports Racer
Bugatti, 1930, Touring
Buick, 1928, Town Brougham
Buick, 1941, Convertible Coupe
Buick, 1982, Indy Pace Car
Cadillac, 1908, Runabout
Cadillac, 1915, Touring
Cadillac, 1932, Sport Phaeton
Cadillac, 1941, Sedan
Cadillac, 1971, Convertible
Cadillac, 1975, Convertible
Chandler, 1916, Touring
Chandler, 1926, Comrade Roadster
Chevrolet, 1931, Sedan
Chevrolet, 1956, Corvette
Chevrolet, 1963, Corvette
Chevrolet, 1964, Corvair
Chitty Bang Bang II, 1921, Sport Tourer
Chrysler, 1935, Airflow Sedan
Chrysler, 1948, Sedan
Cleveland, 1920, Roadster
Columbus, 1908, Motor Buggy
Cord, 1937, Phaeton
Crawford, 1912, Touring
DeLorean, 1981, Coupe

Dodge, 1922, Touring
Duryea, 1910, Electra
Elmore, 1908, Touring
Ferrari, 1967, Spyder
Ford, 1907, Model K
Ford, 1908, Model S
Ford, 1909, Model T
Ford, 1914, Model T
Ford, 1915, Couplet
Ford, 1924, Model T
Ford, 1929, Model A
Ford, 1934, Deluxe Coupe
Ford, 1936, Touring Sedan
Ford, 1940, Convertible Club Coupe
Ford, 1949, Convertible
Ford, 1955, Thunderbird
Ford, 1964, 2dr Hardtop
Ford, 1973, Mustang
Franklin, 1905, 5-Passenger Light Tonneau
Franklin, 1928, Sedan
Gardner-Serpollet, 1899, Steam Carriage
Honda, 1977, Civic
Hupmobile, 1909, Runabout
Hupmobile, 1911, Touring
Imperial, 1958, Limousine
Isotta-Fraschini, 1927, Brougham
Jaguar, 1937, SS

Jaguar, 1973, Roadster
Jordan, 1920, Roadster
Jordan, 1929, Speedboy Phaeton
Krieger, 1906, Landaulet
Lincoln, 1921, Touring
Lincoln, 1940, Panel Brougham
Lincoln, 1956, Continental
Lincoln, 1966, Continental
Lincoln, 1967, Custom Limousine
Lincoln, 1971, Continental
Locomobile, 1919, Sportif
Lotus, 1956, LeMans
McLaren, 1969, Formula 5000
Mercedes, 1912, Gran Prix
Mercedes-Benz, 1940, Cabriolet F
Mercedes-Benz, 1956, 300 SL
Mercer, 1920, Raceabout
MG, 1950, Midget
Minerva, 1929, Custom Limousine
Oldsmobile, 1902, Runabout
Owen-Magnetic, 1916, Touring
Packard, 1901, Runabout
Packard, 1911, Phaeton
Packard, 1919, Sport Runabout
Packard, 1926, Roadster
Packard, 1930, Dual Cowl Sport Phaeton
Panhard et Levassor, 1897, Coupe
Peerless, 1905, *Roi De Belges* Touring
Peerless, 1914, Touring
Peerless, 1932, Touring Sedan
Pierce, 1902, Motorette
Pierce-Arrow, 1912, Runabout
Pierce-Arrow, 1916, Custom Raceabout
Pierce-Arrow, 1929, Convertible Coupe
Pontiac, 1984, Fiero
Rambler, 1913, Touring
Rauch & Lang, 1917, Coach

Red Bug, 1924, Buckboard
Rollin, 1924, Coupe DeLuxe
Rollin, 1925, Touring
Rolls-Royce, 1928, Dual Cowl Phaeton
Rolls-Royce, 1930, Dual Windshield Phaeton
Royal Tourist, 1904, Rear-entrance Tonneau
Sears, 1909, Motor Buggy
Simplex, 1909, Double Roadster
Stanley, 1905, Gentleman's Speedy Steamer
    Roadster
Stearling-Knight, 1925, 5-Passenger Sedan
Stearns, 1910, Touring
Stearns-Knight, 1917, Cloverleaf Roadster
Stevens-Duryea, 1910, 7-Passenger Touring
Studebaker, 1964, 2dr Hardtop
Studebaker-Garford, 1907, Landaulet
Studebaker-Garford, 1910, Touring
Stutz, 1914, Torpedo Roadster
Templar, 1922, Roadster
Toledo, 1901, Stanhope
Tri Moto, 1900, Crescent
Vauxhall, 1925, Tourer
Volkswagen, 1947, Sedan
Waltham, 1904, Orient Buckboard
White, 1904, Touring
White, 1906, Limousine
White, 1917, Town Car
Willys, 1944, Army Jeep
Winton, 1898, Phaeton
Winton, 1899, Phaeton
Winton, 1902, *Bullet No. 1*
Winton, 1902, *Bullet No. 2*
Winton, 1903, Touring Roadster
Winton, 1907, Touring
Winton, 1921, Touring
Woods Mobilette, 1916, Roadster

National Road-Zane Grey Museum
8850 East Pike, Norwich, Ohio 43767
(614) 872-3143

Two seemingly disparate subjects are the focus of this museum, but there is a thin connection. Zane Grey's great grandfather, Ebenezer Grey, built the first public road in Ohio, known as Zane's Trace, a forerunner of the National Road.

The National Road was financed by the United States and was the nation's busiest land route to the West until the advent of the railroads in the 1850s. The government spent over six million dollars on the road, which started in Cumberland, Maryland, and terminated in Vandalia, Illinois. In 1926 the road became a section of US 40, another well-traveled route with the increase of auto and truck traffic. Construction of I-70, which parallels the road, has drawn a great deal of traffic from the road. Through a series of dioramas and exhibits, the museum provides the visitor a look at life along the road from its construction to the automobile age. An 1899 Steamer, 1914 Chevrolet, 1916 Ford Model T and 1927 Buick are integrated into the highway scenes.

DIRECTIONS TO MUSEUM: From I-70 take Exit 164 and travel approximately 3/4 mile on US 40 to museum.

ADMISSION COST: Adults $3.00; senior citizens $2.40; children $1.00.

HOURS OF OPERATION: May-September: open Monday-Saturday 9:30am-5pm; Sunday noon-5pm. March, April, October and November: open Wednesday-Saturday 9:30am-5pm; Sunday noon-5pm. Closed December, January and February.

MUSEUM NOTES: There are vending machines onsite and a restaurant is nearby. Film is available in the gift shop.

A brochure is available.

Pro Team Classic Corvette Collection

P.O. Box 606, Napoleon, Ohio 43545
(419) 592-5086

Pro Team specializes in collecting and selling Corvettes, usually possessing approximately 100 'Vettes. Virtually all model years are found in the inventory, which provides the visitor an overview of the history of General Motors only sports car.

The centerpoint of the collection is the CERV I (Chevrolet Experimental Racing Vehicle). Introduced to the public in 1960, the car's creator was the legendary engineer Zora Arkus-Duntov. CERV was never entered in racing competition, but served as a platform for testing high performance engines and chassis components. The car has been valued between $1.2 and $2 million.

DIRECTIONS TO MUSEUM: Pro Team is located on Rt. 108 just south of US 6/24 Bypass.

ADMISSION COST: Free.

HOURS OF OPERATION: Open daily 9am-5pm.

MUSEUM NOTES: There are restaurants nearby. Pro Team has a gift shop, but film is not available.

A brochure is available.

1960 CERV I. *The CERV was built with a space frame surrounding a mid-engine mounted small-block Chevrolet V-8. The independent rear suspension laid the groundwork for the later Corvette rear drive configuration. Top speed on a closed course was clocked at 206 mph.*

Chickasha Automobile & Transportation Museum

18th Street & Chickasha Avenue, Chickasha, Oklahoma 73023
(405) 222-4222

The museum offers a collection of cars ranging from 1900 to 1970, as well as, collections of license plates, crests, hubcaps, tools and other memorabilia.

The earliest car on display is a White steam car that was built in Cleveland, Ohio. The museum car's vintage is 1900-01, one of the first built by the White brothers. Before gasoline-engine powered cars dominated the market, White steam cars were significant sellers, outselling the well-known Stanley steam cars two to one. In 1905 a racing version of the White held the speed record for the mile. The first U.S. president to drive an automobile was Theodore Roosevelt at the wheel of a White in 1906. But the appeal of steam-powered cars waned, and White offered gasoline engines in 1910, switching totally in 1911. In 1918 White ceased car production to concentrate on the highly successful truck line.

DIRECTIONS TO MUSEUM: Museum is on west side of Chickasha. From Hwy. 62 travel south on 9th St. to Chickasha Ave. Turn right on Chickasha Ave. and follow to museum on left.

ADMISSION COST: Free.

HOURS OF OPERATION: Open Saturday and Sunday 2-4pm.

MUSEUM NOTES: There is a restaurant nearby. Film is not available.

Display Automobiles

Cadillac, 1949, Convertible
Cadillac, 1969, Convertible
Ford, 1922, Model T 4dr Sedan
Ford, 1925, Model T Depot Hack
Ford, 1930, Model A Coupe
Ford, 1934, Coupe

Ford, 1957, Skyliner
Ford, 1957, Thunderbird
Hupmobile, 1928, 4dr Sedan
Lincoln, 1937, Coupe
MG, 1935, Open Touring
White, 1900-01, Stanhope

Lewis Museum

816 S.E. 1st Street, Lawton, Oklahoma 73501
(405) 357-8942

The museum presents an extensive collection of trucks, many of which are fire trucks. Also displayed are a collection of saddles, Civil War artifacts, a railroad caboose, a 110 horsepower steam engine and Avery and Rumley tractors.

Among the 23 cars in the collection are five examples of luxury automobiles built by British auto makers, four Rolls-Royces and a Bentley. Rolls-Royce purchased the bankrupt Bentley company in 1931 and offered the Bentley car line as an alternative to the staid, but opulent Rolls. The Bentleys were generally sportier and less expensive than the Rolls.

DIRECTIONS TO MUSEUM: Call museum for directions.

ADMISSION COST: Free.

HOURS OF OPERATION: Call ahead.

MUSEUM NOTES: There is a restaurant nearby. Film is not available.

Display Automobiles

Ahrens-Fox, 1930, Fire Truck
American LaFrance, 1922, Fire Truck
American LaFrance, 1927, Fire Truck
American LaFrance, 1946, Ladder Fire Truck
American LaFrance, 1954, Foam-Dispensing Truck
American LaFrance, 1954, Rescue Truck
American LaFrance, 1956, Ladder Rescue Truck
Austin, 1962, Princess 4dr Sedan
Bentley, 1956, 4dr Sedan
Cadillac, 1978, Seville 4dr Sedan
Cadillac, 1989, Fleetwood 4dr Sedan
Chevrolet, 1929, Stake Bed Truck
Chevrolet, 1947, Pickup Truck
Coleman, 1930, Truck
Consolidated, 1955/56, Truck
Diamond T, 1919, Truck
Dodge, 1918, Touring
Dodge, 1928, Victory 6 4dr Sedan Deluxe
Dodge, 1961, Army Truck
Ford, 1914, Model T Racer
Ford, 1923, Model T Pickup Truck
Ford, 1924, Model T
Ford, 1925, Model T Fire Truck
Ford, 1926, Model T Doctor's Coupe
Ford, 1926, Model T Truck

Ford, 1930, Pickup Truck
Ford, 1931, Model A Coupe
Ford, 1933, Model B Truck (two)
Ford, 1947, Panel Truck
Ford, 1950, Truck
FWD, 1929, Cattle Truck
FWD, 1951, Truck
GMC, 1919, Fire Truck
GMC, 1951, Army Truck
GMC/American LaFrance, 1924, Fire Truck
Hudson, 1953, Hornet 4dr Sedan
Imperial, 1973, LaBaron 4dr Hardtop
International, 1921, Gravel Truck
International, 1925, Truck
International, 1929, Truck
International, 1933, Truck
International, 1952, Crash Car
Lincoln, 1923, 4dr Sedan
Lincoln, 1991, Town Car
Mack, 1925, Truck
Mack, 1925, Truck
Mack, 1928, Fire Truck
Mack, 1931, Flatbed Truck
Mack, 1941, Fire Truck
Mercury, 1950, Sport Sedan
Oshkosh, 1928, Truck
Porsche, 1979, 928 Coupe

Reo, 1914, Speedwagon
Reo, 1918, Express Truck
Reo, 1920, Fire Truck
Reo, 1921, Fire Truck
Reo, 1923, T6 4dr Sedan
Reo, 1927, Fire Truck
Reo, 1930, Fire Truck
Rolls-Royce, 1927, Phantom II Town Limousine
Rolls-Royce, 1934, Phantom II Landaulet
Rolls-Royce, 1948, Silver Wraith Hearse
Rolls-Royce, 1961, Phantom V Touring
    Limousine

Sayers & Scovill, 1922, Fire Truck
Seagraves, 1929, Fire Truck
ST Divco, 1961, Milk Truck
Sterling, 1924, Fire Truck
Studebaker, 1914, Touring
Traffic, 1917, Stake Bed Truck
White, 1915, Fire Truck
White, 1920, Fairmont Van
White, 1924, Fire Truck
Willys, 1947, Jeep
Willys, 1958, 4dr Sedan

Museum of Special Interest Autos

13700 Hiway 177, Shawnee, Oklahoma 74801
(405)-275-5877

The Museum of Special Interest Autos comprises approximately 40 cars on display indoors and an equal number outdoors. The vintages range from a 1913 Ford Model T to cars in the 1960s. Types of cars range from the unique, like an Amphicar, to classic cars. Several seldom seen marques are on display, including Alvis, Falcon-Knight, Riley and Muntz. For fans of circa-World War II Chrysler products there are six Chryslers, two DeSotos and a Dodge in the collection.

DIRECTIONS TO MUSEUM: From I-40 exit onto US 177 and travel south approximately 1 1/2 miles.

ADMISSION COST: Adults $2.00; children $1.00.

HOURS OF OPERATION: Call ahead.

MUSEUM NOTES: There are restaurants nearby. Film is not available.

Display Automobiles

NOTE: This is a partial list.

Alvis, 1935, 4dr Tourer
Amphicar, 1965, 2dr Convertible
Buick, 1938, Century 4dr Sedan
Cadillac, 1942, Series 67 Sedan
Chevrolet, 1928, Touring
Chevrolet, 1963, Impala SS Convertible
Chrysler, 1942, New Yorker Convertible
Chrysler, 1947, New Yorker Coupe
Chrysler, 1947, Windsor Sedan
Chrysler, 1948, New Yorker 4dr Sedan
Chrysler, 1948, Royal Coupe
Chrysler, 1948, Windsor Sedan
DeSoto, 1939, 4dr Sedan
DeSoto, 1942, LWB Sedan

Dodge, 1948, Coupe
Falcon-Knight, 1928, 4dr Sedan
Ford, 1913, Model T Roadster
Ford, 1919, Model T Touring
Ford, 1926, Model T Touring
Ford, 1928, Roadster
Ford, 1939, 2dr Sedan
Jaguar, 1952, XK-120 Roadster
Lincoln, 1962, Convertible
MG, 1953, TD Roadster
Muntz, 1951, Jet 2dr Convertible
Oldsmobile, 1938, 2dr Sedan
Packard, 1949, 4dr Sedan
Riley, 1951, 4dr Sedan

'77 Grand Prix Museum

16355 S.E. Yamhill, Portland, Oregon 97233
(503) 252-5863

The museum focuses on the Pontiac through the display of artifacts and memorabilia related to that marque from 1927 to present. Particular emphasis is placed on the Pontiac Grand Prix series.

The Pontiac Grand Prix offered sporty luxury in the mid-price car market and the museum has two examples, a 1972 Grand Prix and a 1977 Grand Prix. Two Pontiac Luxury LeMans are also displayed, a 1972 and a 1973. License plates and other auto memorabilia are exhibited.

DIRECTIONS TO MUSEUM: Call museum for directions.

HOURS OF OPERATION: By appointment only.

ADMISSION COST: Free.

MUSEUM NOTES: There is a restaurant nearby. Film is not available.

Alan Dent Antique Auto Museum

Box 254, Lightstreet, Pennsylvania 17839
(717) 784-4927 or 784-9174

The Dent collection focuses on the two marques that have dominated the American market, Chevrolet and Ford. The Fords exhibited are primarily early models, while later model years make up the Chevrolet segment. Several other makes on display add variety to the collection, including examples of upscale marques Cadillac, Packard and Lincoln.

The production race between Chevrolet and Ford has been long lasting, at times lopsided, but often close. Ford was overwhelming leader during the first quarter century, but in 1927 Chevrolet out-produced its competitors, the first change in leadership since Ford's ascendancy in 1906. Chevrolet led the field into World War II, except for years 1929 and 1930 when the Ford Model A vaulted Ford into first place. Although Chevrolet remained the leader after the war, the counting method left no clear-cut winner in some years (the number juggling continues today in the domestic truck market between Ford and Chevrolet).

DIRECTIONS TO MUSEUM: The museum is approximately mile from I-80 Exit 35N.

ADMISSION COST: Donation requested.

HOURS OF OPERATION: Open Monday-Friday 9am-5pm, Saturday 9am-3pm. Call ahead on Sunday and holidays.

MUSEUM NOTES: There are restaurants nearby.

Display Automobiles

Buick, 1960, Electra 225 Convertible
Cadillac, 1941, Model 61 2dr Fastback
Cadillac, 1941, Model 61 4dr
Chevrolet, 1930, 2dr
Chevrolet, 1930, Coupe
Chevrolet, 1940, 2dr
Chevrolet, 1948, 2dr
Chevrolet, 1957, 2dr
Chevrolet, 1957, 4dr
Chevrolet, 1957, Bel Air 2dr
Chevrolet, 1961, Impala Convertible
Chevrolet, 1964, Corvette
Chevrolet, 1967, Corvette
Chevrolet, 1967, Malibu 2dr
Chevrolet, 1969, Camaro
Chevrolet, 1969, Corvette Convertible
Chevrolet, 1971, Cheyenne

Chevrolet, 1971, Impala Convertible
Chevrolet, 1971, Malibu 4dr
Chevrolet, 1971, Monte Carlo
Chevrolet, 1971, Nova
Chevrolet, 1987, Monte Carlo Aero Coupe
Chrysler, 1950, Town & Country
DeSoto, 1955, Fireflite 2dr Hardtop
Edsel, 1959, Pacer 4dr
Ford, 1915, Model T
Ford, 1923, Model T Coupe
Ford, 1924, Model T 2dr
Ford, 1926, Model T 2dr
Ford, 1926, Model T 4dr
Ford, 1926, Model T Touring
Ford, 1927, Model T Coupe
Ford, 1927, Model T Pickup Truck
Ford, 1927, Model T Roadster

Ford, 1928, Model A Roadster
Ford, 1929, Model A 2dr
Ford, 1930, Model A Coupe
Ford, 1931, Model A 2dr
Ford, 1931, Model A Coupe
Ford, 1934, 4dr
Ford, 1935, 2dr
Ford, 1937, 2dr
Ford, 1941, 2dr
Ford, 1964 1/2, Mustang Convertible

Graham Brothers, 1927, Panel Truck
Hudson, 1938, Terraplane 4dr
Kaiser, 1954, Special 4dr
Lincoln, 1924, Sedan
Packard, 1921, 4dr Pullman Body
Packard, 1954, Clipper 4dr
Plymouth, 1936, Deluxe Coupe
Plymouth, 1939, Special Deluxe 4dr
Studebaker, 1953, Commander 4dr

Boyertown Museum of Historic Vehicles

28 Warwick Street, Boyertown, Pennsylvania 19512
(215) 367-2090

The museum's purpose is to collect, preserve, restore and exhibit vehicles of historic significance to the southeastern Pennsylvania region. The majority of the vehicles were constructed by craftsmen in the region in the 1800s and 1900s. On display are automobiles, trucks, carriages, wagons, bicycles, sulkies, fire equipment and sleighs, one of which dates from 1763.

Among the region's earliest automobile manufacturers was Duryea. In 1895 Duryea was the first company organized in America to manufacture automobiles. Formed by Charles and J. Frank Duryea, the brothers split in 1898. Charles unsuccessfully built cars under the Duryea nameplate while J. Frank collaborated with the J. Stevens Arms & Tool Company to produce the Stevens-Duryea automobile until 1927.

DIRECTIONS TO MUSEUM: At intersection of Rt. 73 and Rt. 100, go west on Rt. 73 to fifth traffic light and turn left. Museum is 1 1/2 blocks on left.

ADMISSION COST: Adults $4.00; senior citizens $3.50; children $2.00.

HOURS OF OPERATION: Open Tuesday-Friday 9am-4pm; Saturday and Sunday 10am-4pm. Closed Monday. Closed Christmas.

MUSEUM NOTES: There is a restaurant nearby. The museum has a gift shop, but film is not available.

A brochure is available.

Display Automobiles

Acme SGV, 1909
Adams
Boss, 1905, Steam Car
Daniels, 1918-19, Touring
Daniels, 1919, Convertible Coupe
Daniels, 1920, Touring Sedan
Daniels, 1922, Touring
Detroit Electric, 1920, Coupe
Dile, 1912, Sport Roadster
Duryea, 1902, Phaeton
Duryea, 1903, Swan
Duryea, 1904, Phaeton
Duryea, 1907, Buggyaut
Duryea, 1908, Buggyaut
Duryea, 1916, GEM
Ford, 1914, Model T
Ford, 1914, Model T
Ford, 1915, Model T
Ford, 1928, Model A
Ford, 1930, Model A
Ford, 1930, Station Wagon
Ford, 1932, Victoria
Hill
International, 1907, Buggy-wagon
International, 1916, Auto Wagon
Jaguar, 1938, SS
Lincoln, 1963, Continental
Masano, 1953, Sports Car
Middleby, 1909, Roadster
NSU, 1969, 2dr Sedan
Packard, 1920, Touring Sedan
Pierce, 1902, Motorette
Reading, 1901-02, Steamer
Renault, 1960, Kilowatt Car
SGV, 1914, Roadster
Studebaker
Volkswagen, 1981, Rabbit

Gast Classic Motorcars Exhibit

Route 896, 421 Hartman Bridge Road, Strasburg, Pennsylvania 17579
(717) 687-9500

The Gast collection is broad-based both in variety and vintage. Domestic and foreign marques are displayed, ranging from well-known to lesser-known. The earliest auto on display is a 1910 Ford and the latest is a 1987 Lamborghini. The central theme of the collection is the winning quality of the cars — over half of the cars have earned awards in show competition.

Some highlights of the collection include: the first and last MGs imported to the United States, the first was a 1929 MG purchased by Edsel Ford and the last was a 1980 MGB bought by Henry Ford II; a 1953 Corvette with 9,122 miles; a 1948 Tucker; a 1966 Ford 427 Cobra; a 1938 Packard Super 8 Convertible Sedan; a 1918 Cadillac Touring; a 1953 Nash Healey Roadster; and a fuel-injected 1957 Pontiac Bonneville Convertible.

DIRECTIONS TO MUSEUM: From US 30 travel south on Rt. 896 approximately 2 1/2 miles. Gast is on left.

ADMISSION COST: Adults $6.00; children (7-12 yrs.) $3.50.

HOURS OF OPERATION: May-October: open daily 9am-9pm. November-April: open Sunday-Thursday 9am-5pm; Friday and Saturday 9am-9pm. Closed Christmas Eve and Christmas.

MUSEUM NOTES: There are restaurants nearby. Gast has a gift shop and film is available.

A brochure is available.

1948 Tucker 4dr Sedan. *First noticed in a front view of the Tucker is the center headlight. When the steering wheel is turned, the center headlight traverses to point in the same direction. Although not apparent, the windshield was designed to pop out on impact. The car included many innovations, but financial problems thwarted Preston Tucker's dream of becoming an auto manufacturer.*

Display Automobiles

American Austin, 1930, Deluxe Roadster
Amphicar, 1967
BMW-Isetta, 1957, Model 300
Cadillac, 1918, Touring
Cadillac, 1956, Eldorado Biarritz Convertible
Cadillac, 1959, Eldorado Seville Coupe
Chevrolet, 1940, Special Deluxe Convertible
Chevrolet, 1950, Deluxe Fleetline
Chevrolet, 1953, Corvette
Chevrolet, 1957, Bel Air Convertible
Chevrolet, 1957, Cameo Pickup Truck
Chevrolet, 1961, Corvette
Chevrolet, 1964, Corvair Monza Spyder
Chevrolet, 1966, Corvette
Chevrolet, 1967, Camaro SS/RS Convertible
Crosley, 1947, Pickup Truck
DeLorean, 1982
Dodge, 1969, Hemi Charger Daytona
Edsel, 1958, Citation 2dr Hardtop
Ford, 1910, Model T Tourabout
Ford, 1912, Model T Speedster
Ford, 1929, Model A Sport Coupe
Ford, 1932, Deluxe Roadster
Ford, 1938, Deluxe Convertible Club Coupe
Ford, 1950, Custom Deluxe Convertible Club
    Coupe
Ford, 1956, Fairlane Crown Victoria
Ford, 1957, Thunderbird
Ford, 1959, Galaxie 500 Sunliner

Ford, 1959, Skyliner
Ford, 1964 1/2, Mustang Coupe
Ford, 1966, Cobra
Ford, 1969, Mustang Boss 302
Jaguar, 1950, Mk.V Coupe
Jaguar, 1963, XK-E Coupe
Kurtiss-Offenhauser, 1958, Indy Race Car
Lamborghini, 1981, Countach
Lamborghini, 1987, Countach - 2/3 scale
Lincoln, 1938, Zephyr V-12 Club Coupe
Mason-Dixon, 1913, Mail Coach
Mercury, 1940, Convertible
Messerschmitt, 1957
MG, 1929, Type M
MG, 1947, TC Roadster
MG, 1980, B Roadster
Nash-Healey, 1953, Roadster
Oakland, 1929, Coupe
Packard, 1938, Super 8 4dr Convertible Sedan
Plymouth, 1940, Club Coupe
Pontiac, 1935, 8-cylinder Cabriolet
Pontiac, 1957, Bonneville Convertible
Porsche, 1960, 356 Coupe
Riley, 1934, Imp Roadster
Rolls-Royce, 1971, Silver Shadow II
Studebaker, 1950, Commander Regal Deluxe
    Starlite Coupe
Tucker, 1948, 4dr Sedan

JEM Classic Car Museum
Route 1, Box 120C, Andreas, Pennsylvania 18211
(717) 386-3554

The museum is the culmination of the collecting efforts of John E. Morgan. He has spent over thirty years building and refining his collection that is now offered for public viewing. The collection spans almost fifty years of automaking and is valued at $1.5 million.

The collection contains four early Chryslers, three of 1929 vintage. Chrysler sought upscale buyers and introduced the Imperial in 1926, and catering to the buyer seeking distinction. In 1929 Chrysler also offered bodies customized by LeBaron, Dietrich and Locke, many of them highly prized by collectors. The museum's 1929 Chrysler Imperial roadster is fitted with a Locke designed body.

DIRECTIONS TO MUSEUM: The museum is 10 miles west of Lehighton on Rt. 443. The museum is not in Andreas.

ADMISSION COST: Adults $4.00; senior citizens $3.50; children $2.50.

1929 Chrysler Imperial Roadster. *This top-of-the-line Imperial has a body designed by Locke. A six-cylinder engine producing 110 hp provided power, while four-wheel hydraulic brakes stopped the car.*

HOURS OF OPERATION: Open May 30-October 31 Monday-Friday 10am-4pm; Saturday, Sunday and holidays noon-4pm.

MUSEUM NOTES: There is a restaurant nearby and a gift shop onsite. Film is not available.

A brochure is available.

Display Automobiles

Auburn, 1931, Model 8-98 Boattail Speedster
Auburn, 1932, Model 8-100 Phaeton
Buick, 1932, Model 50 Sport Phaeton
Cadillac, 1931, Imperial Cabriolet
Cadillac, 1931, Model 355A Dual Windshield Phaeton
Chevrolet, 1933, Eagle Roadster
Chrysler, 1929, Imperial Roadster Locke Body
Chrysler, 1929, Model 75 Roadster
Chrysler, 1931, Dual Cowl Phaeton
Chrysler, 1935, Airflow Sedan
Chrysler, 1929, Imperial Sedan
Cord, 1930, L-29 Sedan
DeSoto, 1929, Series K Phaeton
Federal, 1954, Fire Truck
Ford, 1904, Model C Runabout
Ford, 1912, Model T Touring
Ford, 1932, Model B Roadster
Ford, 1934, Express Truck
Ford, 1936, Model 68 Phaeton
Franklin, 1932, Model 16 Airman Sedan
Gardner, 1927, Roadster
Graham Paige, 1930, Model 837 LeBaron Dual Cowl Phaeton
Hudson, 1931, Boattail Speedster

Hupmobile, 1929, Roadster
Lincoln, 1930, Model L Phaeton
Lincoln, 1956, Continental Hardtop
Locomobile, 1927, Junior 8 Phaeton
Marmon, 1930, Phaeton
Marmon, 1932, Coupe
Maxwell, 1906, Model N Runabout
Maxwell, 1924, Convertible
Milburn Electric, 1921
Nash, 1932, Victoria
Oakland, 1931, Model 301 Convertible Cabriolet
Oldsmobile, 1902, Curved Dash
Packard, 1929, Model 640 Dual Cowl Phaeton
Peerless, 1929, Roadster
Pierce-Arrow, 1935, Model 845 Sedan
Plymouth, 1932, PB Roadster
Reo, 1931, Royale Victoria
Rickenbacker, 1924, Model C Coupe
Sears, 1910, Model P
Star, 1927, Model M Roadster
Studebaker, 1930, President Roadster
Stutz, 1929, Black Hawk Roadster
Wills Sainte Claire, 1926, Model W-6 Roadster

State Museum of Pennsylvania

Third Street & North Street, P.O. 1026, Harrisburg, Pennsylvania 17108
(717) 787-4978

The State Museum of Pennsylvania presents exhibits depicting the history of Pennsylvania and its citizens. Areas covered include the arts, archaeology, wildlife, military, industry and technology.

As might be expected of a state with a substantial industrial base, well over two hundred Pennsylvania companies have attempted auto manufacturing, most unsuccessfully. The museum has on display two cars built by Pennsylvania firms, a 1905 Autocar and a 1913 Kearns. Autocar was located in Ardmore, Pennsylvania, and began production in 1901. Autocar was one of the first companies to use a shaft drive instead of the standard chain drive system of the day. The last Autocar pleasure car was constructed in 1912 when the firm decided to produce commercial vehicles exclusively.

The Kearns company followed a path similar to Autocar. First producing automobiles in 1909 in Beavertown, Pennsylvania, the Kearns Motor Buggy Company found that manufacturing commercial vehicles was profitable. In 1916 the last car was built by Kearns and the company concentrated on the production of trucks and fire engines.

DIRECTIONS TO MUSEUM: The museum is located in the William Penn Memorial Building at the corners of Third St. and North St. in Harrisburg.

ADMISSION COST: Free.

HOURS OF OPERATION: Open Tuesday-Saturday 9am-5pm; Sunday noon-5pm. Closed major holidays.

MUSEUM NOTES: The museum has a gift shop and there is a restaurant nearby. Film is available.

A brochure is available.

Display Automobiles

Autocar, 1905, Roadster
Gardner-Serpollet, 1902, Steamer Touring
General Vehicle, 1910, Electric Ice Truck
Kearns, 1913, Lulu Roadster

Packard, 1948, 2200 Series Touring
Rolls-Royce, 1909, Silver Ghost Landaulet
Zimmerman, 1909, I Surrey Touring

Station Square Transportation Museum
One Station Square, Suite 450, Pittsburgh, Pennsylvania 15219
(412) 471-5808

The museum concentrates on road vehicles, artifacts and memorabilia with particular emphasis on transportation history in the Pittsburgh area. Among the artifacts are cars, motorcycles, carriages, model cars, planes and trains, toys and a gasoline-engine powered pogo stick. Current expansion of the museum will add a genuine 1950s diner and a 1965 Westinghouse "Skybus" that will be used as a mini-theater.

The cars on display are on loan and rotated periodically. One of the cars displayed is an 1898 Panhard et Levassor, owned by the Heinz family and reportedly the first car in Pittsburgh. Before building their own cars, the French company Panhard et Levassor built Benz, Deutz and Daimler engines. Car production began in the early 1890s. The company developed the widely copied Panhard system that consisted of a steering wheel, a front engine and chain drive to the rear wheels. The company's presence in automobile manufacturing gradually faded and Citroen purchased the company in 1965. Production of Panhard cars ceased in 1967.

DIRECTIONS TO MUSEUM: The museum is located in Station Square, which is at the south end of the Smithfield St. Bridge.

ADMISSION COST: Adults $2.00; children free.

HOURS OF OPERATION: Open 11am-8pm Tuesday-Sunday. Closed Monday.

Closed New Year's Day, Thanksgiving and Christmas.

MUSEUM NOTES: There are a restaurant and a gift shop onsite. Film is available.

A brochure is available.

Display Automobiles

American Austin, 1936, Coupe
American Austin, 1936, Roadster
American Bantam, 1940, Roadster
Baker Electric, 1910
Buick, 1910, Sport Touring

Chevrolet, 1968, Corvair Monza Convertible
Foster/Artzberger, 1901, Steam Surrey
Panhard et Levassor, 1898
Standard, 1914, Touring

Swigart Museum

Museum Park Box 214, Huntingdon, Pennsylvania 16652
(814) 643-0885

The Swigart Museum is the oldest auto museum in the country. W. Emmert Swigart established the museum in 1920 to preserve examples of car manufacturers who had impacted the young auto industry. Rapidly changing technology and shifts in customer preferences left many cars obsolete and manufacturers bankrupt. Mr. Swigart collected cars primarily built prior to 1914, an era of intense inventiveness and entrepreneurship.

The collection of early one- and two-cylinder cars is one of the most diverse in the country. Included among the exhibits are several of the most popular autos sold at the turn of the century — Locomobile, Cadillac, Rambler, Franklin. Although the collection focuses on the early years of automotive history, notable examples of the classic era are on display, such as Duesenberg, Pierce-Arrow, Marmon, DuPont, Cord and Packard. There are usually 40-48 cars on display.

Among the artifacts on display is the world's largest display of auto nameplates, the identifying crests and emblems attached to front of the car. Also displayed are extensive collections of license plates, lights, horns and other accessories, as well as early Americana.

DIRECTIONS TO MUSEUM: The museum is located in Museum Park on US 22 approximately 4 miles east of Huntingdon.

ADMISSION COST: Adults $4.00; children (6-12 yrs.) $2.00. Group prices available.

HOURS OF OPERATION: Open July and August daily 9am-5pm. Open June, September and October on weekends 9am-5pm. Call (814) 643-3000 ext. 221 for weekday group tour arrangements.

MUSEUM NOTES: A list of display automobiles was unavailable due to rotation of cars exhibited. There is a restaurant nearby. The museum has a gift shop, but film is not available.

A brochure is available.

Schoolhouse Antiques Museum

517 Flat Rock Road, Liberty, South Carolina 29657
(803) 843-6827

The museum claims to be the "largest varied collection in the southeast." Found in the museum are artifacts dating from the 1600s to the 1900s, including items such as a fainting couch, grandfather clocks, porcelain dolls, canopy beds, dentist's equipment, toys, 100-year-old vacuum cleaners, gowns and a glass spittoon.

The auto collection consists of several marques rarely seen elsewhere, if at all, namely Argyll, Armac, Merz, Woods and Woods Mobilette. There are also three three-wheeled cars exhibited, an A.C. (Autocarrier), BSA and Morgan. Three-wheeled cars have had limited success, usually being offered by small specialty manufacturers. Morgan was the most successful builder with over forty years spent constructing three-wheeled cars. When inexpensive cars such as Volkswagon, Citreon and Renault proliferated after World War II, purchasers were less inclined to buy a three-wheeler. Morgan dropped the line in favor of conventional four-wheel cars in 1952.

DIRECTIONS TO MUSEUM: The museum is located three miles east of Liberty at the corner of Flat Rock Rd. and Hwy. 135.

ADMISSION COST: Adults and children over 11 yrs. $2.50; senior citizens $2.00.

HOURS OF OPERATION: Open Wednesday-Saturday llam-5pm; Sunday 1-5pm.

MUSEUM NOTES: There is a restaurant nearby and an antique shop onsite. Film is not available.

A brochure is available.

Display Automobiles

A.C., 1912, 3-Wheeler Sociable
Argyll, 1908, Landaulet Limousine
Armac, 1905, Runabout
BSA, 1934, 3-Wheeler
Custer, 1928, Electric Runabout
Maxwell, 1916, Touring
Merz, 1914, Tandem Roadster
Metz, 1913, Roadster
Morgan, 1936, 3-Wheeler
Overland, 1915, Touring

Reo, 1916, Center-door Sedan
Rolls-Royce, 1920, Landaulet Limousine
Rolls-Royce, 1921, Salmanca
Saxon, 1917, B5R Roadster
Sears, 1908
Studebaker, 1929, Housecar
Woods, 1915, Electric Brougham
Woods Mobillette, 1913, Model 3
Woods Mobillette, 1914, Model 3
Woods Mobillette, 1915, Roadster

Stock Car Hall of Fame
Joe Weatherly Museum

P.O. Box 500, Darlington, South Carolina 29532
(803) 393-2103

The museum is located adjacent to the front entrance of Darlington Raceway, the oldest superspeedway on the NASCAR circuit and host for NASCAR's oldest superspeedway race, the Southern 500. Constructed in 1951, the 1.36-mile track is considered the toughest track on the circuit by most drivers.

The Hall of Fame commemorates the individuals who made significant contributions to stock car racing. The honorees' achievements are documented and artifacts reflecting their achievments are displayed. In the museum several race cars, engines and other racing artifacts and memorabilia are exhibited. This is an interesting collection for anyone interested in motorsports, particularly stock car racing.

DIRECTIONS TO MUSEUM: The museum adjoins Darlington Raceway, which is on Hwy. 34/151 just west of Darlington and about 1/2 mile west of US 52 bypass.

ADMISSION COST: Adults $2.00.

HOURS OF OPERATION: Open daily 9am-5pm.

MUSEUM NOTES: The museum has a gift shop and there is a restaurant nearby.

The Joe Weatherly Museum and Stock Car Hall of Fame are adjacent to Darlington Motor Speedway.

Museum of Wildlife, Science & Industry

Box 461, Webster, South Dakota 57274
(605) 345-4751

The museum occupies 12 acres on which are several historical buildings and later structures. In the museum are antique cars, tractors, horse-drawn equipment, tools and mounted animals. The auto collection comprises 12 cars and trucks dating from 1919 to 1967.

Two Oldsmobile Toronados are a part of the collection, one a 1966, the introductory year. The Toronado was a significant accomplishment for Oldsmobile, and earned the marque the *Motor Trend* magazine "Car of the Year" award. The front-wheel-drive system on the Toronado was the first application of front-wheel drive since the Cord in 1937. Oldsmobile sold over 40,000 1966 Toronados.

DIRECTIONS TO MUSEUM: The museum is one mile west of the intersection of US 12 and Rt. 25.

ADMISSION COST: Donation requested.

HOURS OF OPERATION: May-September: open Monday-Friday 9am-5pm; Saturday and Sunday 1-5pm. October-April: open Monday-Friday 9am-4pm.

MUSEUM NOTES: There are restaurants nearby. Film is not available.

A brochure is available.

Display Automobiles

Dodge, 1947, 4dr Sedan
Ford, 1919, Truck
Ford, 1959, Skyliner
Hupmobile, 1930
International, 1924, Truck
Lincoln, 1956, Premiere
Mercury, 1947

Oldsmobile, 1966, Toronado
Oldsmobile, 1967, Toronado
Packard, 1937, Model 120 4dr Sedan
Packard, 1953, Caribbean Convertible
Packard, 1953, Custom Convertible
Packard, 1956, Custom Clipper
Plymouth, 1930, Coupe

Pioneer Auto Show & Antique Town
P.O. Box 76, Murdo, South Dakota 57559
(605) 669-2691

Pioneer Town is a group of turn-of-the-century buildings housing a wide variety of items including: music boxes, glassware, toys, guns, gems and fossils. Also displayed is an extensive vehicle collection that comprises autos, trucks, motorcycles and tractors.

With over 220 cars and trucks displayed, the collection is vast. All the more recognized marques are displayed, Buick, Cadillac, Chevrolet, Ford, Oldsmobile, Packard, Pontiac, Studebaker, but some cars infrequently seen are here as well. On display are a Cole, Brush, De Vaux, Fuller, Gardner, Moon, Sears, Velie, and others. Many of these cars passed from the scene, not because they were poorly constructed, but due to other factors, usually financial.

DIRECTIONS TO MUSEUM: From I-90 take either Exit 191 or 192 to Hwy. 16. Follow signs.

ADMISSION COST: Adults $5.00; senior citizens $4.50; children (6-13 yrs.) $2.50.

HOURS OF OPERATION: Open April and May daily 8am-6pm; June, July and August daily 7am-10pm; September and October daily 8am-6pm. Remainder of year call ahead.

MUSEUM NOTES: A cafe is located on-site and a restaurant is nearby. There is a gift shop and film is available.

A brochure is available.

Display Automobiles

AMC, 1966, Marlin
AMC, 1970, AMX Convertible
AMC, 1976, Pacer
Amhpicar, 1965
Argo Electric, 1913
Auburn, 1909, Touring
Auburn, 1929, Sedan
Auburn, 1935, Speedster
Brush, 1909
Buick, 1924, Roadster
Buick, 1925
Buick, 1956, Century
Buick, 1970, Electra 225
Cadillac, 1912, Touring
Cadillac, 1938
Cadillac, 1959, Eldorado
Cadillac, 1960, Eldorado
Cadillac, 1964, Convertible
Chalmers, 1918
Chandler, 1921, Roadster

Chevrolet, 1918
Chevrolet, 1918
Chevrolet, 1926, Sedan
Chevrolet, 1929, Sedan
Chevrolet, 1935, Sedan
Chevrolet, 1939, Business Coupe
Chevrolet, 1946, Pickup Truck
Chevrolet, 1947, Coupe
Chevrolet, 1955, Cameo Pickup Truck
Chevrolet, 1957, Convertible
Chevrolet, 1960, Corvair
Chevrolet, 1963, Corvair Convertible
Chevrolet, 1966, Chevelle
Chevrolet, 1967, Camaro
Chevrolet, 1968, Camaro Convertible
Chrysler, 1948, Windsor Convertible
Chrysler, 1960, 300 Convertible
Chrysler, 1965, Crown Imperial
Cole, 1921
Cord, 1937

Cord, 1937, Model 812
Crosley, 1939, Pickup Truck
Crosley, 1941
Crosley, 1949
Crow-Elkhart, 1917
Cunningham, 1928
Dart, 1919
De Vaux, 1931
Diamond T, 1938, Fire Truck
Diamond T, 1949, Pickup Truck
Dodge, 1918
Dodge, 1946
Dodge, 1969, Charger
Dodge, 1971, Challenger
Dort, 1923
Elgin, 1922, Touring
Erskine, 1926, Convertible Coupe
Essex, 1920
Flanders, 1920, Roadster
Ford, 1906, Model N
Ford, 1909, Model T
Ford, 1912, Model T Panel Delivery
Ford, 1917, Model T Touring
Ford, 1920, Model T Fire Truck
Ford, 1921, Sedan
Ford, 1922, Model T Coupe
Ford, 1925, Model T Wrecker
Ford, 1926, Model T Touring
Ford, 1926, Model T Truck
Ford, 1927, Model T
Ford, 1927, Model T Roadster
Ford, 1928, Model A Phaeton
Ford, 1929, Model A Pickup Truck
Ford, 1929, Model A Roadster
Ford, 1929, Model A Truck
Ford, 1931, Model A
Ford, 1932, Model B Pickup Truck
Ford, 1934, 4dr Sedan
Ford, 1936, Sedan
Ford, 1939, 4dr Sedan
Ford, 1949, Coupe
Ford, 1950, Courier Del Sedan
Ford, 1951, 2dr Sedan
Ford, 1951, Marmon-Harrington
Ford, 1955, Crown Victoria
Ford, 1955, Thunderbird
Ford, 1958, Skyliner
Ford, 1958, Thunderbird
Ford, 1959, Country Sedan
Ford, 1964, Hardtop
Ford, 1965, Convertible

Ford, 1965, Mustang
Ford, 1965, Mustang Convertible
Ford, 1966, Bronco
Ford, 1966, Mustang
Ford, 1967, Mustang
Ford, 1968, Mustang
Ford, 1968, Shelby, GT
Ford, 1969, Torino Cobra
Ford, 1981, Electric
Franklin, 1919, Touring
Franklin, 1921
Frazer, 1951, 4dr Sedan
Fuller, 1904, Touring
Gardner, 1920
Go Go Mobile, 1952
Grant, 1917, Touring
Haynes, 1921, Touring
Henderson, 1914
Henderson, 1929
Henry J., 1951
Hudson, 1916, Touring
Hudson, 1949, 2dr Sedan
Hudson, 1951, Pacemaker Coupe
Hupmobile, 1913, Touring
Hupmobile, 1917, Roadster
Hupmobile, 1922
IHC, 1925, Truck
Indiana, 1937, Truck
Isetta, 1958
J.I. Case, 1921, Touring
Jeepster, 1951
Jewell, 1902, Roadster
Jordan, 1924, Playboy
Kaiser, 1951, 4dr Sedan
Kaiser, 1954, Darin Convertible
Kaiser, 1954, Manhattan
King Midget, 1967
Lafayette, 1935
LaSalle, 1928, Roadster
Lexington, 1921
Lincoln, 1940, Zephyr
Lincoln, 1958
Lincoln, 1969, Continental Convertible
Locomobile, 1926
Marquette, 1928
Maxwell, 1909, Roadster
Maxwell, 1918, Truck
Maxwell, 1922, Touring
Mercer, 1920, Touring
Mercury, 1941
Mercury, 1949

Mercury, 1956
Mercury, 1958, Hardtop
Mercury, 1959, 4dr Sedan
Mercury, 1969, Cougar Convertible
Metropolitan, 1954
Metropolitan, 1959
Metz, 1908
Metz, 1912, Cutaway Display
Mickey Rooney, 1940, Movie Car
Mitchell, 1922, Touring
Moon, 1921, Touring
Nash, 1926
Nash, 1948, Wheeler
Nash, 1948, Wrecker
Oldsmobile, 1903, Curved Dash
Oldsmobile, 1940, 2dr Sedan
Oldsmobile, 1966, Toronado
Oldsmobile, 1970, 4-4-2
Oldsmobile, 1972, Cutlass Convertible
Overland, 1909, Runabout
Overland, 1913
Overland, 1916, Touring
Overland, 1917, Country Club
Overland, 1925, Mystery B1 Coupe
Packard, 1931, Convertible
Packard, 1953, Carribean Convertible
Paige, 1928
Patterson, 1919, Touring
Peerless, 1928, 4dr Sedan
Pierce-Arrow, 1929, Sedan
Pierce-Arrow, 1930, Roadster
Pierce-Arrow, 1931
Plymouth, 1949, Coupe
Plymouth, 1950
Plymouth, 1964, Valiant
Plymouth, 1970, Superbird
Pontiac, 1929, 4dr Sedan
Pontiac, 1934, 4dr Sedan
Pontiac, 1950
Pontiac, 1955, Safari Wagon
Pontiac, 1955, Starfire Convertible
Pontiac, 1967, GTO

R.C.H., 1913, Touring
Rambler, 1960
Rambler, 1964, Convertible
Rambler, 1966, Ambassador
Rambler, 1969, SC/Rambler
Reo, 1908
Rickenbacker, 1923, 2dr Sedan
Rockne, 1933, Opera Coupe
Rolls-Royce, 1937
Saxon, 1914, Roadster
Schact, 1904, Roadster
Scripps-Booth, 1922
Sears, 1909, Roadster
Skoda, 1960
Smith Air Car, 1954
Spacke, 1913, Roadster
Stanley, 1925, Steamer
Star, 1922, Touring
Stoddard-Dayton, 1911
Studebaker, 1936, Coupe
Studebaker, 1950, Sedan
Studebaker, 1951, Coupe
Studebaker, 1952, Commander
Studebaker, 1955, Coupe
Studebaker, 1962, GT Hawk
Stutz, 1921, Touring
Sunbeam, 1967, Convertible
Terraplane, 1933
Terraplane, 1936
Triton II, 1983, Domino's Pizza Delivery Car
Tucker, 1948
Velie, 1910, Touring
Velie, 1911, Speedster
Volkswagen, 1956
Whippet, 1927
White, 1921, Motorhome
White-Packard, 1932, Touring Phaeton
Willys, 1948, Jeep
Willys, 1955
Willys-Knight, 1920, Touring
Windsor, 1929, White Prince

Car Collectors Hall of Fame

1534 Demonbreun Street, Nashville, Tennessee 37203
(615) 255-6804

The cars in the collection are owned by E. Howard Brandon. Over half of the collection consists of restored Chevrolet and Ford automobiles. A gallery displaying cars owned or associated with famous people, usually country and western stars, highlights the collection.

In the collection are a 1962 Lincoln Continental used by President Kennedy, a 1976 Cadillac Eldorado owned by Elvis Presley, a 1975 Chrysler Imperial owned by Roy Acuff, a 1953 MG-TD owned by Louise Mandrell, a 1982 Buick Riviera owned by Tammy Wynette, a 1934 Packard limousine owned by Marty Robbins, and a 1962 Pontiac Bonneville owned by Webb Pierce (approximately one hundred fifty silver dollars are inlaid in the upholstery).

DIRECTIONS TO MUSEUM: From I-40 take Exit 209. Facility is across from the Country Music Hall of Fame. Parking is available behind buildings on Demonbraun.

ADMISSION COST: Adults $4.85; children $3.25.

HOURS OF OPERATION: Open May-September daily 8am-9pm; October-April daily 8am-5pm. Closed Thanksgiving, Christmas Eve and Christmas.

MUSEUM NOTES: There is a restaurant nearby. Film is available in the gift shop.

A brochure is available.

1962 Lincoln Continental. *The Lincoln four-door convertible was often selected when an open, spacious car was needed for special occasions. The museum's car was provided for President Kennedy on a trip to Camp Stewart, Georgia.*

1960 Chevrolet Impala 2dr Hardtop. *After the controversial design of the 1959 models, Chevrolet toned down the styling of the 1960 models. The rear fins were flattened and the front grill area was smoother. The Impala was the dressiest version of the model line.*

Display Automobiles

Buick, 1982, Riviera Convertible
Cadillac, 1959, 4dr Hardtop
Cadillac, 1976, Eldorado Coupe
Chevrolet, 1925, Superior 2dr Coach
Chevrolet, 1934, Standard 4dr Sedan
Chevrolet, 1938, Master Deluxe 2dr Sedan
Chevrolet, 1939, Master Sport 4dr Sedan
Chevrolet, 1941, Special Deluxe 2dr Sedan
Chevrolet, 1950, Bel Air 2dr Hardtop
Chevrolet, 1955, Bel Air Convertible
Chevrolet, 1955, Bel Air Nomad Station Wagon
Chevrolet, 1956, Bel Air 2dr Hardtop
Chevrolet, 1957, Bel Air 4dr Sedan
Chevrolet, 1957, Cameo Pickup Truck
Chevrolet, 1957, Convertible
Chevrolet, 1958, Impala 2dr Hardtop
Chevrolet, 1960, Impala 2dr Hardtop
Chevrolet, 1968, Camaro Z/28
Chevrolet, 1978, Corvette Pace Car

Chrysler, 1975, Imperial 4dr Hardtop
DeLorean, 1981
Dodge, 1918, Touring
Dodge, 1966, 2dr Hardtop
Dodge, 1970, Charger R/T
Edsel, 1960, Ranger 2dr Sedan
Ford, 1903, Model A
Ford, 1910, Model T Pickup Truck
Ford, 1928, Model AR Phaeton
Ford, 1934, 2dr Sedan
Ford, 1935, Deluxe Phaeton
Ford, 1956, Thunderbird
Ford, 1971, Mustang Convertible
Ford, 1990, Mustang Convertible
King Midget, 1958
Lincoln, 1962, Continental
MG, 1953, TD Roadster
Packard, 1934, Limousine
Pontiac, 1962, Bonneville Convertible

Dixie Gun Works Old Car Museum

P.O. Box 130, Union City, Tennessee 38261
(901) 885-0700

The museum is the creation of Turner Kirkland, owner of the Dixie Gun Works, a firm that specializes in parts and accessories for antique guns and rifles. Thirty-six cars are presented for viewing as well as a vast assortment of antique car parts. Also on display are more than one thousand antique guns and an early American gunsmith shop constructed of logs.

The centerpiece of the collection is a 1924 Marmon Touring owned by Reagor Motlow, the last family president of the Jack Daniels Distillery. The car was restored in 1961 and subsequently placed on display. Rivaling other upscale cars, approximately 2,500 Marmons were sold in 1924.

DIRECTIONS TO MUSEUM: The museum is on the east side of US 51 on south side of Union City.

ADMISSION COST: Adults $2.00; children free.

HOURS OF OPERATION: Open Monday-Friday 8am-5pm; Saturday 8am-noon. Closed Sunday and major holidays.

MUSEUM NOTES: There is a restaurant nearby. The museum has a gift shop, but film is not available.

A brochure is available.

Display Automobiles

Cadillac, 1912, Touring
Edsel, 1959, Sedan
Ford, 1914, Model T Speedster
Ford, 1914, Model T Touring
Ford, 1914, Snowflyer
Ford, 1915, Model T Touring
Ford, 1925, Model T Touring
Ford, 1926, Model T Roadster
Ford, 1927, Model T Coupe
Ford, 1928, Pickup Truck
Ford, 1930, Model A Touring
Ford, 1932, Coupe
Ford, 1934, Convertible Coupe
Ford, 1935, Convertible Sedan
Ford, 1936, Convertible Coupe
Ford, 1937, Sedan
Ford, 1938, Convertible Coupe

Ford, 1939, Convertible Coupe
Ford, 1940, Sedan
Ford, 1941, Sedan
Ford, 1942, Woody Station Wagon
Ford, 1946, Convertible Coupe
International, 1909, Highwheeler
Marmon, 1924, Touring
Maxwell, 1908
Overland, 1916, Touring
Packard, 1930, Limousine
Packard, 1936, Limousine
Pierce-Arrow, 1927, Roadster
Studebaker, 1921, Sedan
Studebaker, 1928, Victoria
Waverly, 1910
Whippet, 1926, Convertible
Willys, 1950, Jeepster

Elvis Presley Automobile Museum

3764 Elvis Presley Boulevard, Memphis, Tennessee 38116
(901) 332-3322; outside TN (800) 238-2000

The Elvis Presley Automobile Museum is located at Graceland, the home of Elvis Presley for 20 years. Opened to the public in 1982, Graceland houses memorabilia of "The King of Rock 'n' Roll." Graceland is an entertaining 90-minute tour for anyone interested in popular music (the auto museum is a separate attraction from the Graceland tour).

The auto museum contains cars and other vehicles owned by Elvis. He was keenly interested in cars and motorcyles. Presley was known to wake an auto dealer late at night so he could purchase a car that had caught his eye.

Two examples of the Stutz Blackhawk are on display. Built in 1971 and 1973, these cars are unrelated to the earlier Stutz automobiles. Latter day Blackhawks were built using a customized Pontiac Grand Prix body with a modified engine. The original price ranged from $22,500 for a 1971 model to $41,500 for a 1975 model.

DIRECTIONS TO MUSEUM: Graceland is approximately ten miles south of downtown Memphis. From I-55 take exit 5B onto US 51 (Elvis Presley Blvd.) and go south one mile to Graceland.

ADMISSION COST: Auto museum: adults $4.50; children (4-12 yrs.) $2.50. All attractions package: adults $15.95; children (4-12 yrs.) $10.95.

HOURS OF OPERATION: Open seven days a week except closed Tuesday from November 1 through February. Closed New Year's Day, Thanksgiving and Christmas.

Opening time: May-August 8am; September-April 9am.Closing time: September-May 6pm; June-August 7pm (until 8pm June 15-August 11). Last tour of Graceland begins one hour prior to closing time.

The 1973 Stutz Blackhawk in the foreground sports a leather interior trimmed in 18 karat gold. The 1955 Cadillac Fleetwood in the background is painted pink.

MUSEUM NOTES: Film can be purchased in gift shop. Graceland has a restaurant.

A brochure is available.

Display Automobiles

Cadillac, 1955, Fleetwood 4dr Sedan
Cadillac, 1956, Eldorado Convertible
Dune buggy
Ferrari, 1975, Dino 308GT4
Lincoln, 1956, Continental

Mercedes-Benz, 1970, 280 SL
Stutz, 1971, Blackhawk
Stutz, 1973, Blackhawk
Willys, 1960

Music Valley Car Museum
(Cars of the Stars)

2611 McGavock Pike, Nashville, Tennessee 37214
(615) 885-7400

Reflecting the collection's name, Cars of the Stars, most of the cars in the collection were owned by media personalities, more specifically, country and western stars. Here are found cars owned by such Nashville luminaries as Dolly Parton, Randy Travis, Hank Williams and Hank Snow.

As evidenced by the appearance of several Cadillacs in the collection, Cadillac has been the selected automobile of many stars. Cadillac's position as king of luxury cars attracts customers seeking both value and status. Cadillacs have been produced almost ninety years, incorporating innovation, styling and the financial resources of General Motors to outlast its many competitors, leaving the Lincoln as its only domestic adversary. However, foreign manufacturers with considerable resources may test Cadillac's dominance of the luxury car market.

DIRECTIONS TO MUSEUM: From Hwy. 115 take Exit 12 onto McGavock Pike and travel east to museum.

ADMISSION COST: Adults $3.50; senior citizens $3.00; children (6-12 yrs.) $1.50.

1966 Ford Thunderbird Convertible. *The museum's Thunderbird has an optional fiberglass tonneau cover installed over the rear seats. Introduced in 1962, the cover's purpose was to provide a "sportier" image. Ford sold a little over 69,000 1966 Thunderbirds.*

1950 Ford Custom 2dr Sedan. *Minor changes were made by Ford for 1950 after the substantial body and suspension changes on the 1949 model. The only functional changes were a recessed gas filler neck and push-button door handles. The basic body style lasted through the 1954 models.*

HOURS OF OPERATION: Open June-Labor Day daily 8am-10pm; After Labor Day-May 9am-5:30pm. Closed Thanksgiving, Christmas Eve and Christmas.

MUSEUM NOTES: There is a restaurant nearby. Film is available in the gift shop.

A brochure is available.

Display Automobiles

Bentley, 1956, Model S-1
Bricklin, 1975
Buick, 1941, Super Convertible
Buick, 1948, Super Convertible
Cadillac, 1949, Series 62 Convertible
Cadillac, 1959, Coupe de Ville
Cadillac, 1972, Eldorado 2dr Hardtop
Cadillac, 1972, Fleetwood Limousine
Cadillac, 1973, Coupe de Ville
Cadillac, 1973, Fleetwood 4dr Sedan
Cadillac, 1974, Eldorado Convertible
Cadillac, 1975, Fleetwood 4dr Sedan

Cadillac, 1981, Eldorado Convertible
Cadillac, 1982, Fleetwood 4dr Sedan
Chevrolet, 1949, Truck
Chevrolet, 1950, 4dr Sedan
Chevrolet, 1955, Bel Air Convertible
Chevrolet, 1956, Bel Air Convertible
Chevrolet, 1957, Bel Air Convertible
Chevrolet, 1957, Bel Air Convertible
Chevrolet, 1959, Corvette
Chevrolet, 1962, Impala SS 2dr Hardtop
Chevrolet, 1968, Corvette
Chevrolet, 1978, Corvette

Edsel, 1959, Ranger 4dr Sedan
Ford, 1914, Model T
Ford, 1930, Model A Coupe
Ford, 1934, Roadster
Ford, 1942, Super Delivery
Ford, 1950, Custom 2dr Sedan
Ford, 1955, Thunderbird
Ford, 1956, Thunderbird
Ford, 1959, Station Wagon
Ford, 1965, Mustang Convertible
Ford, 1966, Thunderbird Convertible

GMC, 1953, Panel Truck
King Midget, 1962
Lincoln, 1956, Continental
Lincoln, 1959, Continental Convertible
MG, 1949, TC Roadster
Nash, 1961, Metropolitan
Nissan, 1983, Limousine
Oldsmobile, 1972, Hurst Cutlass 2dr Hardtop
Plymouth, 1938, 4dr Sedan
Plymouth, 1948, Special Deluxe Convertible
Studebaker, 1950, 4dr Sedan

Smoky Mountain Car Museum

P.O. Box 1385, Pigeon Forge, Tennessee 37868
(615) 453-3433

The museum exhibits over 30 vehicles powered by gas, electricity and steam. Also displayed are collections of gas pump globes, spark plugs and dolls.

Several cars are noteworthy for their association with famous people and include Elvis Presley's Mercedes-Benz, Al Capone's bullet-proof Cadillac and Hank Williams Jr.'s "Silver Dollar" car. The deadly Aston-Martin that James Bond drove in the *Goldfinger* and *Thunderball* movies resides in the museum.

DIRECTIONS TO MUSEUM: The museum is located at 2970 Parkway near the intersection with Pickel St. (near Magic World).

HOURS OF OPERATION: Open daily July-Labor Day 9am-8pm. Call ahead for operating hours from early spring to late fall.

ADMISSION COST: Adults $5.00; children $2.00.

MUSEUM NOTES: There are restaurants nearby. The museum has a gift shop.

Alamo Classic Car Museum

Route 6, P.O. Box 546, New Braunfels, Texas 78130
(512) 620-4311

The museum houses the auto collection of Carl Van Roekel. Included in the collection of over 150 cars are modern cars such as a 1967 Ford Mustang named "Wildfire" that cost $125,000 to build, as well as classic cars such as a 1927 Cadillac Dual Cowl Phaeton.

A highlight of the collection is a one-of-a-kind 1924 Oldsmobile Boattail Speedster that was built to suit the particular needs of its moonshiner owners. Along with other features unique to the car is a two-compartment gas tank. Gasoline occupied one part of the tank while the other part held moonshine. A 169 cubic-inch engine powers the car, which is equipped with disc wheels, rather than the more common spoke wheels.

Also displayed are collections of engines, tools and hubcaps. The museum claims the collection of "monkey wrenches" is probably the largest in existence.

DIRECTIONS TO MUSEUM: From south-bound I-35 take Exit 182 onto Engel Rd. and cross I-35 to museum. From north-bound I-35 take Exit 180 onto Schwab Rd. and follow to museum.

ADMISSION COST: Men $5.00; women $4.00; children (10-15 yrs.) $2.50.

HOURS OF OPERATION: Open Friday-Tuesday 10am-6:30pm. Closed Wednes-day and Thursday. Call museum for holiday hours.

MUSEUM NOTES: There is a restaurant nearby. Film is not available.

A brochure is available.

Bolin Wildlife & Antique Exhibit

1028 N. McDonald, McKinney, Texas 75069
(214) 542-2639

W. Perry Bolin opened the facility in 1980. Bolin is a rancher, businessman and big game hunter who offers for public viewing the artifacts reflective of his life and the residents of Collin County. Among the items on display are home furnishings, farm tools and equipment, an old country store, and wildlife specimens.

Bolin was an oil distributor and several items from early service stations are displayed, including a 1928 Ford fuel delivery truck. In the auto collection are a 1913 Ford Model T Touring, a 1915 Ford Model T Roadster, a 1925 Ford Model T Coupe and a 1930 Ford Model A Roadster.

DIRECTIONS TO MUSEUM: From US 75 exit onto US 380 and travel east to Hwy. 5 (McDonald St.). Turn right and go one block.

ADMISSION COST: Free

HOURS OF OPERATION: Open Monday-Friday 9am-noon, 1-4pm.

MUSEUM NOTES: There is a restaurant nearby. Film is not available.

A brochure is available.

Central Texas Museum of Automotive History

P.O. Box 160, Rosanky, Texas 78953
(512) 237-2635

The museum's purpose is to trace the development of the automobile, as well as the social and economic impact it caused. The collection contains over 100 cars and ranges from the economical Crosley to the expensive Rolls-Royce, from the utilitarian Ford Model T Truck to the sporty Jaguar XK-140.

Among the more common marques found in the collection, such as Chevrolet, Ford, Dodge, Packard and Studebaker, sits a Bugmobile. Perhaps the hierarchy of the Bugmobile Company of America thought a memorable name would at least draw customers to the showroom to see what a Bugmobile actually looked like. Few lookers actually purchased Bugmobiles, however, and 1908 and 1909 were the only years they were built. Whatever the reason for Bugmobile's demise, the car buyers of the 1950s and 1960s proved that the name is not the overriding purchasing factor by buying thousands of "Beetles."

DIRECTIONS TO MUSEUM: Rosanky is located approximately 12 miles south of Bastrop on Rt. 304.

ADMISSION COST: Adults $2.50; children (6-12 yrs.) $1.50.

HOURS OF OPERATION: Open April 1-September 30 Wednesday-Saturday 9am-5pm; Sunday 2-5pm; closed Monday and Tuesday. Open October 1-March 31 Friday and Saturday 9am-5pm; Sunday 2-5pm; closed remainder of week.

MUSEUM NOTES: There are no restaurants nearby. The museum has a gift shop and film is available.

A brochure is available.

Display Automobiles

NOTE: This is a partial list.

American LaFrance
Auburn
Bugmobile
Buick
Cadillac
Chevrolet
Crosley
Dodge
Duesenberg
Edsel
EMF
Excalibur
Ford
Franklin
Haynes
Holsman
Hudson
Hupmobile
International Harvester
Jaguar
LaSalle
Licorne
MG
Packard
Plymouth
Regal
Rolls-Royce
Stearns Knight
Studebaker

Panhandle-Plains Historical Museum

P.O. Box 967, WT Station, Canyon, Texas 79016
(806) 656-2244

The museum is the oldest and largest state museum in Texas. The museum was established in 1933 with the intent of preserving the history of the Panhandle region. With over 2 million artifacts, areas of concentration include art, Native Americans, ranching, pioneers, paleontology, geology, transportation and oil exploration and production.

The Panhandle region of Texas is one of the top oil producing areas in the country. Exhibits outline the geologic origin of oil, its discovery and production, and its distribution as characterized by a 1930s style gas station, complete with a hand-operated gas pump. Among the vehicles in the transportation is a 1903 Ford Model A, which according to the museum, is the oldest surviving car built on an assembly line.

DIRECTIONS TO MUSEUM: Museum is located on Fourth Ave. one block east of US 87.

ADMISSION COST: Donation requested.

HOURS OF OPERATION: June-August: Monday-Saturday 9am-6pm; Sunday 2-6pm. September-May: Monday-Saturday 9am-5pm; Sunday 2-6pm.

MUSEUM NOTES: The museum has a snack area and gift shop. A restaurant is located nearby. Film is available.

A brochure is available.

Display Automobiles

Buick, 1930, Coupe
Cadillac, 1930, Touring
Chevrolet, 1948, Club Coupe
Detroit Electric, 1915
Ford, 1903, Model A

Ford, 1915, Model T Touring
Ford, 1926, Model T
Ford, 1929, Model A Roadster
Nash, 1954, Metropolitan
Pierce-Arrow, 1933, Limousine

Pate Museum of Transportation

P.O. Box 711, Fort Worth, Texas 76101
(817) 396-4305

The Pate Museum of Transportation has on exhibit an impressive collection of automobiles and aircraft, as well as artifacts and memorabilia reflecting transportation in the United States. Begun in 1969, the museum is sponsored by a foundation that provides funds for the expansion and improvement of the museum.

Among the cars in the museum's collection is a Pierce-Arrow Silver Arrow. The car is a 1934 model equipped with a twelve-cylinder engine. Originally built as show cars for the 1933 New York Automobile Show, the Silver Arrows appeared as production cars only in 1934 and 1935 while the company was in the last years of existence. In May 1938 the last car company that was building only luxury cars closed its doors. Pierce-Arrow was known for leading the industry in its use of aluminum, integrating headlights into the fenders, and introducing hydraulic tappets. The Silver Arrows are among the most prized of the Pierce-Arrows with values exceeding $100,000.

DIRECTIONS TO MUSEUM: The museum is just north of Cresson on US 377.

ADMISSION COST: Free.

HOURS OF OPERATION: Open 9am-5pm Tuesday-Sunday. Closed Monday and major holidays.

1929 Packard Dual Windshield Phaeton. *The museum's award-winning seven-passenger phaeton features a custom body built by famous designer Raymond Dietrich. A 105-hp inline eight-cylinder engine powers the 4,800-pound car.*

MUSEUM NOTES: There are no restaurants nearby. Film is not available.

A brochure is available.

Display Automobiles

Aston Martin, 1935, Mark II Roadster
Brewster, 1934, Town Car
Buick, 1953, Skylark Convertible
Cadillac, 1933, Coupe
Cadillac, 1938, Limousine
Cadillac, 1959, Convertible
Chrysler, 1957, Ghia Limousine
Daimler, 1937, Salon
Ford, 1924, Model T Touring
Ford, 1931, Pickup Truck
Ford, 1937, Convertible Sedan
Ford, 1957, Thunderbird
Ford, 1967, Shelby GT500
Franklin, 1926, Coupe

Hupmobile, 1938, Sedan
Jaguar, 1973, XK-E Roadster
Lincoln, 1933, Sedan
Lincoln, 1940, Zephyr Coupe
Lincoln, 1959, Continental Convertible
Lincoln, 1967, 4dr Convertible
Packard, 1929, Sport Touring
Packard, 1937, Club Sedan
Pierce-Arrow, 1934, Silver Arrow
Rolls-Royce, 1927, Phantom I Town Car
Rolls-Royce, 1938, Phantom III Town Car
Schacht, 1904, Runabout
Studebaker, 1933, Touring
Z.I.M., 1950, Sedan

Bonneville Speedway Museum
1000 Wendover Boulevard, Wendover, Utah 84083
(801) 665-7721

The museum serves to commemorate the achievements made on the nearby salt flats, as well as displaying artifacts and equipment related to Bonneville racing. The museum also presents a broad-based auto collection that ranges from Volkswagon to Rolls-Royce.

What was once vast Lake Bonneville — approximately the size of Lake Michigan and 1,000 feet deep — is now the Great Salt Lake Desert, a portion of which is the Bonneville Salt Flats, mecca for seekers of pure speed. Miles of unobstructed, flat surface provide the ideal surface for attempting land speed records. For over 75 years, racers like Ab Jenkins, Sir Malcolm Campbell, John Cobb, Gary Gablich, Mickey Thompson and Craig Breedlove have steered record-setting cars across the salt.

Each summer at a time when salt conditions are suitable, hundreds of racers congregate for the National Speed Trials. All types of vehicles make runs across the salt, from high-tech streamliners to low-buck homebuilts. The object is to go as fast as possible; the goal is to beat the record. The event generally occurs in the latter portion of summer (contact the museum for dates).

DIRECTIONS TO MUSEUM: The museum is housed in the easternmost building in Wendover.

ADMISSION COST: Adults $2.00; children $1.00.

HOURS OF OPERATION: Open June-September daily 10am-6pm.

MUSEUM NOTES: There is a restaurant nearby. Film is not available.

Display Automobiles

American La France, 1914, Fire Truck
Cadillac, 1971, Eldorado Convertible
Chevrolet, 1962, Impala Convertible
Chevrolet, 1963, Corvair
Chevrolet, 1975, Caprice Convertible
Dodge, 1915, Touring
Essex, 1928, Boattail Roadster
Ford, 1926, Model T Runabout
Ford, 1937, Pickup Truck
Ford, 1957, Skyliner
Ford, 1957, Thunderbird
Ford, 1962, Thunderbird

Jaguar, 1959, 4dr Coupe
Lincoln, 1956, Continental
Lincoln, 1967, 4dr Convertible
Lincoln, 1968, Limousine
MG, 1948, TC Roadster
Rauch & Lang, 1909, Electric
Rolls-Royce, 1935, Sedanca De Ville
Rolls-Royce, 1963, Silver Cloud III
Studebaker, 1953, Coupe
Studebaker, 1963, Avanti
Volkswagen, 1973, Convertible
Volkswagen, 1979, Convertible

Classic Cars International

355 West 7th South Street, Salt Lake City, Utah 84101
(801) 582-6883

The museum contains over 200 antique, classic and special interest cars, but not all are on display. The cars are constantly rotated to provide an ever-changing exhibit.

Several Packards are on display, including a 1936 Packard with a Victoria convertible body built by Dietrich. Early cars were a combination of two builders, the chassis manufacturer and the body constructor. Car companies gradually started their own body building facilities, bought a body builder or contracted the work. Some body companies, however, remained independent and built special, custom bodies. Smaller car companies, particularly upscale marques, built cars using custom bodies. Greater prestige was usually attached to a car having a custom body. Although Packard possessed a facility to build bodies, the buyers of expensive Packards often sought bodies listed in the catalogs of firms such as Dietrich, LeBaron, Judkins, Holbrook and Fleetwood.

1948 Lincoln Continental Club Coupe. *The post-war Continentals were essentially the same as the pre-World War II versions. Acclaimed for its styling, Continental sales nevertheless were low, and Continental was dropped from the Lincoln line in 1949. Continental returned in 1956 as the Mark II.*

DIRECTIONS TO MUSEUM: From I-15 and I-80 take Exit 310 to 6th South St. Turn right at 3rd West St. and follow to museum.

ADMISSION COST: $3.00 donation to Utah Boys Ranch.

HOURS OF OPERATION: Call ahead.

MUSEUM NOTES: There is a restaurant nearby. Film is not available.

A brochure is available.

Union Station Museum
2501 Wall Avenue, Ogden, Utah 84401
(801) 629-8535

The museum houses selected automobiles from the Browning car collection. Also exhibited at the museum are railroad artifacts, the Browning firearms collection, art, antiques, gems and minerals.

Several classic Pierce-Arrows are on display. The marque did not become Pierce-Arrow until 1909. Arrow models were first built in 1904 by the Pierce Company, which in its ancestry had manufactured household appliances, bicycles and bird cages. The company proved adept at auto manufacturing and the marque became one of the most prestigious of the early era. But the management that directed the company's ascent left shortly after World War I and a steady decline ensued.

DIRECTIONS TO MUSEUM: The museum is located at the intersection of 25th St. and Wall Ave.

ADMISSION COST: Adults $2.00; senior citizens $1.50; children 50¢.

HOURS OF OPERATION: Open Monday-Saturday 10am-6pm. Closed Sunday. Closed Thanksgiving and Christmas.

MUSEUM NOTES: There is a restaurant nearby and a gift shop onsite. Film is not available.

A brochure is available.

Display Automobiles

Cadillac, 1930, Sports Sedan
Cadillac, 1932, Limousine
Ford, 1932, Roadster
Isotta-Fraschini, 1929, Type 8A Convertible Coupe
Knox, 1911, Model S Raceabout
Lincoln, 1926, Touring
Lincoln, 1931, Dual Cowl Phaeton
Lincoln, 1931, Landaulet
Lincoln, 1933, Sports Phaeton
Marmon, 1931, Club Sedan
Oldsmobile, 1901, Curved Dash Runabout
Oldsmobile, 1910. Special Roadster
Oldsmobile, 1911, Touring
Oldsmobile, 1912, Autocrat Roadster
Packard, 1912, Phaeton

Packard, 1928, Convertible
Packard, 1929, Runabout
Packard, 1933, Phaeton
Packard, 1934, Coupe
Packard, 1939, Limousine
Pierce-Arrow, 1909, Touring
Pierce-Arrow, 1915, Touring
Pierce-Arrow, 1929
Pierce-Arrow, 1929, Convertible Sedan
Pierce-Arrow, 1929, Touring
Pierce-Arrow, 1931, Club Sedan
Pierce-Arrow, 1931, LeBaron Convertible Sedan
Pope-Hartford, 1909
Simplex, 1910, Runabout
Stearns, 1909, 30/60 Touring

Westminster MG Car Museum

Route 5, Westminster, Vermont 05158
(802) 722-3708 or (603) 756-4121

The collection of Gerard J. Goguen comprises the automobiles on display at the Westminster MG Car Museum, and it is "the worlds largest private exhibit of a single marque." As the name of the museum specifies, all of the museum's cars were built by the British manufacturer MG.

Cecil Kimber, a garage manager in Oxford, England, began the line by constructing cars from components purchased from chassis and body builders. He soon identified his cars as "M.G.," the name of the garage, Morris Garage, and in 1928 the MG Car Company was created. Although MGs were constructed in a variety of body styles, they are best known in the United States for the sports cars.

The museum contains a wide variety of models and vintages representative of the MG marque. Among the rare cars on display is a 1933 J-4 supercharged racer (only nine built), a 1927 14/28 Tourer Flatnose (only six exist), a 1930 Type M roadster (only three exist), and a prototype for the MGA.

DIRECTIONS TO MUSEUM: From I-91 take Exit 5 to Rt. 5.

ADMISSION COST: Adults $2.50; senior citizens $2.00; children (6-16 yrs.) $1.00.

HOURS OF OPERATION: Open Memorial Day. Open weekends during June. Open July and August Tuesday-Sunday 10am-5pm. Open Labor Day weekend and Columbus Day weekend.

MUSEUM NOTES: There is a restaurant nearby. The museum has a gift shop, but film is not available.

A brochure is available.

Display Automobiles

MG, 1927, 14/28 Tourer Flatnose
MG, 1930, 18/80 Mk I Speed Model
MG, 1930, Sportsman Coupe
MG, 1930, Type M Roadster
MG, 1932, F3 Magna Salonette
MG, 1933, J4 Supercharged Racer
MG, 1933, L2 Magna Roadster
MG, 1934, PB Airline Coupe
MG, 1934, PB Trials Car
MG, 1937, SA Saloon
MG, 1938, SA Tourer
MG, 1939, VA Tickford Drophead Coupe
MG, 1948, TC Roadster
MG, 1952, TD Roadster
MG, 1953, TD Arnolt Bertone Coupe

MG, 1953, TD Inskip Roadster
MG, 1953, TD Roadster
MG, 1953, YB, Saloon
MG, 1955, EX 182 Prototype
MG, 1955, TF Roadster
MG, 1955, ZA Magnette Sedan
MG, 1956, A Coupe
MG, 1956, A Roadster
MG, 1963, B Roadster
MG, 1965, Mk IV Magnette Sedan
MG, 1969, C Roadster
MG, 1971, Midget Mk III Gan 5 Roadster
MG, 1975, B GT Coupe
Wolseley, 1954, 4/44 Sedan

Glade Mountain Museum
Route 1, Box 360, Atkins, Virginia 24311
(703) 783-5678

The museum is a potpourri of regional historic artifacts and memorabilia that includes firearms, farm implements, household goods and other items, some dating from the Civil War.

The cars listed below are located inside the museum. Some cars are stored outside. Behind the museum is a salvage yard made up of vehicles from approximately 1935 to 1969 that is open for browsing or parts buying.

DIRECTIONS TO MUSEUM: From I-81 take Exit 18 and travel one mile west on US 11. Turn onto Rt. 708 and go south one mile. Turn onto Rt. 615 and go east mile to museum.

ADMISSION COST: Donation requested.

HOURS OF OPERATION: Open May-August Sunday 1-8pm. Other times by appointment.

MUSEUM NOTES: There is a restaurant nearby. Film is not available.

Display Automobiles

Ford, 1926, Touring
Ford, 1927, Doctor's Coupe
Ford, 1928, 2dr Sedan
Ford, 1929, Pickup Truck
Ford, 1930, Roadster
Ford, 1931, Briggs 4dr Sedan
Ford, 1937, 4dr Sedan

Ford, 1939, 4dr Sedan
Ford, 1940, Truck
Ford, 1945, Jeep
Ford, 1946, Fire Truck
Ford, 1947, Pickup Truck
Studebaker, 1948, Coupe

Historic Car & Carriage Caravan

Luray Caverns, P.O. Box 748, Luray, Virginia 22835
(703) 743-6551

This collection of cars, carriages, coaches and other modes of transportation is a portion of the Luray Caverns complex. Centerpiece of the facility are the Luray Caverns, the most popular cave system in the East.

The transportation exhibits comprise over 144 items that include cars, coaches, carriages and costumes that date back over 350 years. The oldest vehicle on display is a 1625 Berline Coupe de Gala.

1908 Baker Electric. *Baker was the preeminent builder of electric cars in the world. It was the first American car equipped with shaft drive, and the first car purchased by Thomas Edison. This 1908 version was propelled by 48-volt electric motor and could operate 60-70 miles before requiring a battery charge. Although electric cars were somewhat successful early on, their attraction waned when gasoline-engined cars became more civilized.*

1927 Mercedes-Benz SS Sports Touring. *Designed by Ferdinand Porsche, the Mercedes SS offered fast, eye-catching transportation for the well-heeled buyer. The SS was a more powerful version of the S. All of the Mercedes S, SS and SSK series cars are prized by collectors.*

Several of the autos were built in the early years of the automobile era, including a 1892 Benz, one of the oldest cars in America that is still in running condition. Karl Benz is the acknowledged constructor of the first car that later reached production. Benz built a vehicle designed to use an engine he also built. Other experimenters installed engines in existing horse carriages. Sporadic initial sales grew to over 600 by 1900, but disagreements with corporate management forced the conservative Karl Benz from the company he founded. The company prospered as a car manufacturer and engine builder and merged with Daimler in 1926. The merger created Mercedes-Benz.

DIRECTIONS TO MUSEUM: Luray Caverns is east of Luray on US 211. Follow signs.

ADMISSION COST: Includes admission to Luray Caverns — Adults $10.00; senior citizens $8.50; children $4.50.

HOURS OF OPERATION: Open daily at 10am. Auto exhibit closes 1 1/2 hours after last tour of caverns.

MUSEUM NOTES: There are a restaurant and a gift shop in the complex. Film is available.

A brochure is available.

Display Automobiles

Baker Electric, 1908
Bugatti, 1927
Buick, 1907
Buick, 1910
Cadillac, 1904
Cadillac, 1906
Chevrolet, 1915
Cord, 1930
Daimler, 1946
Delaunay-Belleville, 1908
Dodge, 1915
Ford, 1906
Ford, 1910, Touring
Ford, 1914, Milk Wagon
Ford, 1915
Ford, 1915, Delivery Truck
Ford, 1929
Ford, 1931, Coupe
Franklin, 1922
Graham Brothers, 1925, Paddy Wagon
Hispano-Suiza, 1935
Hudson, 1912
International, 1907

International, 1913
Knox, 1903
Lincoln, 1941
Locomobile, 1914
Maxwell, 1910
Mercedes-Benz, 1927
Metz, 1912
Middleby, 1909
Morgan, 1931, Super Sports
Oldsmobile, 1900
Orient, 1903
Packard, 1928
Paige, 1922
Pierce-Arrow, 1931
Riley, 1903
Rolls-Royce, 1925
Schacht, 1906
Sears, 1908
Speedwell, 1903
Stanley, 1913, Steamer
Westcott, 1914
Willys-Knight, 1922
Winton, 1903

Roaring Twenties Antique Car Museum
Rt. 1, Box 576, Hood, Virginia 22723
(703) 948-6290

The museum presents cars, trucks, stationary engines, horse-drawn equipment, farm tools, household goods and other Americana.

Several marques that did not survive in the marketplace are exhibited in the museum. Examples of Carter, Stephens, Cleveland, Star, Hupmobile, Paige, Essex and Nash cars are on display. Among the unique cars is a 1948 Playboy. Like the post-war Crosley, also exhibited, the compact Playboy failed to attract sufficient cost-conscious buyers. The small, single-seat, three-passenger convertible was only built from 1947 to 1951.

DIRECTIONS TO MUSEUM: The museum is located on Rt. 230 in Hood, which is south of Madison.

ADMISSION COST: Adults $5.00; children $3.00.

HOURS OF OPERATION: By appointment only.

MUSEUM NOTES: There is a restaurant nearby. Film is not available.

A brochure is available.

Display Automobiles

American LaFrance, 1914, Fire Engine
Buick, 1922, Model 6-44 Roadster
Cadillac, 1924, 4dr
Carter, 1904, Motorette Electric
Chandler, 1925, Big Six 4dr
Chrysler, 1928, Model 72 Rumble Seat
Cleveland, 1924, 4dr
Crosley, 1947, 2dr
Dodge, 1920, 4dr
Essex, 1927, Pickup Truck
Ford, 1931, 4dr
Hudson, 1922, 4dr
Hudson, 1929, Super Six Rumble Seat
Hupmobile, 1925, Boattail Rumble Seat
Hupmobile, 1936, Model 618 2dr
Nash, 1927, 400 Series 2dr

Nash, 1929, Advanced 6 4dr
Oakland, 1926, 2dr
Packard, 1941, Model 160 4dr
Paige, 1925, Model 6-70 4dr
Peerless, 1929, Model 6-61 4dr
Playboy, 1948, Model A-48 2dr
Plymouth, 1931, PA Series 4dr
Reo, 1933, Model S-2 4dr
Star, 1925, Taxi
Stephens, 1923, 4dr
Studebaker, 1925, Duplex Roadster
Studebaker, 1929, Dictator Rumble Seat
Surlesmobile, 1945, 2dr
Whippet, 1928, Model 98 4dr
Whippet, 1929, Model 96A Rumble Seat
Willys, 1931, Model C-100 Pickup Truck

U.S. Army Transportation Museum

Building 300, Besson Hall, Fort Eustis, Virginia 23604
(804) 878-1182

Fort Eustis is home for the Army Transportation Center and School. Army personnel are trained at Fort Eustis in all aspects of the vast transportation system of the Army. The museum presents an historical overview of the complex worldwide system used to supply the Army.

While there are no shiny, concours examples of classic autos on display, anyone interested in how the Army has managed to move people and supplies over the last two centuries should find the Army Transportation Museum interesting. Over 90 pieces of equipment are on display, including trucks and other wheeled vehicles, aircraft, boats and rail equipment.

DIRECTIONS TO MUSEUM: Fort Eustis is adjacent to Newport News. From either US 60 or I-64, exit onto Fort Eustis Blvd. and travel west to Fort Eustis. Directions to the museum will be provided by the guard at the gate.

ADMISSION COST: Free.

HOURS OF OPERATION: Open daily 9am-4:30pm. Closed Easter and all federal holidays.

MUSEUM NOTES: There are no restaurants nearby. Film is available in the gift shop.

A brochure is available.

Lynden Pioneer Museum

217 Front Street, Lynden, Washington 98264
(206) 354-3675

The museum was established in 1977 to document the history of Lynden and environs by preserving artifacts and mementos from the region. Items on display include horse-drawn vehicles, cars, trucks, tractors, military artifacts, Indian artifacts and other smaller displays.

A considerable portion of cars on display are early model Chevrolets. The Chevrolet was the brainchild of William "Billy" Durant, founder of General Motors, but ousted in 1910. Durant wanted another auto company and contracted with Louis Chevrolet to build a French type automobile. But the design goals of Durant and Chevrolet did not agree. Durant envisioned a light, inexpensive car, but Chevrolet built a large, sturdy automobile that couldn't be manufactured at Durant's desired price. The association was severed with Durant keeping the Chevrolet name and the car. Durant combined the good features of the Chevrolet and another car, the Little, into a new Chevrolet that proved to be successful in the marketplace. The long-running battle with Ford was underway.

DIRECTIONS TO MUSEUM: Museum is on Front St. in Lynden, which is approximately 22 miles north of Bellingham on Hwy. 439.

ADMISSION COST: Adults $1.00; children free.

HOURS OF OPERATION: April-October: open Monday-Saturday 10am-5pm. November-March: open Thursday, Friday and Saturday noon-4pm.

MUSEUM NOTES: There are restaurants nearby. The museum has a gift shop, but film is not available.

A brochure is available.

Display Automobiles

Chevrolet, 1914, Baby Grand Touring	Ford, 1914, Speedster
Chevrolet, 1915, Royal Mail Roadster	Ford, 1923, Depot Hack
Chevrolet, 1918, Model 490 Touring	Ford, 1925, Touring
Chevrolet, 1919, Truck	Ford, 1930, Model A Coupe
Chevrolet, 1920, Sedan	International, 1928, Truck
Chevrolet, 1921, Model 490 Touring	Lincoln, 1936, 4dr Sedan
Chevrolet, 1922, Model 490 Roadster	Nash, 1950, 4dr Sedan
Chevrolet, 1925, Touring	Overland, 1914, Touring
Chevrolet, 1927, Roadster	Reo, 1929, Truck
Chevrolet, 1928, Touring	Star, 1923, Truck
Chevrolet, 1931, Cabriolet	Stoddard-Dayton, 1910, Touring
Chevrolet, 1931, Coupe	Studebaker, 1926, Coupe
Dodge, 1936, Truck	Stutz, 1928, Speedster
Fiat, 1937, Topolino Cabrio	

Brooks Stevens Automotive Museum

10325 N. Port Washington Road, Mequon, Wisconsin 53092
(414) 241-4185

The museum bears the name of one of the world's foremost industrial designers, Brooks Stevens. The design skills of Brooks Stevens, and the staff of his firm, have been responsible for the design of over forty automobiles. Over the last fifty years, Stevens has designed such diverse machinery as toasters and railroad trains, bottles and manufacturing plants.

In assembling the cars for his collection, Stevens concentrated on cars that feature a mechanical or styling highpoint. Among the cars is a 1922 Premier that used a preselective shift mechanism invented by Brooks Stevens' father, William Stevens. There are also design prototypes of the Excalibur II and Studebaker cars developed by Stevens' design firm.

Created in 1965, the Excalibur II was a blend of classic styling and modern mechanical components. The body resembled a 1928-1929 Mercedes-Benz SSK. A Studebaker convertible chassis supported the car while a Chevrolet V-8 provided power. A phaeton body style was added in 1967. Prices ranged from $7,250 in 1965 to $62,000 in 1985.

DIRECTIONS TO MUSEUM: From I-43 exit onto Port Washington Rd. and travel north on Port Washington Rd. to museum.

HOURS OF OPERATION: Open daily 10am-5pm. Closed Tuesday and Thursday from Labor Day to Memorial Day.

ADMISSION COST: Adults $5.00; senior citizens $3.50; children $1.75.

MUSEUM NOTES: A restaurant is located nearby. Film is not available.

A brochure is available.

Display Automobiles

Alfa Romeo, 1950, Touring Coupe
Bugatti, 1925, Brescia Modifee Speedster Type 23
Buick, 1913, Touring
Cadillac, 1905, Roadster
Cadillac, 1926, Sedan
Cadillac, 1956, 2dr Die Valkyrie
Chrysler, 1959, Scimitar Hard Top Convertible
Cord, 1930, L-29 Speedster
Detroit Electric, 1915
Duetsch, 1956, Bonnett
Excalibur, 1952, XJ100 Race Car
Excalibur, 1956, Race Car

Excalibur II, 1963, SSK Roadster Prototype
Ferrari, 1953, Europa
Ford, 1955, Thunderbird
Ford, 1956, Victoria
Frazer, 1951, Convertible Sedan
Gutbrod, 1953, Superior E S-L246
Hispano-Suiza, 1927, Town Car
Hoffman, 1936, X001 Rear Engine Sedan
Hudson, 1952, Hornet
Isetta, 1955, Coupe
Jaguar, 1939, SS-100 Roadster
Jaguar, 1950, XK-120
Kaiser, 1955, Manhattan

Marmon, 1914, Roadster
Marmon, 1933, Special HCM Prototype V-12
Mercedes-Benz, 1928, Phaeton
Metz, 1910
MG, 1949, TC Roadster
Oldsmobile, 1937, Custom Coupe
Packard, 1920, Phaeton
Packard, 1934, Dual Cowl Phaeton
Paige, 1919, Daytona Roadster
Premier, 1922, Touring
Rolls-Royce, 1925, Phaeton
Rolls-Royce, 1954, Silver Wraith Town Car
Studebaker, 1929, Erskine
Studebaker, 1932, Indy Race Car

Studebaker, 1963, Excalibur Hawk
Studebaker, 1964, Gran Turismo Hawk
Studebaker, 1964, Sedan Prototype
Studebaker, 1964, Skyview Station Wagon
   Prototype
Studebaker, 1965, Sliding Roof Station Wagon
Studebaker, 1966, 4dr
Studebaker, 1966, 4dr Sedan Prototype
Studebaker, 1966, Sceptre Coupe
Talbot-Lago, 1938, Figoni Filashi Coupe
Velie, 1918, Model 38 Touring
Willys, 1948, Jeepster
Willys, 1963, Aero 2600 Sedan

David V. Uihlein Antique Race Car Museum

232 Hamilton Drive, Cedarburg, Wisconsin 53012
(414) 377-0987

Uihlein's collection of early race cars will appeal to any motorsports enthusiast, or anyone interested in early automobiles.

Among the cars are such noteworthy racers as the 1966 Lola that Graham Hill drove to
victory in the 1966 Indianapolis 500, the Wisconsin Special car that set the world land
speed record of 180 mph in 1922, the MORS French Grand Prix racer, and the Gallivan
1925 sprint car that set the Milwaukee track record.

There are several race cars equipped with Miller engines. Harry Miller was the major
force in American oval racing during the 1920s. In championship racing, Miller cars
won every event in 1923, 1928 and 1929, and only lost 16 times during that time
span. Miller designed the engine (later marketed as the Offenhauser) that dominated
Indy car racing for nearly 40 years.

DIRECTIONS TO MUSEUM: From I-43
take Exit 89 onto Rt. C. Go west two
miles to Green Bay Rd. (first stop sign).
Turn right and follow Green Bay Rd. for
four city blocks to museum (Green Bay
Rd. becomes Hamilton Dr.).

ADMISSION COST: Adults $3.00; senior
citizens and children $1.00.

HOURS OF OPERATION: Open during
summer months Wednesday-Saturday
10am-5pm; Sunday 1-5 pm. Closed Monday and Tuesday.

MUSEUM NOTES: There is a restaurant
nearby. Film is not available.

A brochure is available.

Display Automobiles

Auto-Shippers, 1947-49, Indy Car
Dreyes-Miller, 1935, Sprint Car
Gallivan, 1922, Sprint Car
Gallivan, 1925, Sprint Car
Hispano-Suiza, 1918, Dragster
Lola-Ford, 1966, Indy Car
Marchere, 1947, Midget Racer

Marchese, 1937-51, Indy Car
Miller, 1923
Miller, 1931, Indy Car
Mors, 1908, Grand Prix Car
Thorne-Sparks, 1937-46, Indy Car
Uihlein MG, 1954, Sports Car Racer
Wisconsin Special, 1922, Land Speed Car

Dells Auto Museum

804 N. Main Street, Lake Mills, Wisconsin 53551
(608) 764-5050

The vintages in Dells collection date from 1901 to 1988. The collection contains over 200 cars that are rotated periodically for viewing. Approximately 25 cars are usually displayed.

Featured at Dells are convertibles, with special interest in Indianapolis 500 pace cars. Early in the history of the Indianapolis 500, a suitable car was selected the day of the event to lead the race cars around the track on their pace lap. The selection became a noteworthy honor for the auto manufacturer, an award that became advertising ammunition. Chevrolet more than other manufacturers has attempted to gain the most from the award by selling pace car replicas during the years when one of its models was selected. The value of these limited-run cars is generally greater than other models, depending on how many the manufacturer produced.

DIRECTIONS TO MUSEUM: From I-90/94 take Exit 87 onto Hwy. 13 and travel to second stop light. Turn right onto Hwy. 23 and go 1/2 mile to museum.

ADMISSION COST: Adults $4.00; children $2.00.

HOURS OF OPERATION: Open mid-May through mid-October daily 9am-9pm.

MUSEUM NOTES: There is a restaurant nearby and a gift/antique shop onsite. Film is available.

A brochure is available.

Display Automobiles

There are approximately 25 cars on display. The cars are rotated frequently and selected from an inventory of over 200 cars housed elsewhere. Contact museum for information on cars not displayed.

FWD Museum

105 E. 12th Street, Clintonville, Wisconsin 54929
(715) 823-2141

Clintonville, Wisconsin, is headquarters for the FWD Corporation, a major truck manufacturing firm and direct descendant of the Four Wheel Drive Auto Company founded in 1909.

Two machinists in Clintonville, Otto Zachow and William Besserdich, developed a four-wheel-drive system that was originally used in an automobile. While attempting to market an automobile, the firm also began building trucks using the four-wheel-drive system. Manufacturing trucks proved successful so automobile production was aborted at an early stage to concentrate on truck production.

The museum reflects the history of the FWD Corporation and its predecessors. Several vehicles produced by the company are on display including the *Battleship*, the first gasoline-engine powered car produced by FWD, the *Nancy Hank*, the last car built by the firm (1911) and driven in company service for 35 years, the *Miller FWD Special* that raced in the Indianapolis 500 race in the mid-1930s, and early trucks manufactured by FWD.

DIRECTIONS TO MUSEUM: The museum is at the corner of 11th St. and Memorial St.

ADMISSION COST: Donation requested.

HOURS OF OPERATION: Open Memorial Day through Labor Day on Saturday and Sunday 1-4pm.

MUSEUM NOTES: There is a restaurant nearby.

A brochure is available.

Hartford Heritage Auto Museum

147 N. Rural Street, Hartford, WI 53027
(414) 673-7999

The museum has over 70 automobiles on display, but the emphasis is on a car manufactured in Hartford, the Kissel.

The Kissel family owned several businesses in Hartford and in 1906 two of the brothers organized the Kissel Motor Car Company. Originally named the Kissel Kar, it was an "upscale" car that was built from 1907 to 1931. In deference to anti-German feelings during World War I, the name was shortened to Kissel. The design of the car lured such noteworthy owners as Al Jolson and Amelia Earhart, but sales dropped from 1926 until 1930 when the company went into receivership. The firm reorganized and subsequently manufactured outboard motors. The plant was sold and made outboards for West Bend, and later for Chrysler.

DIRECTIONS TO MUSEUM: The museum is two blocks north of Rt. 60 on Rural St., which is two blocks west of Main St.

ADMISSION COST: Adults $4.00; senior citizens & students $3.50; children (7-12 yrs.) $1.00.

HOURS OF OPERATION: May-September: open Monday-Saturday 10am-5pm; Sunday and holidays noon-5pm. October-April: open Wednesday-Saturday 10am-5pm; Sunday noon-5pm; closed holidays.

MUSEUM NOTES: There is a restaurant nearby and a gift shop at the museum. Film is not available.

A brochure is available.

1920 Kissel Touring. *The Kissel Motor Car Company only built 506 cars in 1920 while the company struggled during the recession following World War I. To promote the upscale image of Kissels, the company called all models in the line "Custom-Built". A 61-horsepower, six-cylinder engine powered all 1920 Kissels.*

Zunker Auto Museum

3722 MacArthur Drive, Manitowoc, Wisconsin 54220
(414) 684-4005

The museum has on display over 40 antique and special interest cars, as well as, an antique gas station, memorabilia, antique motorcycles and bicycles, and a collection of dolls and children's lunch boxes.

The museum possesses two Whippets, a 1928 roadster and a 1930 coupe. Whippets were manufactured by the Willys-Overland Company and were very successful. The first year of production resulted in 110,000 cars sold, placing the company in third place behind Chevrolet and Ford. In 1928 Whippet sales exceeded 300,000, the best annual sales for the marque. Whippets were the smallest U.S. cars built at the time and cost less than comparable Fords. Available with a four-cylinder or eight-cylinder engine, the Whippet provided many features at an economical price. But the Depression forced Willys-Overland to change direction. In 1931 the Whippet was dropped so the company could concentrate on production of the Willys Model 77.

DIRECTIONS TO MUSEUM: From southbound I-43 take Exit 151 onto Waldo Blvd. Follow Waldo to County Rd. R and turn right. Follow County Rd. R to Broadway and turn left. Follow Broadway to MacArthur Dr. and turn right. Museum is on the right.

From northbound I-43 take Exit 149 onto Hwy. 151. Follow Hwy. 151 to Rapids St. and turn left. Follow Rapids St. to Custer St. and turn right. Follow Custer St. to MacArthur Dr. and turn left. Museum is on left.

ADMISSION COST: Adults $2.50; senior citizens $2.50; students (14-18 yrs.) $1.50; children (6-13 yrs.) 50¢.

HOURS OF OPERATION: Open May-October 10am-5pm.

MUSEUM NOTES: There is a restaurant nearby. Film is not available.

A brochure is available.

Display Automobiles

AMC, 1965, Marlin
Auburn, 1929, 4dr Brougham
Buick, 1924, Coupe
Chevrolet, 1919, Touring
Chevrolet, 1931, Coupe
Chevrolet, 1932, 4dr Sedan
Chevrolet, 1964, Corvair Pickup Truck
Chevrolet, 1965, Corvair Corsa Convertible
Chrysler, 1930, Coupe
Crosley, 1948, Station Wagon
Crosley, 1950, Convertible

Crosley, 1950, Station Wagon
Diamond, 1940, Fire Truck
Dodge, 1924, Touring
Durant, 1922, 4dr Sedan
Edsel, 1959, Convertible
Essex, 1920, Touring
Ford, 1915, Model T Pickup Truck
Ford, 1925, Model T Coupe
Ford, 1926, 2dr Sedan
Ford, 1930, Model A Sport Coupe
Ford, 1937, Coupe

Ford, 1947, Woody Station Wagon
Ford, 1958, Thunderbird
Frazer, 1951, Vagabond 4dr Sedan
Hudson, 1947, Pickup Truck
Hudson, 1951, Pacemaker Convertible
Kaiser, 1953, Manhattan 4dr Sedan
Marquette, 1930, Roadster
Metropolitan, 1961, Hardtop
Nash, 1929, Model 470 4dr Sedan
Nash, 1936, Model 400 2dr Sedan

Packard, 1937, Model 110 4dr Sedan
Plymouth, 1934, Deluxe Coupe
Rambler, 1966
Saxon, 1916, Touring
Studebaker, 1917, Touring
Studebaker, 1941, Pickup Truck
Studebaker, 1956, Skyhawk
Whippet, 1928, Roadster
Whippet, 1930, Coupe
Willys, 1950, Jeepster

Bibliography

Angelucci, Enzo and Bellucci, Alberto. *The Automobile*. McGraw-Hill, New York, 1974.

Automobile Quarterly's World of Cars. Automobile Quarterly, New York, 1971.

Baldwin, Nick, Georgano, G.N., Sedgwick, Michael and Laban, Brian. *The World Guide to Automobile Manufacturers*. Facts On File Publications, New York, 1987.

Boyne, Walter J., *Power Behind The Wheel.* Stewart, Tabori & Chang, New York, 1988.

Burness, Tad. *Cars of the Early Twenties*. Chilton, Philadelphia, 1968.

Clymer, Joseph Floyd. *Treasury of Early American Automobiles*. McGraw-Hill, New York, 1950.

Cunningham, Briggs S. *Racing, Sports & Touring Cars*. Walker and Company, New York, 1979.

Flammang, James M. *Standard Catalog of American Cars 1976-1986*. Krause Publications, Iola, WI 1989.

Georgano, G.N., ed. *The Complete Encyclopedia of Motorcars*, 2nd ed. E.P. Dutton and Company, New York, 1973.

Gunnell, John A., ed. *Standard Catalog of American Cars 1946-1975*. Krause Publications, Iola, WI, 1987.

——, ed. *Standard Catalog of Light Duty American Trucks 1896-1986*. Krause Publications, Iola, WI, 1987.

Kimes, Beverly Rae, and Clark, Henry Austin, Jr., *Standard Catalog of American Cars 1805-1942*, 2nd ed. Krause Publications, Iola, WI, 1988.

Lawrence, Mike. *A-Z of Sports Cars*. Bay View Books, Bideford, Devon, England, 1991.

Neville, Bill. *Real Steel*. Running Press, Philadelphia, 1975.

Robson, Graham. *Classic Cars*. Salamander Books, London, 1982.

Stein, Ralph. *The American Automobile*. Random House, New York, 1975.

——. *The Treasury of the Automobile*. Golden Press, New York, 1961.

Wilkie, David J., *Esquire's American Autos And Their Makers.* Esquire, New York, 1963.

Photograph Credits

Front cover courtesy The Behring Auto Museum
Back cover (upper) courtesy Auburn-Cord-Duesenberg Museum
Back cover (center) courtesy Historic Car & Carriage Caravan
Back cover (bottom) courtesy Museum of Transportation
1, 27, courtesy R.E. Olds Transportation Museum
11, courtesy International Motorsports Hall of Fame
19, 20, courtesy The Behring Auto Museum
23, 24, 25, courtesy Deer Park Auto Museum
28, 29, courtesy Hays Antique Truck Museum
31, courtesy Natural History Museum of Los Angeles County
32, courtesy San Diego Automotive Museum
46, courtesy Smithsonian Institution Photo No. 49,442
48, 49, courtesy Bellm's Cars and Music of Yesterday
52, 53, 54, courtesy Collier Automotive Museum
56, courtesy Don Garlits Museum of Drag Racing
63, courtesy Katheryn Doty
72, courtesy McDonald's Corporation
75, 76, courtesy Museum of Science and Industry
78, courtesy Volo Antique Auto Museum
81, 82, courtesy Auburn-Cord-Duesenberg Museum
90, 91, courtesy Don Brayton, Photoart
92, courtesy Studebaker National Museum
99, courtesy Van Horn's Antique Truck Collection
109, 110, 111, 112, courtesy Owls Head Transportation Museum
119, courtesy Museum of Transportation
121, courtesy Alfred P. Sloan Museum
126, 127, 128, courtesy Gilmore-CCCA Museum
130, 131, 132, courtesy Henry Ford Museum
146, 147, 148, 149, courtesy Towe Ford Museum
155, 156, courtesy Imperial Palace Auto Collection
159, 160, 161, courtesy National Automobile Museum
164, 165, courtesy Grand Manor Antique & Classic Car Museum
180, courtesy Canton Classic Car Museum
182, courtesy Carillon Historical Park
184, 186, courtesy Henry Austin Clark, Jr.
185, courtesy Western Reserve Historical Society
189, courtesy Pro-Team Classic Car Collection
198, courtesy Gast Classic Motorcars Exhibit
200, courtesy JEM Classic Car Museum
214, courtesy Estate of Elvis Presley/Hud Andrews-Memphis
224, courtesy Pate Museum of Transportation
227, courtesy Classic Cars International
232, 233, courtesy Historic Car & Carriage Caravan
243, courtesy Hartford Heritage Auto Museum

Index

Alamo Classic Car Museum, 220
Alan Dent Antique Auto Museum, 195
Alfred P. Sloan Museum, 121
Amphicar, 135
Antique Auto And Music Museum, 60
Apperson brothers, 85
Arkus-Duntov, Zora, 189
Auburn Speedster, 81
Auburn-Cord-Duesenberg Museum, 81
Auto Memories, 167
Autocar, 202
Automotive Hall of Fame, 123
Autos of Yesteryear, 140

Backing Up Classics, 173
Baker Electric, 232
Barrett, Stan, 13
Barris, 103
Behring Auto Museum, 19
Bellm's Cars & Music of Yesterday, 48
Bentley, 191
Benz, 76
Benz, Karl, 76, 233
Besserdich, William, 242
Birthplace of Speed Museum, 51
Bluebird, 12
BMW (Bayerische Motoren Werke), 168
BMW Gallery, 168
Bolin Wildlife & Antique Exhibit, 221
Bonneville Salt Flats, 226
Bonneville Speedway Museum, 226
Boothbay Railway Village, 105
Bortz Auto Collection, 65
Boyertown Museum of Historic
   Vehicles, 197
Bricklin, 48
Bricklin, Malcom, 48
Brooks Stevens Automotive Museum, 238
Budweiser Rocket Car, 13
Buick *Bug,* 121
Buick Roadmaster Skylark, 66
Buick Touring, 178

C. Grier Beam Truck Museum, 175
Cadillac, 18, 216
Cadillac Automobile Company, 36
Cadillac Convertible Sedan, 126
Cadillac Fleetwood, 214
Cadillac Series 452C All-Weather
   Phaeton, 161
Cadillac V-8 Sport Phaeton, 185
Campbell, Sir Malcolm, 12, 51
Canton Classic Car Museum, 180
Car Collectors Hall of Fame, 211
Carillon Historical Park, 182
Cars of the Stars, 216
Case, 68
Central Texas Museum of Automotive
   History, 222
CERV I, 189
CGV, 119
Challenger, 103
Chevrolet, 195, 237
Chevrolet Bel Air Convertible, 164
Chevrolet Fleetline, 151
Chevrolet Impala 2dr Hardtop, 212
Chevrolet, Louis, 87, 237
Chevrolet Nomad, 151
Chevyland U.S.A., 151
Chickasha Automobile & Transportation
   Museum, 190
Chinetti, Luigi, 78
Chrysler, 200
Chrysler 300C 2dr Hardtop, 25
Chrysler Airflow, 115
Chrysler Imperial Airflow Sedan, 186
Chrysler Imperial Roadster, 200
Chrysler Town and Country, 156
Citreon 2CV, 143
Classic Car Club of America, 126
Classic Cars International, 227
Climber, 17
Cole Land Transportation Museum, 107
Cole, 97
Cole, Joseph, 97
Collectors Cars Museum, 169

Collier Automotive Museum, 52
Cord, Errett Lobban, 81
Cord L-29 Cabriolet, 90
Covert, 172
Crawford, Frederick C., 184
Crosley, 70
Crosley, Powel, 70

Daimler, 75
Daimler, Gottlieb, 75
Dale's Classic Cars, 66
Darrin, Dutch, 166
David V. Uihlein Antique Race Car
   Museum, 240
Dayton Engineering Laboratories, 182
Dayton, Ohio, 182
Daytona Beach, 51
de Dion-Bouton, 113
Deer Park Auto Museum, 23
Delco, 182
Dells Auto Museum, 241
DeLorean, John, 27
Dennis Mitosinka's Classic Cars, 27
DeSoto Airflow, 115
Detroit Automobile Company, 36
Detroit Historical Museum, 124
Diana, 74
Dixie Gun Works Old Car Museum, 213
Dodge, 103
Dodge brothers, 146 - 147
Dodge Charger, 179
Dodge Coupe, 16
Domino's Classic Car Collection, 125
Don Garlits Museum of Drag Racing, 56
Drag racing, 103
Duesenberg brothers, 87
Duesenberg Model J, 31
Duesenberg Model J Convertible, 91
Duesenberg Model J Speedster, 83
Duesenberg Motors Company, 81
Duffy's Collectible Cars, 95
Durant, William, 144, 237
Duryea, 80
Duryea, Charles, 197

Duryea, J. Frank, 197
Duryea Motor Carriage, 46

Eckhart, Frank, 81
Eckhart, Morris, 81
Edaville Railroad, 117
Elliott Museum, 59
Elvis Presley Automobile Museum, 214
Elwood Haynes Museum, 85
Estes, Pete, 27

Flint, 144
Ford, 195
Ford 2dr Sedan, 174
Ford *999*, 131
Ford Club Convertible, 112
Ford Coupe, 173
Ford Custom 2dr Sedan, 217
Ford, Edsel, 180
Ford, Henry, 36, 87, 108, 109, 180
Ford Model A, 45, 146, 147
Ford Model A Runabout, 148
Ford Model A Sport Coupe, 23
Ford Model K, 109
Ford Model K 6-40 Roadster, 149
Ford Model N, 108, 142
Ford Model T, 36, 108
Ford Model T Touring, 146
Ford Motor Company, 36, 108, 146
Ford Skyliner, 23, 24
Ford Thunderbird Convertible, 216
Ford trucks, 105
Ford V-8 Sportsman, 36
Ford Woody Station Wagon, 37
Forney Transportation Museum, 41
Four Wheel Drive Auto Company, 242
Foyt, A.J., 88
Foyt-Gilmore Coyote Indy Car, 88
France, Bill, Sr., 11
Frederick C. Crawford Auto-Aviation
   Museum, 184
Front Wheel Drive Auto Museum, 44
FWD Museum, 242

Garford, 92
Garlits, Don, 56
Gast Classic Motorcars Exhibit, 198
General Motors, 121, 144, 237
Gilmore-Classic Car Club Museum, 126
Glade Mountain Museum, 231
Glide, 80
Grand Manor Antique & Classic Car
    Museum, 164
Grant Hills Antique Auto Museum, 68
Gray's Ride Through History Museum, 69
Greensboro Historical Museum, 176

Hanson, 60
Harrah, William "Bill", 159
Harroun, Ray, 87
Hartford Heritage Auto Museum, 243
Hartung's Automotive Museum, 70
Hastings Museum, 152
Haynes-Apperson, 85
Hays Antique Truck Museum, 28
Henry Ford Company, 36
Henry Ford Museum & Greenfield
    Village, 130
Heritage Plantation of Sandwich, 118
Himes Museum of Motor Racing
    Nostalgia, 170
Hispano-Suiza H6c Boulogne, 54
Historic Car & Carriage Caravan, 232
Holsman, 140
Hupmobile Touring, 60

Imperial, 200
Imperial Palace Auto Collection, 155
Indianapolis 500, 86, 241
Indianapolis 500 pace cars, 241
Indianapolis Motor Speedway Hall of
    Fame Museum, 86
International Motorsports Hall of Fame, 11

Jaguar SS 4dr Sedan, 38
Jay Hill Antique Auto Museum, 108

Jeffery, 153
Jeffery, Charles, 153
Jeffery, Thomas, 153
JEM Classic Car Museum, 200

Kaiser-Frazer, 166
Kearns, 202
Kelsey's Antique Cars, 141
Kettering, Charles, 182
Kimber, Cecil, 230
King Midget, 107
Kissel Motor Car Company, 243
Kissel Touring, 243
Knudsen, Bunkie, 27

Leata Sedan, 63
Leland, Henry, 180
Lewis Museum, 191
Liberace Museum, 158
Lincoln Continental, 211
Lincoln Continental Club Coupe, 227
Lincoln KB Touring, 180
Linn, 29
Locomobile, 114
Lozier Touring, 128
Lynden Pioneer Museum, 237

Mack Truck, 99
Malcomson, Alexander, 109
Marmon, 86, 90
Max Nordeen's Wheels Museum, 71
McClaren Indy Car, 20
McDonald's Des Plaines Museum, 72
Mercedes, 109
Mercedes-Benz 540K, 19
Mercedes-Benz Model S Cabriolet, 110
Mercedes-Benz SS Sports Touring, 233
Mercury Convertible, 132
Miller FWD Special, 242
Miller, Harry, 240
Mississippi Valley Historic Auto Club
    Museum, 74

Moon, 74
Morgan, 205
Morris Garage, 230
Motorsports Hall of Fame, 134
Muscle cars, 103
Museum of Alaska Transportation &
    Industry, 15
Museum of Automobiles, 16
Museum of Science and Industry, 75
Museum of Special Interest Autos, 193
Museum of Transportation, 119
Museum of Wildlife, Science &
    Industry, 207
Music Valley Car Museum, 216

NART, 78
Nash, Charles, 153
National Association of Stock Car
    Racing (NASCAR), 11
National Automobile Museum, 159
National Museum of American History, 46
National Museum of Transport, 142
National Road, The, 188
National Road-Zane Grey Museum, 188
Natural History Museum of Los Angeles
    County, 31
North Carolina Transportation
    Museum, 177

Old Idaho Penitentiary, 63
Old Rhinebeck Aerodrome, 171
Oldfield, Barney, 131, 184
Olds, Ransom E., 51, 101, 137
Oldsmobile, 137
Oldsmobile Boattail Speedster, 220
Oldsmobile Curved Dash Runabout, 137
Oldsmobile Curved Dash, 101
Oldsmobile Toronado, 207
Olson Linn Museum, 97
Ormond Beach, 51
Oscar's Dreamland, 145
Owls Head Transportation Museum, 109

Packard, 177
Packard 1607 Convertible Coupe, 160
Packard Dual Cowl Phaeton, 184, 224
Packard, James, 126
Packard Motor Company, 126
Packard Phaeton, 165
Packard Speedster, 127
Packard Super 4dr Sedan, 177
Packard Victoria, 165
Packard, William, 126
Panhandle-Plains Historical Museum, 223
Panhard et Levassor, 111, 203
Pate Museum of Transportation, 224
Patee House Museum, 144
Pebble Hill Plantation, 62
Petty, Lee, 179
Petty, Richard, 179
Pierce Motor Company, 68
Pierce-Arrow, 224, 229
Pierce-Arrow Silver Arrow, 224
Pioneer Auto Show & Antique Town, 208
Playboy, 235
Plymouth, 103, 139
Plymouth Fury 2dr Hardtop, 103
Poll Museum of Transportation, 135
Pontiac, 27
Pope, Col. Albert, 118
Pope-Hartford, 118
Porsche, Ferdinand, 52, 110, 233
Porsche, Ferry, 53
Porsche RS60 Spyder, 52
Porsche RS61L Spyder, 52
Porsche-Behra Formula II Race Car, 53
Pro Team Classic Corvette Collection, 189

R.E. Olds Transportation Museum, 137
Rambler, 153
Reed's Museum of Automobiles, 18
Reo, 137
Reo Antique Auto Museum, 101
Reo Flying Cloud Coupe, 101
Reo Motor Car Company, 101
Reo Touring, 102
Richard Petty Museum, 179

Roaring Twenties Antique Car Museum, 235
Roberts, Fireball, 14
Rockne 2dr Sedan, 92
Rockne, Knute, 92
Rolls, Charles, 34
Rolls-Royce, 34
Rolls-Royce, 191
Royal Gorge Scenic Railway Museum, 45
Royce, Frederick, 34

S. Ray Miller Antique Car Museum, 90
San Diego Automotive Museum, 32
San Sylmar-Merle Norman Classic Beauty Collection, 34
Sawyer's Sandhills Museum, 153
Schield International Museum, 98
Schoolhouse Antiques Museum, 205
Scripps-Booth Bi-Autogo, 124
Seal Cove Auto Museum, 113
Sears, 152
Service station, 182
'77 Grand Prix Museum, 194
Silverado Classic Car Collection, 35
Sloan, Alfred, 121
Smoky Mountain Car Museum, 219
Space Farms Zoo and Museum, 166
Spencer Shops, 177
St. Louis Motor Carriage Company, 142
Stanley, Francis E., 114
Stanley, Frelan Ozro, 114
Stanley Museum, 114
Stanley *Wogglebug*, 64, 114
State Museum of Pennsylvania, 202
Station Square Transportation Museum, 203
Steam cars, 64, 114
Stevens, Brooks, 238
Stock Car Hall of Fame/Joe Weatherly Museum, 206
Studebaker, 177
Studebaker brothers, 92
Studebaker company, 92

Studebaker National Museum, 92
Stuhr Museum, 154
Stutz Blackhawk, 214
Swigart Museum, 204

Thomas Flyer, 159
Towe Ford Museum, 36, 146
Tremulis, Alex, 32
Tucker, 32
Tucker 4dr Sedan, 32, 155, 198
Tucker, Preston, 32, 155

U.S. Army Transportation Museum, 236
Union Station Museum, 229

Van Horn's Antique Truck Museum, 99
Velie, 71
Vintage Wheel Museum, 64
Volo Auto Museum, 78

Wayne County Historical Museum, 94
Wells Auto Museum, 115
Westminster MG Car Museum, 230
Wheels & Spokes, 103
Wheels O' Time Museum, 80
Whippet, 244
White, 190
Willys-Overland Company, 244
Wilson Historical Museum, 172
Winton, Alexander, 51, 184

Ypsilanti Antique Auto, Truck & Fire Museum, 139
Yunick, Smokey, 14

Zachow, Otto, 242
Zunker Auto Museum, 244

Notes

Notes

Notes